STRANDED
OBJECTS

STRANDED
OBJECTS

Mourning, Memory, and Film
in Postwar Germany

ERIC L. SANTNER

Cornell University Press

ITHACA AND LONDON

First published 1990 by Cornell University Press.
First printing, Cornell Paperbacks, 1993.

International Standard Book Number 0-8014-2344-9 (cloth)
International Standard Book Number 0-8014-8162-7 (paper)
Library of Congress Catalog Card Number 89-38522

Printed in the United States of America

*Librarians: Library of Congress cataloging information
appears on the last page of the book.*

⊗ The paper in this book meets the minimum requirements of the American National Standard for Information Sciences—Permanence of Paper for Printed Library Materials, ANSI Z39.48-1984.

For Lotte Lemke and Hans J. Fröhlich
in loving memory of our friendship

Contents

Preface

In 1986, while in the Federal Republic of Germany to begin my
research for this study of postwar political culture and film, I visited
a family I had known as an exchange student years earlier at the
University of Freiburg. During this brief visit a curious thing happened that condensed many of the issues I would face in the months
and years to come. During our midday meal one day I noticed that
the youngest boy in the family—let me call him Ralf—was wearing
a gold chain bearing a Star of David. I had seen young Germans
wearing the Jewish Star before but never had had the opportunity to
question them about their reasons for performing what I perceived
as a highly resonant symbolic act (given the size of the Jewish population in Germany, the majority of these young Germans were not
likely to have been Jewish). I asked Ralf, who was seventeen at the
time, why he, a non-Jew, was wearing the Star of David and what it
meant to him. His reaction was abrupt and defensive. He said that
his girlfriend had been to Israel and had bought it for him as a
souvenir of her trip; he said he could no doubt rehearse an elaborate
political interpretation of its significance but that he had no interest
in such exercises. *Schluß*. At the time I thought it best to drop the
matter. Later that day, however, I asked Ralf's mother, a woman in
her late forties, about her understanding of her son's souvenir and
his vehement reaction to my inquiry. Her response was even more
aggressive than Ralf's. She insisted that the necklace signified noth-

ing beyond the private gesture of affection for his girlfriend. This was, after all, an object intended for tourists, a token that anyone can purchase on the streets of Israel. She then began to accuse me, an American and a Jew, of trying to complicate her son's life unnecessarily and of trying to impose guilt feelings on her son who, she insisted, had the right to feel unencumbered by events that occurred long before he was born. She was tired, she said, of people from the outside telling Germans, especially young Germans, what they should or should not feel, what they should or should not be mindful of. In the course of this tirade, my friend did mention other possible meanings of her son's necklace: a gesture of friendship with a half-Jewish schoolmate; a gesture of solidarity with victims; a gesture of rebellion. (Here I wonder at what or at whom this rebellion might have been directed: at the legacy of the grandfathers? at the radical members of the generation between himself and his parents who in large numbers donned Al Fatah headgear in an act of solidarity with Palestinians against the "fascist" Israelis?) In the end, however, she insisted that these matters were nobody's business but Ralf's. And why after all, she asked, should a young German have to bear burdens of conscience and consciousness that, for example, a young Frenchman or American would not? (At the time, neither of us considered whether it would have even occurred to a young non-Jewish Frenchman or American to wear a Star of David in the first place.)

I told my friend that I understood and appreciated her desire to protect her son's ingenuousness, his *Unbefangenheit*, as the Germans say. I tried to argue, however, that one simply could not wish away the fact that wearing a Star of David in Germany forty years after the end of the war and the Final Solution was a highly complex symbolic gesture, that at this moment in history her son's souvenir functioned as a memory token in a larger and far more ambiguous sense than he or she might like. Needless to say, the matter remained unresolved. When I left town the next day, we all seemed to know, or at least I remember hoping we knew, that our capacity to communicate our thoughts and feelings about these things was far from adequate.

It was clear at the time, and has become all the more so in the intervening years, that this experience belonged to a much broader set of issues and events which have loomed large in German political culture in the eighties. It had been only a year since Ronald Reagan's visit to Bitburg, a year since the controversy surrounding the attempt to stage Rainer Werner Fassbinder's 1975 play *Trash, City, and Death*, a year since Richard von Weizsäcker's historic speech commemorating the fortieth anniversary of the end of the war, but also a year since another speech of commemoration by the cardinal of Cologne, Joseph Höffner, in which he declared that Germans "should not, again and again, exhume past guilt and mutually committed injustices, in constant self-torment."[1] During this period intense and bitter debates took place regarding the idea of building a new museum of German national history in Berlin, and the so-called historians' controversy—the *Historiker-Streit*—began: a remarkable series of debates played out in the German press dealing with the place of the Final Solution in German history (these debates will be discussed in detail in chapter 2). Certainly one of the more remarkable events during this period was the resignation in November 1988 of the speaker of the West German Parliament, Philipp Jenninger, in the wake of the reaction to his speech commemorating the fiftieth anniversary of the *Kristallnacht*. Jenninger had broken certain rules of decorum regarding the shape, structure, and tone of public acts of memorialization. Employing a mode of free indirect discourse, a narrative strategy whereby one speaks the thoughts of others without actual citation or commentary, Jenninger had articulated the enthusiasm and passions that had moved so many Germans to support National Socialism and to stand by while the windows and existences of Jewish neighbors were being shattered. Jenninger went on to claim that the initial triumphs and exuberance of the Nazi movement have, even to this day and, apparently, even at the very moment of recalling the suffering of the victims, not ceased to be a *Faszinosum* for the postwar population. Obviously, there is still tremendous uncertainty and confusion in contemporary German society about how to approach the tasks of mourning and anamnesis with regard to fascism and the Holocaust.

If one tries to give a historical account of the various stages of German efforts to master the past—efforts at *Vergangenheitsbewältigung*—key political and cultural events that have provoked brief periods of intense confrontation with this past come to mind (when one speaks of such confrontations one is speaking of a relatively small segment of the population for whom the imperative to work through the past is a given): the performances of the Anne Frank story in German theaters in the late fifties; the Eichmann trial in 1960–61; the Auschwitz trials in Frankfurt in 1963–65; the student revolts of the late sixties; the broadcast of the American television film *Holocaust* in 1979; the series of public commemorations of significant dates in the history of the Third Reich, the most notorious of which have been the events at Bitburg and the Jenninger speech. One might also think of other domestic political events that have indirectly influenced the discourses of mourning and memory in the Federal Republic. (It is only for pragmatic reasons that I limit my discussion to West Germany. As the Waldheim affair made painfully obvious, uncertainties and confusions in these matters are not limited to West Germany.) Particularly significant here are the various displacements and reconfigurations of the parties and coalitions that have held power in Bonn.

Most observers of the political and cultural scene in Germany do, however, agree that the radical student movement of the late sixties represents a kind of caesura in this history of *Vergangenheitsbewältigung*. The revolts in Germany, unlike those in other European nations and the United States, were, as Peter Schneider has noted, "specifically addressed to the generation responsible for Nazism."[2] That is, the student movement in Germany was, in essence, performing a radical act of *Vergangenheitsbewältigung*. Never before in the postwar period had public discourse about the Nazi past attained such a feverish pitch. In retrospect, however, this explosive effort to condemn and to dissociate oneself from the crimes and morally tainted ways of life of the fathers and mothers seemed only to have numbed temporarily the psychic pain that accompanied the inheritance of a cultural tradition poisoned by the word "Auschwitz." "It is now clear," Schneider notes, ". . . that the protestors were terribly naive and unself-conscious in their anti-fascism. There has probably never been a movement at once so obsessed with language and so incapable of articulating its ideas and desires."[3]

This book is a study of the next long stage in this history of postwar efforts to work through the legacies of fascism and the Holocaust. In this next stage, which carries through to the present, efforts to master the past shift in emphasis. As the perpetrator generation dies out, more properly juridical issues of guilt and complicity yield to more inchoate questions of historical memory and of the mediation and transmittal of cultural traditions and identities. In this next stage the fundamental issue becomes, in a sense, what it means to identify oneself as a German, what it means to say *"ich"* and *"wir"* in a Germany that still finds itself under the shadow of the Final Solution. What are the strategies and procedures by which a cultural identity may be reconstituted in post-Holocaust Germany?

The task of integrating damage, loss, disorientation, decentered-ness into a transformed structure of identity, whether it be that of an individual, a culture, or an individual as a member of a cultural group, is, as I shall argue in these pages, one of the central tasks of what Freud called *Trauerarbeit*, or the "work of mourning." In the following pages I shall look at the successes and failures of various attempts at such *Trauerarbeit* in German political and film culture of the seventies and eighties. In the chapters dealing with film, I focus on the work of two contemporary filmmakers, Edgar Reitz and Hans Jürgen Syberberg. I have chosen to look at filmmakers, and these two filmmakers in particular, for several reasons. Reitz and Syberberg have, with their films *Heimat* and *Our Hitler* respectively, produced the two most ambitious attempts by recent German artists to create works of national elegiac art: works that make use of the procedures and resources of mourning to reconstitute something like a German self-identity in the wake of the catastrophic turns of recent German history. In each case the task of mourning involves the labor of recollecting the stranded objects of a cultural inheritance fragmented and poisoned by an unspeakable horror.

But I have chosen filmmakers for another reason as well. Each of the films I analyze points up the particular significance of the medium of film in the successes of German fascism to mobilize and to sustain collective fantasies of omnipotence and community. In a word, cinema is seen as being somehow implicated in the constitution of fascism as *Faszinosum*. In both cases, cinema is itself interrogated as an important and highly ambiguous site of communal and individual identity formation.

As will become evident especially in the first two chapters, I have made an effort to situate the historical tasks of mourning which face Germans of the second and third postwar generations within a larger context of mourning tasks. This context, I shall argue, defines the cultural space that has come to be called the "postmodern." In this respect, the theoretical framework of my entire project could be considered a reworking and expansion, in a postmodern context, of Margarete and Alexander Mitscherlich's groundbreaking work on the question of mourning in postwar German society. I have tried to broaden the range of the Mitscherlichs' study to include contemporary cultural and political phenomena and concerns that can no longer be viewed as exclusively German because they are shared widely by Western societies. I hope to show that the postmodern destabilization of certain fundamental cultural norms and notions, above all those dealing with self-identity and community, cannot be understood without reference to the ethical and intellectual imperatives of life after Auschwitz. For if the postmodern is, in a crucial sense, about the attempt to "think difference," we take on this task in the knowledge of what can happen if a society turns away from such labors.

Before all, I thank Hans Jürgen Syberberg and Edgar Reitz for their generosity as artists and as interlocutors. I thank the American Council of Learned Societies and Princeton University for their generous support of this project. I am especially grateful to the following readers of early sections of the book: David Bathrick, Stanley Corngold, Michael Jennings, Peter Schneider, Saul Friedländer, Frederic Morton, Maria DiBattista, Gail Finney, Marc Kaminsky, Kristin Koptiuch and the reader who remained anonymous. I thank Meredith Monk for (unknowingly) providing me with my title, *Stranded Objects*, and for all that I have learned through her art about the dramaturgy of mourning. Other artists who have helped me in this regard are Arthur Strimling and Diane Dowling. I am most grateful to Ingrid Scheib-Rothbart of the Goethe Haus, New York, for her advice and for making so many films available to me. I also thank my editors at Cornell University Press—especially Bernhard Kendler and Emily Wheeler—for their support and always generous and expert counsel. I owe a special debt to Richard Campbell for all his guidance in the course of this project, and not just this one. Finally, my largest debt is to Pamela K. Pascoe, who helped to make the work on these difficult and often disturbing matters a life-affirming project.

Wherever possible, references have been made to accessible English editions of texts. Unless otherwise indicated, translations are my own. With the exception of those cases where a film has become well known under a particular English title, I have provided more or less literal translations of German titles of films.

ERIC L. SANTNER

Princeton, New Jersey

STRANDED
OBJECTS

Postwar / Post-Holocaust / Postmodern: Some Reflections on the Discourses of Mourning

When Alexander and Margarete Mitscherlich published their groundbreaking study *The Inability to Mourn* in 1967, they were struck by the apparent absence of any sustained emotional confrontation with the Nazi past in postwar German society. Deep feelings of contrition and a genuine urge to heal injury had not followed upon recognition of complicity in horrific crimes performed in the name of the fatherland; shame had not followed upon loss of face among nations; the desire to remember had not followed upon the testimonies of survivors of the Final Solution. But what struck the Mitscherlichs even more was the fact that the population of the new Federal Republic had avoided what might—and in a certain sense should—have been the psychological reaction to the defeat in 1945, the direct confrontation with the facts of the Holocaust and, above all, the loss of Hitler as *Führer*, namely a massive fall into depression and melancholy:

> To millions of Germans the loss of the "Führer" (for all the oblivion that covered his downfall and the rapidity with which he was renounced) was not the loss of someone ordinary; identifications that had filled a central function in the lives of his followers were attached to his person. As we said, he had become the embodiment of their ego-ideal. The loss of an object so highly cathected with libidinal energy—one about whom nobody had any doubts, nor dared to have any, even when the country was being reduced to rubble—was in-

deed reason for melancholia. Through the catastrophe not only was
the German ego-ideal robbed of the support of reality, but in addition
the Führer himself was exposed by the victors as a criminal of truly
monstrous proportions. With this sudden reversal of his qualities, the
ego of every single German individual suffered a central devaluation
and impoverishment. This creates at least the prerequisites for a melancholic reaction.[1]

This remarkable diagnosis offered a new framework of interpretation, one that promised to extend the reach of the analysis and moral
evaluation of social and political behavior in postwar Germany.

The Mitscherlichs are referring here, of course, to Freud's distinction between two different patterns of bereavement: mourning and
melancholy. According to Freud, mourning occurs when an object
that one had loved for its intrinsic qualities as separate and distinct
from oneself is lost. The pleasures that derive from this form of love
depend on a capacity to tolerate the potentially painful awareness
that "I" and "you" have edges, and that inscribed within the space
of this interval are the possibilities of misunderstanding, disappointment, even betrayal. According to Freud, the loss of an object loved
in this manner typically results in mourning (*Trauer*):

> Reality-testing has shown that the loved object no longer exists, and it
> proceeds to demand that all libido shall be withdrawn from its attach-
> ments to that object. . . . Normally, respect for reality gains the day.
> Nevertheless its orders cannot be obeyed at once. They are carried out
> bit by bit, at great expense of time and cathectic energy, and in the
> meantime the existence of the lost object is psychically prolonged.
> Each single one of the memories and expectations in which the libido
> is bound to the object is brought up and hyper-cathected, and detach-
> ment of the libido is accomplished in respect of it.[2]

At the completion of this process of *Trauerarbeit*, the ego "becomes
free and uninhibited again"[3] and capable of cathecting new love-
objects. In the case of melancholy, the pattern by which loss is
worked through is different because the loved object fulfilled a
rather different function in the psychological life of the bereaved. A
melancholic response to loss, the symptomology of which is a severe, often suicidal depression, ensues when the object was loved
not as separate and distinct from oneself, but rather as a mirror of
one's own sense of self and power. The predisposition to love in this

2

manner obtains when the self lacks sufficient strength and cohesion to tolerate, much less comprehend, the reality of separateness (this is the situation of both the primary narcissist, the infant, and the secondary narcissist, the adult melancholic). The paradox of this narcissism is that the narcissist loves an object only insofar and as long as he or she can repress the otherness of the object; narcissistic love plays itself out in the (non-)space where "I" and "you" are not perceived as having hard edges.[4] The grieving that occurs in melancholy is thus more primitive than what occurs in "healthy" mourning, since what is at stake is nothing less than the constitution of the boundaries between self and other, and the integration of that painful awareness of the dangers of separateness alluded to above.[5] What melancholy must work through is not so much the loss of a particular object that one had loved and cared for—an object that had appealed to one's pleasure principle—but rather the loss of a fantasy of omnipotence. As Freud says, "In mourning it is the world which has become poor and empty; in melancholia it is the ego itself."[6] The melancholic grieves not so much for the loss of the other as for the fact of otherness and all that that entails. Melancholy, one might say, is the rehearsal of the shattering or fragmentation of one's primitive narcissism, an event that predates the capacity to feel any real mourning for a lost object, since for the narcissist other objects do not yet really exist.

In reality, pure forms of either mode of grieving are considered rare. Since love inevitably seems to include an element of narcissism, understood here in the most general sense as a residual resistance to the perception of the separateness of self and other, it might make more sense to speak of a continuum or a layering of more primitive and more mature modes of mourning in any specific experience of loss. The shock of mortal loss, which is the shock of definitive separateness, therefore necessarily recapitulates the more fundamental task of reestablishing the boundaries of the self. Given, however, the predominance of the narcissistic element in the communal fabric of Nazi Germany, the Mitscherlichs insist on the priority of the more primitive tasks of mourning facing the postwar population. Before Germans could really begin to perceive the full magnitude of the crimes committed in the name of the fatherland and to mourn for the victims of Nazism, they would first have to work through the traumatic shattering of the specular relations they

3

had maintained with Hitler and the *Volksgemeinschaft*. In a word, a sense of self would first have to be reconstituted on the ruins of this narcissism.

But as the Mitscherlichs insist over and over again, this process, which would have required a willingness to experience and work through a potentially debilitating melancholy, never in fact took place in postwar Germany, thanks to the remarkably efficient deployment of a set of defense mechanisms that served to burn affective bridges to the past. Foremost among the defenses were derealization of the past, the sudden and radical shift of (narcissistic) identifications with Hitler to the democratic allies, and finally, identification with the victim:

> The Federal Republic did not succumb to melancholia; instead, as a group, those who had lost their "ideal leader," the representative of a commonly shared ego-ideal, managed to avoid self-devaluation by breaking all affective bridges to the immediate past. . . . This rejection of inner involvement in one's own behavior under the Third Reich prevented a loss of self-esteem that could hardly have been mastered, and a consequent outbreak of melancholia in innumerable cases.[7]

And as the authors are quick to point out, these breaks in the continuity with the past are not achieved once and for all but, rather, have to be maintained—have to be broken over and over—at enormous psychic cost. It is, the Mitscherlichs argue, this unconsciously sustained rupture with the past—a gap that was, to a certain extent, filled by the manic achievements of the "economic miracle"—that has been responsible for much of the psychic and political immobility of large segments of the German population. Here one must keep in mind that these breaks with the past are essentially defenses against a massive narcissistic injury:

> That so few signs of melancholia or even of mourning are to be seen among the great masses of the population can be attributed only to a collective denial of the past. The very grimness with which the job of clearing away the ruins was immediately begun—which, in oversimplification, was taken as a sign of German efficiency—itself betrayed a manic element. Perhaps this manic defense also explains why news of the greatest crimes in Germany's history was received with so few indications of outward emotion.[8]

4

In a talk delivered in 1959, Theodor Adorno touched on many of the themes later elaborated by the Mitscherlichs, including their central thesis of the narcissistic foundation of the Germans' relation to Hitler and to the ideals of National Socialism. Adorno's analysis is harsher and rather more disturbing than that of the Mitscherlichs. According to Adorno, the postwar population was never really in danger of falling into a melancholic depression for the simple reason that it never fully abandoned its identifications with the old order:

> On the subjective side, the collective narcissism in the human psyche—national vanity, in a word—was immeasurably exalted by National Socialism. . . . This collective narcissism was grievously damaged by the collapse of the Hitler regime; a damage which, however, occurred in the realm of simple fact, without each individual becoming conscious of it and thereby getting over it. That is the social-psychological relevance of the talk about an unmastered past. Also lacking is the panic that, according to Freud's theory in *Group Psychology and the Analysis of the Ego*, sets in where collective identifications break down. If the great psychologist's theory isn't to be thrown out, there remains only one conclusion: secretly, unconsciously smoldering and therefore especially powerful, these identifications as well as a group narcissism were not destroyed but continue to exist.[9]

Like the Mitscherlichs, Adorno believed that the German population had narcissistically identified with Hitler and the ideology of National Socialism. This globally deployed narcissism projected difference and otherness as something that intervenes from the outside, something that could and should be purged from an otherwise pure system seamlessly continuous with itself. In Lacanian terms, the Jews were assigned the role of the ones who intrude into and disrupt the Imaginary, akin to evil fathers who brutally uproot the children from their native matrix and maroon them in the cold and abstract space of the Symbolic. To eliminate the Jews would allow for a fantasy of return to the purity of a self-identity unmediated by any passage through alterity. The destruction of the Jews becomes, according to this logic, part of a broad group psychological strategy designed to "undo" or reverse the passage through that more primitive labor of mourning by which the boundaries between self and other are consolidated on the ruins of primary, that is, infantile, narcissism. The ideology of National Socialism and the narcissistic

5

identification with Hitler thus promised a utopian world in which one was free to destroy what threatened the claustral intimacy afforded by this narcissism. This was a world where the mournful labor that opens up the space between "I" and "thou," "here" and "there," "now" and "then," could be banished as degenerate (*entartet*) and Jewish. A "respecularization" of identity, that is, the simulation of a pure, specular reciprocity between self and other, was achieved by finding those one could blame for having disturbed this utopian exchange of gazes. In such a utopia, needless to say, a mature self could never really develop. The paradoxical task faced by the postwar population was thus to mourn for losses incurred in the name of a society that was in its turn founded on a fundamental denial of mourning in its (self-)constituting capacities. Germans had to mourn *as Germans* for those whom they had excluded and exterminated in their mad efforts to produce their "Germanness."

One fairly common strategy of circumventing this complex layering of mourning tasks (and thereby remaining within the closure of narcissism) was to identify with the victim, to become the one who helplessly and innocently suffered the deceptions and ravages of the fascist utopia as well as the destruction wrought by the allied forces:

> Identification with the innocent victim is very frequently substituted for mourning; this is above all a logical defense against guilt. . . . To the conscious mind the past then appears as follows: We made many sacrifices, suffered the war, and were discriminated against for a long time afterward; yet we were innocent, since everything that is now held against us we did under orders. This strengthens the feeling of being oneself the victim of evil forces; first the evil Jews, then the evil Nazis, and finally the evil Russians. In each instance the evil is externalized. It is sought for on the outside, and it strikes one from the outside.[10]

The identification with the victim on the basis of a continued refusal to work through a narcissistic pattern of object relating—evil remains that which intervenes from the outside into an otherwise pure and innocent inside—perpetuates an incapacity to perceive or feel for the suffering of the real victims of Nazism:

> In these attempts to shake off guilt, it is remarkable how little attention is paid to the victims. . . . Now there is only feeling enough for the cathexis of one's own person, hardly for any kind of sympathy

6

with others. If somehow, somewhere, one finds an object deserving of
sympathy, it usually turns out to be none other than oneself.[11]

The capacity to feel grief for others and guilt for the suffering one
has directly or indirectly caused, depends on the capacity to experience empathy for the other *as other*. This capacity in turn depends on
the successful working through of those primitive experiences of
mourning which first consolidate the boundaries between self and
other, thereby opening up a space for empathy. According to the
Mitscherlichs, the failure to perform these primitive mourning tasks
not only provided the psychic foundation of the narcissistic identification with Hitler but continue to block any true feelings of sympathy and guilt for the victims of Nazism.

Since the publication of *The Inability to Mourn* in the late sixties, a
body of critical discourses has emerged which appears to address
questions of mourning very close to those the Mitscherlichs raise. I
am thinking here of the rhetoric of mourning which has come to
occupy the semantic field of so much critical theory in recent years.
By the "rhetoric of mourning" I mean the recurrence, in so many
postmodern theoretical discourses, of a metaphorics of loss and impoverishment.[12] The appeal, in these discourses, to notions of shattering, rupture, mutilation, fragmentation, to images of fissures,
wounds, rifts, gaps, and abysses, is familiar enough. These discourses, primarily poststructuralist in inspiration, appear committed to the vigilant and radical critique of what are taken to be the
narcissisms and nostalgias central to the project of modernity—
namely Enlightenment faith in progress—and the Western tradition
more generally. These discourses propose a kind of perpetual leave-
taking from fantasies of plenitude, purity, centrality, totality, unity,
and mastery. Such fantasies and their various narrative performances, whether cast in the rhetoric of totalization or of liberation,
are in turn seen as the primary sources of violence in history, the
Third Reich being only the most extreme example in a long historical
series. These discourses aim to empower the "survivors" of European modernity to creatively, and even playfully, inhabit the heterogeneous language games that constitute the modest forms of community which mark the postmodern landscape. Postmodern critics
invite readers to mourn the shattered fantasy of the (always already)
lost organic society that has haunted the Western imagination, and

7

to learn to tolerate the complexities and instabilities of new social arrangements as well as more hybrid, more "creole," forms of personal, sexual, cultural, and political identity. It is a matter of learning to live as a nomad, as one disabused of notions of roots and rootedness and as one who has learned that survival is a constant improvisation.

In a recent text, Jean-François Lyotard, certainly the most well-known proponent of the postmodern agenda to which I have been referring, makes the link between the inability to tolerate the nomadism characterizing the habits and habitations of postmodern selves, and an inability, symptomatic especially of German society but also reaching beyond national boundaries, to mourn the losses left in the wake of the Holocaust. Speaking of the various failures of the project of modernity to realize its vision of the "transparency of humanity to itself," Lyotard remarks,

> All these wounds can be given names. Their names are strewn across the field of our unconscious like so many secret obstacles to the quiet perpetuation of the "modern project." Under the pretense of safeguarding that project the men and women of my generation in Germany imposed on their children a forty-year silence about the "Nazi interlude." This interdiction against anamnesis stands as a symbol for the entire Western world. Can there be progress without anamnesis? Anamnesis constitutes a painful process of working through, a work of mourning for the attachments and conflicting emotions, loves and terrors, associated with those names. . . . We have only gotten as far as a vague, apparently inexplicable, end-of-the-century melancholy.[13]

The inability to assume the disorientations and decenteredness of the postmodern, minimally defined as the fragmentation of the modern project, is seen by Lyotard as contributing, in a fundamental way, to an inability to remember a past dismembered under the sign of Auschwitz. In other words, readers are being asked to think the "postwar" under the double sign of the postmodern and the post-Holocaust. And this double "post" is conceived in its turn as an imperative to work through—to mourn—the narcissisms that have, often with lethal consequences, tantalized the Western imagination in the modern period. These postmodern critical discourses represent a kind of translation into more global terms of Adorno's famous dictum that there could be no poetry after Auschwitz. After Auschwitz—after this trauma to European modernity—critical theory becomes in large part an ongoing elaboration of a seemingly endless series of "no longer possibles."[14]

Central to these "no longer possibles," whether they be modes of aesthetic practice, thinking, political practice, or human interaction, is an inability to tolerate difference, heterogeneity, nonmastery. These discursive practices are founded on an inability or refusal to engage in those more primitive tasks of mourning which institute difference on the ruins of (infantile) fantasies of omnipotence. Not unlike the Mitscherlichs, the postmodern discourses of bereavement—of the "no longer possibles"—to which I have been referring, invite readers to mourn these refusals to mourn. Postmodernism, as I am using the term here, may thus be understood as a collection of theoretical and aesthetic strategies dedicated, some directly, some rather more indirectly, to undoing a certain repetition compulsion of modern European history. This compulsion may be seen to have found its ultimate staging in Auschwitz, which can be seen as a sort of modern industrial apparatus for the elimination of difference.

And indeed, much poststructuralist critical practice views the figure of the mourner-survivor as a kind of arch-trope not just for what it means to be a citizen of postwar or postmodern society but, more radically, for what it means to be a member of a linguistic community. To be a speaking subject is to have already assumed one's fundamental vocation as survivor of the painful losses—the structural catastrophes—that accompany one's entrance into the symbolic order. Furthermore, according to poststructuralist readings of the modern project in particular and of Western thinking more generally—what Heidegger called onto-theological and Derrida has variously termed logo-, phono-, phallo-, and ethnocentric thinking—the violence of this tradition may be traced to a repression of these catastrophes, to a disavowal of the opportunities for and necessities of bereaved thinking, speaking, writing. And it is precisely this work of denial and repression of the inherent fragmentation of a life in the symbolic order which produces the pile of wreckage that, in Walter Benjamin's famous thesis on the philosophy of history, grows skyward under the melancholic eyes of the angel of history.[15] The violence of history grows out of a refusal or an inability on the part of the members of a society to assume the vocation of mourner-survivor of what might be called the violence of the signifier. In the writings of numerous poststructuralist theorists, *historical* suffering

9

is believed to spring from a failure to tolerate the *structural suffering*—the always already shattered mirrors of the Imaginary—that scars one's being as a speaking subject.

Commenting, for example, on Husserl's philosophy of signification, a key moment in the tradition that would keep men and women from consciously and creatively inhabiting the ruinous edifice of human discourse, Derrida insists on the testamentary—the proleptically or structurally elegiac—dimension of every linguistic utterance:

> This alone enables us to account for the fact that we understand the word *I* not only when its "author" is unknown but when he is quite fictitious. And when he is dead. The ideality of the *Bedeutung* here has by virtue of its structure the value of a testament. . . . My death is structurally necessary to the pronouncing of the *I*. . . . The statement "I am alive" is accompanied by my being dead, and its possibility requires the possibility that I be dead. . . . This is not an extraordinary tale by Poe but the ordinary story of language.[16]

In "Signature Event Context," an essay in which Derrida is concerned with the citability of any linguistic utterance, written or spoken, he states:

> To be what it is, all writing must . . . be capable of functioning in the radical absence of every empirically determined receiver in general. And this absence is not a continuous modification of presence, it is a rupture in presence, the "death" or the possibility of the "death" of the receiver inscribed in the structure of the mark.[17]

And in *Of Grammatology* Derrida leads readers through a number of key texts in the Western tradition which have sought to diminish this elegiac dimension of language by assigning it the value of a supplement, that is, by attempting to contain it as a feature of the written sign "which . . . must therefore be born out of a primary gap and a primary *expatriation*, condemning it to wandering and blindness, to mourning."[18] It is precisely this mourning that Derrida insists on relocating inside and, indeed, at the very origin of language. *Every* utterance resonates, in this view, with the mythic musical lament Rilke evokes at the close of the first *Duino Elegy*:

> Ist die Sage umsonst, daß einst in der Klage um Linos
> wagende erste Musik dürre Erstarrung durchdrang;

daß erst im erschrockenen Raum, dem ein beinah göttlicher Jüngling
plötzlich für immer enttrat, das Leere in jene
Schwingung geriet, die uns jetzt hinreißt und tröstet und hilft.

(Is the legend meaningless that tells how, in the lament for Linus, /
the daring first notes of song pierced through the barren numbness; /
and then in the startled space which a youth as lovely as a god / had
suddenly left forever, the Void felt for the first time / the harmony
which now enraptures and comforts and helps us.)[19]

That in Derridean discourse every speech act is, in a sense, some
such vibration of the void, has led one critic to the quite radical claim
that, in effect, "all of Derrida's privileged 'undecidable' terms, *sup-
plément, différance, dissémination,* are diacritical avatars of the death
instinct."[20]
As I have been arguing, this obsession with death, loss, and
impoverishment—which may, of course, also be found in numerous
texts of Romantic and modernist writers—is part of a larger, more
properly postmodern project that is equally concerned with the resources of what one might call a playful nomadism. That is, these
discourses of bereavement see in the harrowing labor of mourning
one's various narcissisms and nostalgias a source of empowerment,
play, and even *jouissance.* In these discourses we find the elaboration
of an intellectual habitus that provides for new ways of coming to
terms with difference: of playing with and playing out difference
rather than seeking to resolve or transcend it. It comes as no surprise, then, that Walter Benjamin's book on German baroque *Trauerspiel,* a subject that seems almost magically to condense the two
obsessions of postmodern criticism—the German word for tragic
drama literally means "mourningplay"—has enjoyed a vigorous
second life in recent critical theory. In language anticipating Derrida's critique of Western phonocentrism, Benjamin suggests that
the greatness of the baroque lay precisely in its insight into the
irreducible elegiac dimension of signification, which for Benjamin is
to be seen in the allegorical mode of representation of baroque
Trauerspiel:

For the baroque sound is and remains something purely sensuous;
meaning has its home in written language. And the spoken word is
only afflicted by meaning, so to speak, as if by an inescapable disease;
it breaks off in the middle of the process of resounding, and the

11

damming up of the feeling, which was ready to pour forth, provokes mourning. Here meaning is encountered, and will continue to be encountered as the reason for mournfulness.[21]

In this view, the speaking subject who has entered—or rather fallen—into the order of signification, has crossed over a bar that separates him or her from the benevolence as well as the tyranny of nature and the imaginary relations of myth. She or he is marooned in a world of ruins, fragments, stranded objects that thereby take on a textual aspect: they demand to be read. The allegorical structure of baroque tragedy enacts the fall into the disturbing opacity of a history bereft of all comforting teleologies; this fall is, however, also seen as the promise of knowledge and, as postmodern critics would have it, of the play of *écriture*. Of course postmodern playfulness and *jouissance* are hardly the first things that come to mind when one thinks of Benjamin's work. It is not, however, difficult to see this postmodern potential in the pile of ruins which Benjamin associates with the allegorical sensibility. For in the wake of the disruption of all organicisms and natural relations, "Any person, any object, any relationship can mean absolutely anything else."[22] The fragmentation of all images of organic totality, which Benjamin sees as the mournful point of departure for the baroque, opens up extravagant and excessive possibilities of recollection, recombination, and interpretation. It is in this sense that the baroque allegorist has been regarded as the forbear of the postmodern *bricoleur*. Both engage in signifying practices that depend on a previous dispersion, on a certain state of diaspora. The difference is that the postmodernist, while insisting on this condition of loss and dispersion, tries to move beyond mourning and invest his or her libidinal energies in the process of improvising new associations and correspondences in this open field of semiotic excess. The postmodernist appropriates the Benjaminian analysis of *mourning* play as one of mourning *play*.[23]

But is it the same thing to elaborate a postmodern ethics of impossibility or undecidability, to rehearse the elegiac procedures of leave-taking from the "no longer possibles" of the modern project—which include the very notion of the redemption of modern life through culture[24]—and to engage in a labor of mourning with respect to the "Nazi interlude" and the Holocaust? Are the postmodern critical agendas that direct themselves against the nostalgic dreams of Western man also to be considered adequate modes of assuming the moral and psychological burdens of the post-Holocaust? Is it the same thing to cross over, again and again, that "jagged line of demarcation between physical nature and significance"[25]—a gesture that is at the heart of postmodern theory and aesthetic practice—and to cross over that other line that, to paraphrase Paul Celan, writes asunder history into a time before and a time after the Shoah? To return to Lyotard's remark regarding the relation between amnesia with respect to Auschwitz and the repression of the failures of European modernity more generally to deal with difference, one must wonder whether the elaboration of those failures, which is an essential aspect of so much postmodern critical practice, can also be understood as a gesture of genuine anamnesis and mourning toward the Holocaust and its victims. These questions have recently come into sharp focus thanks to the debates raging over the wartime activities and writings of the postmodern critic most thoroughly identified with bereaved thinking, Paul de Man. That is, since the revelations of his wartime writings, Paul de Man has become a sort of test case for exploring at least a certain strand of contemporary critical discourse and evaluating its potential as a strategy by which one might work through the inability to mourn and come to assume one's place, in a conscious and creative way, in the cultural space of the post-Holocaust and the postmodern.

I

Even a cursory glance at Paul de Man's writings reveals a predominance of the rhetoric of bereavement which, as I have been arguing, informs postmodern theoretical discourses more generally. In Demanian discourse the entrance into the order of the signifier is always presented as a primal disaster or catastrophe. "Writing," says de Man, "always includes the moment of dispossession in favor of the arbitrary power play of the signifier and from the point of view of the subject, this can only be experienced as a dismemberment, a beheading or a castration."[26] The essentially bereft condition of the speaking subject points, for de Man, to a fundamental double bind that defines the linguistic condition: language, and in particular the tropological resources of language, is used to heal wounds that language never ceases to open up. For de Man it is as if language worked like the discourse of a liar trying to undo the effects of an initial, injurious lie. The liar (a male, let us assume) tries to talk his way out of these effects, tries to persuade his wounded interlocutor that harmony now prevails, but the more he speaks the more duplicitous and convoluted his story becomes. This pattern obtains even if there was no actual lie or if the liar was not conscious of having told a lie in the first place, for his discourse is governed by the paradoxical, Kafkaesque law, that, as soon as he begins to speak, his untruth and his guilt show themselves to have already been there. And indeed, to use language is to assume necessarily this "always already" guilty and bereft condition of the order of the signifier. As Derrida has said in the course of his own labor of mourning for de Man: "It will not surprise you when I say that all I have recently read and reread by Paul de Man seems to be traversed by an insistent reflection on mourning, a meditation in which bereaved memory is deeply engraved. Funerary speech and writing do not follow upon death; they work upon life in what we call autobiography."[27]

Put somewhat differently, de Man's critical practice represents an attempt to situate the study of literature, as poetics rather than aesthetics or hermeneutics, *beyond the pleasure principle*. "The aesthetic," de Man says, "is, by definition, a seductive notion that appeals to the pleasure principle." Poetics, on the other hand, is presented as a concern with language to the extent that it is radically, even violently, cut off from its semantic rootedness. Here the "sphinx" in Baudelaire's "Spleen (II)" figures as a cipher for the bereavement that grounds poetics in de Man's sense: "He is the grammatical subject cut off from its consciousness, the poetic analysis cut off from its hermeneutic function, the dismantling of the aesthetic and pictorial world . . . by the advent of poetry as allegory." Here poetry is "the dismemberment of the aesthetic whole into the unpredictable play of the literary letter."[28]

A somewhat less violent characterization of the bereavement from which poetry is born may be found in de Man's commentary on the practice of figuration in Rilke:

> On the level of poetic language this renunciation corresponds to the loss of a primacy of meaning located within the referent and it allows

> for the new rhetoric of Rilke's "figure." Rilke also calls this loss of
> referentiality by the ambivalent term of "inwardness" . . . which then
> does not designate the self-presence of a consciousness but the inevi-
> table absence of a reliable referent. It designates the impossibility for
> the language of poetry to appropriate anything, be it as conscious-
> ness, as object, or as a synthesis of both.[29]

In Demanian discourse the speaking subject is perpetually, constitu-
tionally, in mourning: for the referent, for beauty, for meaning, for
home, for stable terms of orientation, because these losses are always already there as soon as one uses language. As de Man has
said, "Death is a displaced name for a linguistic predicament."[30] The
speaking subject is, as it were, always "celebrating some funeral."[31]

The discovery in 1987 of some 180 articles, mostly book reviews,
interviews, notices of concerts, recitals, and other cultural events,
written by de Man between 1940 and 1942 for the Belgian collaborationist newspaper *Le Soir* and the Flemish-language journal *Het
Vlammsche Land*, has raised numerous questions regarding de Man's
later critical procedures in general and the prevalence of funerary
speech in his later writing in particular. I shall not concern myself
with detailed exegeses of de Man's wartime writings. Much of that
work has already been performed by Derrida in his response to
these discoveries, and there will be opportunity for more now that
the full set of those writings has been published.[32] I will assume that
there is no fundamental disagreement that in at least several pieces
from that period, despite certain ambiguities in formulation and
despite de Man's friendship with members of the Resistance and
with Jews, de Man openly contributed to and even celebrated the
cause of collaboration[33] and that in at least one piece, the most
notorious of the series, "The Jews in Contemporary Literature" (*Le
Soir*, March 4, 1941), de Man criticizes a vulgar form of anti-Semitism
only to give voice to a more refined version of the same racist ideology. In this piece de Man even suggests that "the creation of a
Jewish colony isolated from Europe would not entail, for the literary
life of the West, deplorable consequences." What interests me in the
present context is the relation between a past scarred by these
words, as few as they may be, and the subsequent writings of de
Man which are informed by an uncompromising elegiac rigor.

Many of those who have formally responded to these revelations
have suggested that de Man's mature writings in particular, and
deconstructions in general, be viewed precisely as an ongoing work

of mourning and conscience with respect to "one's" (i.e., Western civilization's) complicity with fascism and the Holocaust. Geoffrey Hartman, one of the first to respond at length to the revelations of de Man's wartime writings, raises the question whether de Man avoided the drama of a public personal confession in order instead to "work out his totalitarian temptation in a purely intellectual and impersonal manner."[34] This would certainly be plausible given the fact that, according to Hartman, deconstruction, as de Man taught and practiced it, "is surely a significant critique of German Idealism ('identity philosophy'), insofar as the latter resulted in various kinds of organicism, including fascism." Given this ongoing critique in the later work of the organicism that ostensibly contributed to the rhetorical foundations of fascism, Hartman notes, "it may yet turn out that in the later essays we glimpse the fragments of a great confession" and that the "postwar writings may constitute an avowal of error, a kind of repudiation in its very methodology of a philosophy of reading." Citing de Man's essay on Benjamin, Hartman even suggests that the radical critique of all forms of nostalgia which de Man elaborates there may be seen as a renunciation of solace in the face of the horror of the Holocaust, that is, as a rejection of any facile declarations of mourning and hope for new beginnings: "De Man does not mention the exceptional Nazi years, and that is an evasion; but he makes a general statement that to mourn the past as lost in order to guarantee ourselves an unencumbered future will not succeed. There cannot be, he suggests, a future that will not prove to have been a past like that." Still within the context of this association of de Man and Benjamin, Hartman concludes his own essay, however, on a note of hope:

> In light of what we now know, however, his work appears more and more as a deepening reflection on the rhetoric of totalitarianism. His turn from the politics of culture to the language of art was not an escape into, but an escape out of, aestheticism: a disenchantment with that fatal aestheticizing of politics, blatant in his own early articles, that gave fascism its false brilliance. De Man's critique of every tendency to totalize literature or language, to see unity where there is no unity, looks like a belated, but still powerful, act of conscience.[35]

Many of these same themes and interpretive strategies crop up in one of the most forceful and articulate responses from a German,

Werner Hamacher's essay "A Continuous Work of Mourning—Paul de Man's Complex Strategy."[36] Responding to polemical attacks on de Man by Jon Wiener and Frank Schirrmacher, Hamacher suggests that de Man's postwar career represents a deep and ongoing commitment to the work of mourning for the guilt of his—and Europe's—failure to resist the Holocaust. Citing a review, written three weeks after the first deportations of Jews from Belgium, of a poem entitled "The Massacre of the Innocents," Hamacher comments: "De Man never ceased to keep the consciousness of this guilt and its inexcusability alive. To excuse oneself with, say, the triumphant gesture of a conversion would only be a further accumulation of guilt in the face of that which can never be excused." Hamacher concludes: "De Man's mature work is a document of an immense labor of mourning. There are few who analyze the dangers of aesthetic totalitarianism and its political consequences with more dedication. There is hardly another body of work that more emphatically denies itself the comforts of moralism." De Man's work thus becomes exemplary for the postwar generations and perhaps, though Hamacher does not say so explicitly, for Germans in particular, since it represents precisely that "continuation of the work of mourning" that has been, as the Mitscherlichs argued, so wanting in German society.[37]

Certainly Jacques Derrida has produced the most detailed and compelling response produced to date. In his long, complex, and deeply emotional essay "Paul de Man's War," Derrida takes great pains to demonstrate that de Man's writings in collaborationist publications are, on closer examination, not nearly as damning as they seemed initially, and indeed, that they often exhibit an insolent, anticonformist tone that could be interpreted as an act of crypto-resistance against the prevailing vulgar forms of fascism and anti-Semitism. At the same time, Derrida insists that de Man broke, in the most radical way possible, with everything his wartime writings and activities represented. Meditating, for example, on why de Man never brought up the issue of his wartime activities, Derrida writes:

> He was aware of having never collaborated or called for collaboration with a Nazism that he never even named in his texts, of having never engaged in any criminal activity or even any organized political activity. . . . Therefore, to provoke spontaneously an explanation on this subject was no longer an obligation. It would have been, more-

over, an all the more distressing, pointlessly painful theatricalization
in that he had not only broken with the political context of 1940–42,
but had distanced himself from it with all his might, in his language,
his country, his profession, his private life.[38]

More interesting in the present context, however, is the way that,
according to Derrida, de Man performed this radical break with
"anything whatsoever that one might suspect in the ideology of the
texts" in question. The form that this rupture took was, beyond the
departure from Europe and, to use Derrida's phrase, "second birth"
in the United States, the very methodology of deconstruction(s): "To
put it in a word, deconstructions have always represented, as I see
it, the at least necessary condition for identifying and combating the
totalitarian risk" that is in question in these debates. In the end, de
Man turns out to be for Derrida the man who most radically resisted
the "terrifying desire for roots and common roots," that is, the regressive, narcissistic longings that contributed so much to the appeal of Nazism. The tireless process of deconstructing the potentially fascist desire for rootedness in the stability of a communally
authorized transcendental signified, which was de Man's life work,
allows Derrida to conclude: "He must have thought that well-tuned
ears knew how to hear him, and that he did not even need to
confide to anyone about the war in this regard. In fact, that is all he
talked about. That is all he wrote about."[39]

Much in these interpretations of the relationship between the early and the late de Man is insightful and compelling. De Man's work
resonates with a whole body of recent critical theory that appears
single-mindedly dedicated to the mournful/liberating labor of dismantling all of those narcissistically charged cultural constructions
that at some point always seem to want to assert their hegemony
over what is perceived as other: the *Volk*, the nation, the clean, the
healthy; but also: man, home, the self, being, and so on. The nomadic
deconstructor helps to transform the loss of these "dwellings," the
shattering of these narcissistic mirrors, into a new kind of habit and
habitation, a sort of postmodern humanism guided by an ironic imperative, the imperative to ironize. In this sense de Man's work in particular, and deconstructive practice more generally, might be viewed as
a strategy of assuming the double "post" of the postmodern and the
post-Holocaust. Or alternatively, the postmodern discourses of be-

reavement of which de Man's writings are in many ways exemplary, attempt to disarticulate the ideologies that provided the psychic bedrock of Nazism and that may, if not continuously deconstructed, serve as a support for future adventures in fascist politics. By teaching how to tolerate the instabilities of the postmodern, these discourses provide an antidote against the contagious appeals of such ideologies. In this sense they would indeed seem to offer a means of overcoming what the Mitscherlichs called the "inability to mourn."

I would, however, like to register certain reservations about the fundamental premise underlying the responses to the de Man revelations discussed thus far. Central to all of these texts is the notion that to attend to, and even in a certain sense to mourn, the death that de Man has explicitly identified as a fundamentally "linguistic predicament," is an adequate mode of coming to terms with one's complicity, however indirect or ambivalent, in a movement responsible for the extermination of millions. Before I can flesh out these reservations, however, I want to look more closely at what I have been calling the "work of mourning."

II

Taking my lead from the Mitscherlichs, the focus of my discussion has been the work of mourning that Freud associated with melancholy. In that process of *Trauerarbeit* it is not a matter of decathecting a lost love-object in accordance with the dictates of the pleasure principle but, rather, of performing a more primitive elegiac procedure whereby an infantile sense of omnipotence—primary narcissism— is fragmented by the realization that "I" and "you" have edges, that "you" have a life and a will that are irreducibly separate from my own. This focus on the more primitive elegiac labor underlying the constitution of the self corresponds with a fundamental shift of focus that has taken place in psychoanalytic theory and practice over the last half-century. This shift, which may be found in the work of a number of neo-Freudian analysts—for example, Lacan, Kohut, and Winnicott—points to a fundamental displacement of concerns since Freud: from the fate of the drives to the vicissitudes of the self, from narratives of libido to the text of desire, from structural conflicts to the whole range of borderline and narcissistic character disorders.

This displacement of paradigms comes in part as an answer to transformations in the the clinical data brought to analysts and therapists
in recent years.[40] That disorders that have to do with unresolved
narcissisms have come to be the most common cause of the suffering
therapists and analysts now see has caused psychoanalytic theory to
shift its focus to those primal scenes *beyond the pleasure principle* in
which a self begins to take shape around its first confrontations with
death and loss.

The most famous presentation of elegiac procedures beyond the
pleasure principle is, no doubt, Freud's discussion of the *fort/da*
("gone"/"here") game that he had observed in the behavior of his
one-and-a-half-year-old grandson. In this game the child is seen to
master his grief over separation from the mother by staging his own
performance of disappearance and return with props that D. W.
Winnicott would call "transitional objects." Bereft by the mother's
absence, and more generally by the dawning awareness that the
interval between himself and his mother opens up a whole range of
unpredictable and potentially treacherous possibilities, he reenacts
the opening of that abyssmal interval within the controlled space of
a primitive ritual. The child is translating, as it were, his fragmented
narcissism into the formalized rhythms of symbolic behavior; thanks
to this procedure, he is able to administer in controlled doses the
absence he is mourning. The capacity to dose out and to represent
absence by means of substitutive figures at a remove from what one
might call their "transcendental signified," is what allows the child
to transform his lost omnipotence into a form of empowerment.
This empowerment is called creativity; it is the capacity for play, for
symbolic behavior in accordance with rules and forms. As Julia
Kristeva has said of literary creation in general:

> Literary creation is that adventure of body and signs that bears wit-
> ness to the affect: to sadness as the mark of separation and the begin-
> nings of the dimension of the symbol, to joy as the mark of triumph,
> placing me in that universe of artifice and symbol which I try to make
> correspond, as best as I can, to my experiences of reality. But this
> testimony is one produced by literary creation in a medium entirely
> different from that of mood, the affect being transposed into rhythms,
> signs, forms.[41]

The dosing out of a certain negative—a thanatotic[42]—element as a
strategy of mastering a real and traumatic loss, is a fundamentally

homeopathic procedure. In a homeopathic procedure the controlled introduction of a negative element—a symbolic or, in medical contexts, real poison—helps to heal a system infected by a similar poisonous substance. The poison becomes a cure by empowering the individual to master the potentially traumatic effects of large doses of the morphologically related poison.[43] In the *fort/da* game it is the rhythmic manipulation of signifiers and figures, objects and syllables representing an absence, that serves as the poison that cures. These signifiers are controlled symbolic doses of absence and renunciation which help the child to survive the negativity of the mother's absence, this first, provisional face of death. As Angus Fletcher has described such a procedure—Fletcher's precursor texts are Frazer's *Golden Bough* and Freud's *Totem and Taboo*—homeopathic or "imitative magic tries to bring real events which the magician wants to control into parallel with symbolic events. The latter are under his direct control."[44]

The homeopathic nature of this primal work of mourning becomes increasingly evident in the oedipal stage, the next strophe in the elegiac text which helps to constitute the self as a member of a symbolic order. (To speak of oedipal scenarios is, of course, to remain within the terms of a patriarchal symbolic order and, perhaps, to address primarily, though I hope not exclusively, the experience of the male child.) In the oedipal drama the child must transform the triangulation of his dyadic relation to the mother into a source of empowerment. This triangulation or partial eclipse of the mother, which already begins with the pre-oedipal awareness of the interval between self and other, here and there, now and then, is now embodied by the father. The homeopathic "poison" that helps facilitate the transmutation of (oedipal) triangulation into empowerment was conceived by Freud as symbolic castration. In his elegant study of the poetics of mourning in the English elegy, a work to which my own thinking on these matters is much indebted, Peter Sacks has remarked on this stage of the homeopathic procedure of self-constitution:

> Henceforth the child's sexual satisfactions and choices of love-objects will necessarily take the form of substitutes for his original desire. He will have to recognize that his sexual power is strictly limited: he cannot *be* the physical object capable of satisfying the desires of his mother, nor can he sexually return to his earlier state of union with his

21

origins. Instead, he now comes to *possess* a castrated, figurative version of such an object or power—the phallus.[45]

Corresponding to this act of renunciation on the part of the child is a symbolic transmutation of the father into a figure or totem, that is, into a symbolic legacy that, if successfully integrated, empowers the child to have a future of his own. Indeed, the necessity of having a future of one's own, of assuming this temporal noncoincidence of self with self, is what protects the child from the regressive desire to merge with the mother. The child reiterates, as unconscious symbolic procedure, the "totem meal" that for Freud in turn commemorates the primordial crime of the father-murder with which civilization took its mythic beginnings. In Juliet Mitchell's words, "In submitting to the completely unreal possibility of castration the little boy acknowledges the situation [unfulfillable desire] and learns that one day he, too, will accede to the father's function. He pays thereby his symbolic debt to the father he has murdered in his rivalrous thoughts."[46] By means of the homeopathy of symbolic castration, the child works at transmuting the desire for presence and possession into a capacity to assume particular subject positions in a symbolic order. (To assume a subject position does not preclude one's desire and, ideally, ability to influence the opportunities it affords and the constraints it imposes; the availability of such influence is, of course, a political matter.)

Numerous examples of the homeopathic pattern of mourning exist in the texts of ancient mythology. One thinks, for example, of the story of Apollo and Daphne in which the object of desire is transformed into the laurel tree from which the god then cuts and fashions a wreath. This construction of a figure or trope bearing the traces of the lost object displaces the desire for possession into a realm of material and formal laws, a realm of play or art. The cutting of the tree together with the weaving of the wreath out of the severed leaves represents an ambivalent troping or turning from the organic matrix into a transitional space organized by the unnatural codes of the Symbolic. The partial "demotivation" of the figure of consolation—its capacity to be exchanged and grafted—is what allows it to become a sign or title of power and vocation: the floating signifier of a legacy. Recall also that it is Peneus, Daphne's father, who, at his daughter's behest, performs the metamorphosis that triangulates the god's desire for possession at the same time that it endows him with the legacy that will help him to master his loss. The story of mourning, in its most primitive form as a drama of self-constitution and as one of self-reconstitution in the face of mortal loss in later life, comes full circle by describing a triangle.

A similar, homeopathically patterned performance of mourning is enacted in Pan's invention of the pipes out of the reeds into which Syrinx had been transformed by her sisters. This story, as Sacks notes, offers a rich portrayal of "one of the most profound issues to beset any mourner," namely "his surviving yet painfully altered sexuality":

> In the story of Pan's invention of the pipes, we have a clear example of how the sexual impulse is continued yet displaced onto a symbol of itself, and onto an instrument for assuaging the sorrow of that displacement. Granted, the pipe or the flute is appropriate to mourning, for it joins a sighing breath to hollowness. At the same time, its phallic nature is obvious, and it is far from arbitrary that the goatlike Pan, associated with Priapus, should be the one to invent this woeful, reedlike intrument; or that he, together with the flute's blend of plaintiveness and oblique sexuality, should be so integral to the elegy.[47]

In each of these mythological performances of "consolatory figuration"[48] the cutting and subsequent shaping of an organic material—its transformation, in other words, into a medium of art—empowers the mourner to survive his loss. In both cases the mourner inherits the power and title of singer and poet. Commenting on the parallels between these ancient tales of successful mourning and patterns of oedipal resolution, Sacks remarks:

> At the core of each procedure is the renunciatory experience of loss and the acceptance, not just of a substitute, but of the very means and practice of substitution. In each case such an acceptance is the price of survival; and in each case a successful resolution is not merely deprivatory, but offers a form of compensatory reward. The elegist's reward, especially, resembles or augments that of the child—both involve inherited legacies and consoling identifications with symbolic, even immortal, figures of power.[49]

The self constitutes itself by homeopathically integrating the loss of its narcissistic fantasies of centrality and omnipotence. By learning to engage in symbolic behavior at a distance from the self through play and through identification with figures of power—totems—the child is able to survive loss and to discover new possibilities and satisfactions of a life in the symbolic order.[50] I have, however, left out what I take to be the essential element that allows these primal scenes of loss and mourning to help consolidate a cohesive and vital self, a self that, when faced with mortal loss, will be able to reenact these elegiac procedures successfully rather than fall into a pathological melancholy. The homeopathic constitution (and reconstitution) of the self takes place not in a vacuum but always in a particular social context. Indeed, the administration of the homeopathic poison/remedy might be said to lead to pathology rather than the consolidation of self-structure if the environment in which this procedure takes place is unempathic to the complex experience of the mourner. In each case the particular "social formation" in which the mourner finds himself safeguards or blocks the transmutation of poison to cure in the homeopathic labor of mourning.

Already in Freud's own account of psychic instances beyond the pleasure principle one finds indications of the importance of the intersubjective context for the mourning process. Freud gives two examples of behavior that suggested the existence of psychological needs more primitive than the attainment of pleasure: the *fort/da* game of his grandson discussed earlier, and the behavior of *Unfallsneurotiker*, individuals who have experienced and then repressed some trauma but return to it over and over again in their dreams. Freud sees in both cases efforts to master shock by symbolic means: in the case of the child, with play; in that of the trauma victim, with dreams. Regarding such dreams, Freud says,

> We may assume . . . that dreams are here helping to carry out another task, which must be accomplished before the dominance of the pleasure principle can even begin. These dreams are endeavouring to master the stimulus retrospectively, by developing the anxiety whose omission was the cause of the traumatic neurosis. They thus afford us a view of a function of the mental apparatus which, though it does not contradict the pleasure principle, is nevertheless independent of it and seems to be more primitive than the purpose of gaining pleasure and avoiding unpleasure.[51]

Given the homologies Freud underlined between the symptoms of the trauma victim and the symbolic behavior of the child at play, it becomes clear that these other, more primitive psychic tasks are the tasks of mourning that serve to constitute the self and that must, at some level, be reiterated with all later experiences of loss or trauma-tic shock (Freud was thinking here of the great number of trau-matized soldiers returning from World War I). Both the child trying to master separateness from the mother and the trauma victim re-turning, in dream, to the site of a shock, are locked in a repetition compulsion: an effort to recuperate, in the controlled context of symbolic behavior, the *Angstbereitschaft* or readiness to feel anxiety, absent during the initial shock or loss. It was Freud's thought that the absence of appropriate affect—anxiety—is what leads to trau-matization rather than loss per se. This affect can, however, be recuperated only in the presence of an empathic witness. In the case of the child playing *fort/da* it is the parent/observer, and in that of the trauma victim the empathic analyst, who co-constitute the space in which loss may come to be symbolically and affectively mastered. Homeopathy without appropriate affect becomes a purely mechan-ical procedure that can never lead to empowerment; without a social space in which this affect can be recuperated, the homeopathic oper-ation becomes a sort of elegiac loop that must repeat itself endlessly.

Winnicott, to whose theory of transitional objects I have already alluded, has similarly stressed the importance of the intersubjective context for the successful working through of the decenteredness that inaugurates the drama of human subjectivity. According to Winnicott, the child is able to make use of transitional objects— those first elegiac tokens that accompany his passionate journey out of a world of continuity into one of contiguity—only insofar as he senses that his play is witnessed by the figure whose separateness he is coming to master:

> As is well known, when the mother or some other person on whom the infant depends is absent, there is no immediate change owing to the fact that the infant has a memory or mental image of the mother, or what we call an internal representation of her, which remains alive for a certain length of time. If the mother is away over a period of time which is beyond a certain limit . . . then the memory or the internal representation fades. As this takes effect, the transitional phenomena become gradually meaningless and the infant is unable to experience them. We may watch the object becoming decathected. Just before loss we can sometimes see the exaggeration of the use of a transitional ob-ject as part of *denial* that there is a threat of its becoming meaningless.[52]

25

Or as Winnicott says elsewhere: "the mental representation in the inner world is kept significant . . . by the reinforcement given through the availability of the external separated-off and actual mother, along with her techniques of child care."[53] The evacuation of meaning from a transitional object may be thought of as a signification trauma, the moment when a transitional object becomes a stranded object thereby destroying the "baby's capacity to use the symbol of the union." In the wake of a traumatic withdrawal on the part of the mother, the infant at play begins to look more like Dürer's allegorical figure of Melancholia surrounded by stranded props and artifacts. This sort of traumatic deprivation is what Winnicott calls madness. "Madness here simply means a *break-up* of whatever may exist at the time of *a personal continuity of existence.*"[54]

Short of traumatic crisis there are the countless examples of "localized spoiling"[55] which are necessary for the child's consolidation of self-structure. It is precisely these localized disruptions of the dyadic relation between mother and child that make play both *necessary*—this is bereavement—and *possible*—this is potential empowerment; in order for the third modality to function, that is, for the potential space of play to feel *real*, a "good enough" facilitating environment must be available. One might summarize these points by way of an aphorism: Mourning without solidarity is the beginning of madness.[56]

III

In conclusion, I would like to return to the reservations I registered about the claim that Paul de Man's mature writings—and the practice of deconstruction more generally—could and should be understood as an extended work of mourning with regard to the narcissisms that otherwise inhibit people's capacities to assume postmodern, post-Holocaust selves. It should now be obvious that de Man's writings do in fact deploy elegiac procedures in their elaboration of a methodology of reading. Much of what de Man has said, for example, about the "task of the translator" in his paper on Benjamin's essay of the same name, corresponds with my presentation of the work of mourning. In de Man's reading of the Benjamin essay, the "task" (*Aufgabe*) of translation succeeds precisely according to the logic of a certain loss or failure (*Aufgabe* in the sense of *aufgeben*).[57] Translation, just like mourning, completes its circuit by way of an interruption. Furthermore, every translation, and for that matter all intralinguistic activities, including critical philosophy, literary theory, and history, exhibit, according to de Man, a pattern remarkably similar to the process of totemization which figures so centrally in the work of mourning. These activities repeat, in essence, the totem meal which is a necessary component in the homeopathy of symbolic castration (the name-of-the-father is, in other words, always in some sense the dead father, the father as figure):

> They disarticulate, they undo the original, they reveal that the original was always already disarticulated. They reveal that their failure, which seems to be due to the fact that they are secondary in relation to the original, reveals an essential failure, an essential disarticulation which was already there in the original. They kill the original, by discovering that the original was already dead.[58]

But for all that de Man rehearses over and over again the procedures of *Trauerarbeit* and institutes them as a paradigm of translation, reading, and being (a speaking subject), he vehemently denies that any of this has anything at all to do with human grief, pain, or survival, with the community of human subjects and their particular, concrete stories and histories. De Man is quite explicit about this. Commenting on the expressions *"jene Nachreife des fremden Wortes"* and *"die Wehen des eigenen"* in Benjamin's essay, de Man says the following: "It [*Nachreife*] has the melancholy, the feeling of slight exhaustion, of life to which you are not entitled, happiness to which you are not entitled, time has passed, and so on. It is associated with another word that Benjamin constantly uses, the word *überleben*, to live, beyond your own death in a sense."[59] De Man continues his commentary by insisting, against the evidence of German morphology, that "death pangs" would be a more accurate translation of *Wehen* than "birth pangs." But what is one to make of this "melancholy," of these "death pangs"? What sort of affect is being invoked here? "It is easy," de Man tells us,

> to say to some extent what this suffering is not. It is certainly not subjective pains, some kind of pathos of a self, a kind of manifestation of a self-pathos which the poet would have expressed as his sufferings. This is certainly not the case, because, says Benjamin, the suffer-

27

ings that are here being mentioned are not in any sense human. . . . This suffering is also not a kind of historical pathos . . . ; it is not this pathos of remembrance, or this pathetic mixture of hope and catastrophe . . . which is present certainly in Benjamin's tone, but not so much in what he says. It is not the pathos of a history, it is not the pathos of what in Hölderlin is called the "dürftiger Zeit" between the disappearance of the gods and the possible return of the gods. It is not this kind of sacrificial, dialectical, and elegiac gesture, by means of which one looks back on the past as a period that is lost, which then gives you the hope of another future that may occur.

It is not any of these things because, as de Man says, "The reasons for this pathos, for this *Wehen*, for this suffering, are specifically linguistic." De Man reiterates this point in even more emphatic terms in response to a query:

What is precisely interesting, I think . . . is that Benjamin's language of pathos, language of historical pathos, language of the messianic, the pathos of exile and so on and so forth, really describes linguistic events which are by no means human. So that what he calls the pains of the original become structural deficiencies which are best analyzed in terms of the inhuman, dehumanized language of linguistics, rather than into the language of imagery, or tropes, of pathos, or drama, which he chooses to use in a very peculiar way.[60]

De Man's rigorously a-pathetic discourse exemplifies here a dilemma alluded to above with regard to the intersubjective dimensions of the tasks of mourning. Performance of the homeopathic procedures of *Trauerarbeit* requires, if it is not to lead to a pathological fragmentation of self-structure, the space of a "good enough" empathic environment. Mourning, if it is not to become entrapped in the desperate inertia of a double bind, if it is to become integrated into a history, must be witnessed. To repeat an earlier formulation, mourning without solidarity is the beginning of madness. By insisting that the "interpersonal rapport" is illegitimate, "since there is, in a very radical sense no such thing as the human,"[61] de Man seems to privilege this madness as the truth of literature. In the absence of the solidarity afforded by the empathic witness, suffering will no doubt always be felt to be unreal, even inhuman, dissociated from the drama of human subjectivity. Depleted of affect, unfolding in the polar stillness of an exquisite isolation, mourning can never be anything but a repetitive looping through the abstract procedures of so many purely structural operations.[62] De Man's discourse might be said to enact a shattering of narcissistic illusions by strategically deploying what at first glance appears to be the most extreme alternative to narcissism: the instabilities of schizophrenia. If narcissism is selfhood at the price of flexibility and play, this discourse of the radically decentered subject teaches play at the cost of selfhood. These are, however, two sides of a single double bind.[63]

But something else happens as well in this radical dissociation and abstraction of mourning from lived human experience. By turning death into a purely linguistic operation, de Man precludes the possibility of distinguishing one victim from any other. Furthermore, the historical victim—the victim of this or that moral shortcoming or failure in the realm of empirical decisions and politics—is overshadowed here by an impersonal and apathetic "dismemberment" at the violent hands of the signifier; to be a victim of history is, in the end, to be a victim of a "purely . . . linguistic complication."[64]

Insofar as deconstruction as practiced by de Man and others privileges a heroism of an abstract mode of bereavement—let me call it a heroism of the elegiac loop—it cannot be considered an adequate response to an earlier complicity, however "abstract" it may have been, in German fascism's hegemony over Europe and all that that entailed. The error of Paul de Man in this historical series was, I suggest, that he sought to *displace* and *disperse* the particular, historical tasks of mourning which for him, as is now known, were substantial and complex, with what might be called structural mourning, that is, mourning for those "catastrophes" that are inseparable from being-in-language. And since so much recent critical theory has followed de Man's lead in reducing historical suffering and catastrophe to a series of structural operations depleted of affect—the appeal to human subjectivity is taken as a sign of lack of rigor, nostalgia, sentimentality—the error of Paul de Man, despite the very particular features of his history, becomes exemplary. The more difficult labor would have been, of course, openly and explicitly to *sediment* these tasks of mourning, to explore the ways in which they might, in the long run, mutually enlighten one another. Much of that work has now been initiated in the various responses to the de Man affair summarized above. Indeed, the rest of my study is intended as an exploration of this very layering or sedimentation of mourning tasks. And in this work I cannot dispense with what Paul de Man has taught in his mature writings about what it means to be a speaking subject, to be in mourning in the structural ways he has elaborated.

Before going on, I would finally like to touch on one more question that has been raised by the de Man case. How, in all of this, have de Man's "heirs" dealt with the bereavement represented by the revelation of his wartime writings? This is a rather important question in the present context, since the discovery of de Man's contributions to collaborationist newspapers places his heirs, many of whom are Jewish academics and intellectuals, in a situation not unlike that of the second and third generation of Germans who are faced with the task of assuming a similarly ambivalent legacy. As I have noted, the construction of a viable, empowering legacy is one of the most important tasks in the mourning process. In what sense is de Man still available for idealization, still a "totemic" resource? That this question has been, and continues to be, crucial in this story, may be gleaned from statements such as Jonathan Culler's remarks regarding journalists who have commented on the de Man affair: "Their innuendoes have cast a shadow over his later work, as if the criticism de Man wrote in America from 1953 to his death in 1983 was somehow tainted"; or Jacques Derrida's categorical declaration: "Paul de Man's legacy is not poisoned, or in any case no more than the best legacies are if there is no such thing as a legacy without some venom."[65] Things are quite a bit more complicated than that.

In the following chapters I shall explore such complications as they afflict the second and third generations in Germany in their efforts to work through the intense ambivalences that they face as heirs to a much tainted, much poisoned legacy. Perhaps, finally, there is also something to learn here with respect to what it could now mean to assume the legacy of Paul de Man.

2

Germany and the Tasks of Mourning in the Second and Third Generations

In chapter 1, I attempted to rewrite the Mitscherlichs' thesis of the "inability to mourn" from a perspective informed by postmodern theorizations of marginality and difference. Such a revision illustrates just how much recent critical theory has been engaged in labors of mourning with respect to structures of thought and behavior—call them logocentric, phallocentric, onto-theological—which were, as many have come to suspect, complicitous in the "successes" of German fascism. By expanding the range of the thesis in this way, I am claiming that the inability to mourn cannot be understood simply as a function of, to use the Mitscherlichs' words, a "German way of loving" (it will not do, in other words, to turn the inability to mourn into a psychoanalytic *Sonderweg*-thesis). Furthermore, such a revision deepens the reach of the Mitscherlichs' thesis and fills in some of the structural detail that their theory, which is caught up in a discourse of instincts, fails to articulate. For as I have argued, when one broaches issues of mourning and melancholy one enters into a realm of psychic mechanisms beyond the pleasure principle which have to do not so much with the economy of drives as with the constitution of the self. As the case of Paul de Man illustrates, there are dangers embedded in this postmodern revision of a thesis that was addressed to a very concrete historical situation. By broadening and deepening the scope of the Mitscherlichs' thesis, I also run the risk of dispersing some of the critical import of their analysis of postwar political culture in Germany; by universalizing key terms of their analysis—most important, *catastrophe* and *victim*—I may end up dehistoricizing the issues at hand and absorbing the horror of the Shoah into the ostensible violence of a universal linguistic operation. By turning my focus to political and film culture in contemporary German society, I hope to show that a reading of the Mitscherlichs informed by a more postmodern awareness of questions of alterity and marginality cannot only avoid such consequences but, even more, provide a guide to understanding the core issues that preoccupy the political unconscious of German society at the present historical moment.

Before beginning, it is necessary to consider carefully how applicable the terms of the discussion are some twenty years after the initial publication of the thesis of the "inability to mourn." Here it is useful to recall the double-edged character of the tasks of mourning in postwar German society. In order to mourn for the victims of National Socialism, the Mitscherlichs claimed, the population of the new Federal Republic (and again, it is for pragmatic reasons only that I limit myself to this case) would first have to work through the more primitive narcissistic injury represented by the traumatic shattering of the specular, imaginary relations that had provided the sociopsychological foundations of German fascism. According to the Mitscherlichs, Nazism had promised a so-called utopian world in which alterity in its multiple forms and dimensions could be experienced as a dangerous Semitic supplement that one was free to push to the margins and finally to destroy. This was a utopia in which a mature self could never really develop. For the complex entity called the human self constitutes itself precisely by relinquishing its narcissistic position and mournfully, and perhaps even playfully, assuming its place in an expanded field of relations and relationality in which "I" and "you," "here" and "there," "now" and "then," signifiers and signifieds, have boundaries, that is, are discontinuous. It is this passage from a realm of continuity into one of contiguities that signals the advent of the uncanny—the *unheimlich*—in human experience. There could be, the Mitscherlichs argued, no real mourning for the victims of Nazism, no genuine perception of the full magnitude of human suffering caused in the name of the *Volksgemeinschaft*, until this more primitive labor of mourning—the mastery of the capacity to say "we" nonnarcissistically, the integration of the *unheimlich* into the first person plural—had been achieved.

By focusing in this way on issues of mourning, I have not intended to reduce a complex historical phenomenon to a series of psychological events and processes. Nazism was certainly more than simply a social machinery for producing individual and group identities. It was, however, at this deep level of identity formation that Nazism was able to exert its most powerful appeal in its mobilization of the population, that the particular modes of address it deployed found their deepest resonances. Not only is this the level at which Nazism achieved some of its more remarkable "successes"; it is also, as Saul Friedländer notes, the level at which it continues to fascinate the postwar generations. (One is reminded here of Philipp Jenninger's later rather uncritical and perhaps vaguely nostalgic allusion to this fascination.) This fascination has, according to Friedländer, generated a "new discourse on Nazism" which organizes itself around the same phantasms, the same seductive modes of address, that proved so powerful during the Third Reich (examples of the new discourse discussed by Friedländer include Michel Tournier's novel *The Ogre*, Joachim Fest's film *Hitler, A Career*, Fassbinder's *Lili Marleen*, George Steiner's *The Portage to San Cristobal of A.H.*, Visconti's *The Damned*, and the film that is the focus of chapter 4, Syberberg's *Our Hitler*). It is at these deep levels of fantasy production and reception so important in the constitution of individual and collective identities that one can begin to explore essential aspects of German fascism (as well as its afterlife in the imaginations of the second and third generations) which remain inaccessible to purely political and socio-economic analyses. As Friedländer has noted, once one moves beyond these other modes of inquiry,

> that leaves the psychological dimension, which, being autonomous, followed its own course. It did not rest on complex arguments nor sometimes on very clear ideological positions. . . . Nazism's attraction lay less in any explicit ideology than in the power of emotions, images, and phantasms. Both left and right were susceptible to them. . . . It seems logical, therefore, to suppose, a priori, that a new discourse on Nazism will develop at the same level of phantasms, images, and emotions. More than ideological categories, it is a matter of rediscovering the durability of these deep-seated images, the structure of these phantasms common to both right and left.[1]

33

In my view the deep structure of these phantasms may best be understood not so much in light of that peculiar admixture of kitsch and death which is the focus of Friedländer's analysis of Nazi phantasmagoria and the "new discourse on Nazism" but, rather, as a matter of blocked or circumvented mourning. And once again I am using the term *mourning* first and foremost to identify those psychic procedures that, in Christa Wolf's words, lay the "patterns of childhood" and thereby ground people's capacity (or incapacity) to tolerate difference and otherness.[2]

In her most recent evaluation of the current state of political culture in West Germany, Margarete Mitscherlich has reiterated the centrality of the psychological dimension in general and the question of mourning in particular for any understanding of the generations born during and after the Nazi period. These generations, born too late to become complicitous in the crimes of Nazism, can still be understood, according to Mitscherlich, in terms of an inability to mourn:

> Since the publication of *The Inability to Mourn*, much has changed in the political landscape of Germany. It is doubtful, however, whether our collective attitude toward the unmastered core of our past has been affected by these transformations. And that is because the working through of the foundations of National Socialism—each individual's involvement in the movement, his or her emotional and spiritual identification with this period—has not yet been achieved. Even those in their twenties today, whose parents passed along their own defenses against the past, continue to live in the shadow of the denial and repression of events that cannot be undone by acts of forgetting.[3]

The postwar generations have in this view inherited not guilt so much as the denial of guilt, not losses so much as lost opportunities to mourn losses. But perhaps more important, along with this negative legacy of denial and repression postwar generations have inherited the psychic structures that impeded mourning in the generations of their parents and grandparents. Foremost among such structures is a thinking in rigid binary oppositions, which forms the sociopsychological basis of all searches for scapegoats. As Margarete Mitscherlich has said in another context,

> You can prohibit Nazi symbols and Nazi organizations; but without a labor of mourning you cannot exorcise *Nazi structures* from the realms

of education and politics, from behavior, from modes of thinking and interpersonal communication. And it is for this reason that we must acknowledge that the younger generation, which feels itself to be innocent, has inherited not a past that has been worked through, but rather its denial and repression.[4]

These remarks suggest that the legacies—or perhaps more accurately: the ghosts, the revenant objects—of the Nazi period are transmitted to the second and third generations at the sites of the primal scenes of socialization, that is, within the context of a certain psychopathology of the postwar family. The postwar generations face the complex task of constituting stable self-identities by way of identifications with parents and grandparents who, in the worst possible cases, may have been directly implicated in crimes of unspeakable dimensions, thereby radically impeding their totemic availability. But even where direct culpability is absent, these elders are individuals whose own self-structures are likely to have been made rigid by a persistent core of repressed melancholy as well as the intense aggressions associated with unmourned narcissistic injuries, namely, the sudden and radical disenchantment of Nazi phantasms. Furthermore, the second and third generations face the task of saying "we" in the knowledge that the social mechanisms and rituals in and through which the signification of this "we" was stabilized in the generation of the elders had catastrophic consequences that continue to resonate in that little pronoun.

There have been extensive studies of the effects of the Holocaust experience on the children of survivors; only in recent years, however, have the effects of the psychic legacy of the Nazi period on the children of the perpetrators begun to be articulated. In one such effort, a series of case studies of the second generation of the perpetrators published in the context of a larger work concerned primarily with the children of Holocaust survivors, remarkable similarities were discovered between the case histories of the children of the oppressed and those of the oppressors. Of particular significance was the responsibility felt, at least by those members of the second generation who sought treatment, to perform the psychic labors of their parents:

The children of both persecutor and persecuted felt called upon to repair the fatal events in the histories of their parents. Since they were burdened with a task stemming from a past reality that was incomprehensible to them they could only act out what had been engraved, but not integrated, in their parents' memories. Thus, a second reality was actualized in the present reality of these children, but they had no insight into its points of reference.[5]

Beginning in the late seventies, a number of German authors began a much belated process of coming to terms with these unintegrated phantoms. These efforts typically took the form of a reconstruction of the father's biography. This biography or literary obituary—in most cases the father was already dead—was woven together with an autobiographical narrative that registered the wounds inflicted on the psyches of the author by the father. Examples of such texts, which together might constitute a subcategory of the new discourse analysed by Friedländer, are: Paul Kersten's *Der alltägliche Tod meines Vaters* (The everyday death of my father; 1978); Ruth Rehmann's *Der Mann auf der Kanzel: Fragen an einen Vater* (The man in the pulpit: Questions for a father; 1979); Sigfrid Gauch's *Vaterspuren* (Traces of a father; 1979); Heinrich Wiesner's *Der Riese am Tisch* (The giant at the table; 1979); Peter Härtling's *Nachgetragene Liebe* (Love in the aftermath; 1980); Christoph Meckel's *Suchbild: Über meinen Vater* (Image for investigation about my father; 1980); Brigitte Schwaiger's *Lange Abwesenheit* (Long absence; 1983); Ludwig Harig's *Ordnung ist das ganze Leben: Roman meines Vaters* (Order is the essence of life: Novel of my father; 1985).[6] In a brilliant analysis of this new genre of *Vater-Literatur*, Michael Schneider proposes Hamlet as the negative patron saint of these authors and indeed of the second generation more generally, especially those members of this generation who participated in the student movement in the late sixties only to fall into the melancholy, passivity, and so-called New Subjectivity of the seventies.[7] Hamlet is so suggestive in the present context because his saturnine disposition clearly derives from blocked mourning. The corrupt familial and political constellation in which Hamlet finds himself offers little opportunity to pass beyond the mere "trappings and . . . suits of woe" (1.2.86); in this world of "maimed rites" Hamlet indeed seems destined to remain captive to an elegiac loop, always hovering between murder and suicide.[8]

The situation of the postwar generations in Germany is, however, rather more complex than that of Shakespeare's melancholic Dane. As these literary biographies suggest, the second generation bears deep psychological wounds left by elders whose own inability to work through the radical disenchantment of narcissistic phantasms predisposed them to seeing their progeny primarily as a resource for the reparation of their depleted sense of self. For these traumatized parents, the family became the primary site where a damaged self could be refurbished, could be respecularized under the mirroring gazes of spouse and offspring. That is, the family was used as a sort of looking glass that would magically make one whole again, give oneself back to oneself, if only as an image. In this way the second generation was blackmailed into complicity with the parents' inability to mourn. As a result of this complicity, which was, after all, the price of emotional survival in such families, these members of the second generation inherited the melancholy that their parents had managed to hold in abeyance by way of a variety of defense mechanisms (these mechanisms were analyzed in detail by the Mitscherlichs in their 1967 study). Schneider characterizes this cultural transmission of psychopathology in the following way:

> The depressive disposition and the high incidence of suicide within the "second lost generation" . . . would lead us to conclude that the post-war generation identified less with the . . . pathos of the reconstruction generation than they did with the latent emotions of that generation, i.e. with the concealed, unspoken, un-"lived-out" and apocryphal side of their sense of self. In a sort of unconscious displacement, the post-war generation appropriated those feelings of melancholy, resignation, and depression which the older generation, in an act of self-preservation, had denied itself, by repressing them through the heroic reconstruction effort.[9]

One of the cruel ironies of this legacy was, as I have already suggested, that the second generation inherited not only the unmourned traumas of the parents but also the psychic structures that impeded mourning in the older generation in the first place. That is, since so many members of the second generation never really had access to the full attention and care of their parents, who were expending enormous amounts of psychic energy to ward off melancholy (these were parents who were, psychologically speaking, always elsewhere), their own psychological growth has in large measure been disrupted. They have tended, as Schneider notes, to fixate on their parents to a remarkable degree. This fixation is the flip side of a "depressive self-obsession," a state of melancholy "which can be attributed less to a sense of sorrow that something has been lost than to an existential feeling that something is missing—a sense of disappointment over something which was never received."[10] And as the history of the parents illustrates, such a condition can heighten people's vulnerability to anxiety in the face of alterity and thereby provide fertile ground for unrealistic and absolutist longings for security, community, and intimacy. Postwar generations in Germany may be predisposed to respond to new postmodern uncertainties and disorientations in the same ways—according to the same "patterns of childhood"—that their elders responded to the economic and political instabilities of the twenties and thirties.

Another recent contribution to the literature on the second and third generations has confirmed many of the suspicions I have aired here regarding the psychological dilemmas facing these generations. It is a series of interviews with children and grandchildren of some prominent as well as some quite "ordinary" Nazis, conducted and edited by the Austrian journalist Peter Sichrovsky.[11]

I

These interviews depict a striking variety of ways in which a legacy of unmourned trauma has cast a shadow over these representatives of the second and third generation. Among the interviewees were those who defended, others who tried to relativize the deeds of their parents; still others refused to consider their parents outside the familial contexts in which they directly experienced them, thereby reinscribing the radical split between the private and the public so characteristic of the Nazi period; and still others were locked in the seemingly endless labor of living out an extended disavowal of their parents, becoming in some ways their mirror image, reversed yet remarkably similar and thoroughly entangled with them and their fate.

Within this wide spectrum of responses, Sichrovsky discovered certain unifying themes and motifs. One of the most striking patterns to emerge from the interviews was that as children the second generation experienced their parents for the most part as victims: "Fleeing advancing armies, bombed out, homeless and unemployed, hidden from the Allied police, arrested and jailed, these parents are remembered by their children as victims of the war, as victims of a lost war" (7). This pattern would typically correct itself in adolescence, that is, once the children had reached an age at which they could understand just what their parents' experience had in fact been. It was then that they began to experience themselves as tragic victims of their own families and familial histories: "Many of the people I interviewed saw themselves in that light, as the victims of a mentality which, even though the war had been lost, fostered a fascistic attitude in the home" (7–8). Occasionally an interviewee would claim a privileged status within a hierarchy of victimization and suffering vis-à-vis Sichrovsky, the son of Austrian Jewish refugees:

> Most of the time they tried to explain to me that because of my relationship to my parents, which undoubtedly was different from theirs, I could not understand what growing up with Nazi parents was like. Occasionally this took the form of almost aggressive attacks and accusations that in my situation, despite the sufferings of my family, I had had an easier time of it than they, the sons and daughters of murderers. I had to agree. The crucial difference between the children of victims and the children of perpetrators is that the former do not have to live with the fear and suspicions of what their parents had done during the war. (12)

These interviews provide a good sampling of voices from the second and third generation. Sichrovsky describes, for example, the case of the thirty-nine-year-old Anna, daughter of a former guard in a death camp; when as a child she finally asks her father why he had been questioned by the authorities, she is met by paranoia, rage, and self-pity on the part of her parents:

> They stood in front of me with angry eyes, one screaming louder than the other, and spoke of their own daughter slandering her parents, of schools that incited children against their own mothers and fathers. Was that the thanks for all their sacrifices and pain, the terrible times they had gone through. . . . Neither yes nor no. No "I'll try to explain it to you." No guilt. No sorrow. No responsibility [Betroffenheit]. (24)

Anna's response to this immobilizing constellation of family history and world-historical horror is to search for an entirely new beginning; neither she nor her husband invite their parents to their wedding: "We wanted to make a fresh start. No witnesses from the past" (27).

Rudolf, born in 1950 in a community of former Nazis living in

South America,[12] is plagued by guilt and self-hate; he relates that his parents felt shame for the first time in their lives when they discovered his homosexuality. He experiences himself as hopelessly contaminated by the past: "I must not have any children. This line must come to an end with me. What should I tell the little ones about Grandpa? I lived with my parents too long, who knows what evil I carry within me? It mustn't be handed down" (46).

In another family, an older sister defends the father, a former high officer in the Wehrmacht, while a brother turns to radical politics in an effort to undo his forbear's crimes. She insists on her right to be proud of her father: "He had the courage to join a movement that held out the promise for a better future" (61). In her defense of her father she even, no doubt unknowingly, paraphrases Himmler's famous Posen speech: "Our father behaved decently throughout. He never took a single item of confiscated Jewish property. He paid for his house out of his own pocket" (59). Her brother on the other hand, lives out an extended disavowal of the same father: "I have always tried my best to become a new type of German, not to be like my father. What's wrong with that?" (63).

And there is the case of the small-town butcher whose understanding of history seems to reiterate the bitter banalities of evil of the Nazi era as well as to suggest the evils of a new banality, characteristic perhaps of the postwar era. Because his father had been the Nazi mayor of the town and another, competing butcher's uncle had been a socialist (and postwar mayor), he is assigned a less favorable location for his butcher shop: "Father always said we were a decent family. He was proud of his children and what they managed to achieve. Only he wasn't allowed to be mayor. And that's too bad, because maybe then I'd have a shop in the pedestrian zone" (87).

Another woman, born shortly after the war to a former SS officer, recognizes the enormity of the task of sorting out her own identity from the family legacy:

My greatest problem is to avoid becoming like my parents, given their past. I know what I have in common with them. And I wasn't able to change, to make myself over, until I stopped thinking of them as victims. I also saw myself as the victim of their upbringing and their past. But as soon as I stopped seeing my parents as victims I became able to distance myself from them. Having looked at the historical record, the books and films, I have become convinced that they must be counted among the perpetrators. But when I was small, as a child, I saw something altogether different. They were refugees with very little money, frightened people living from hand to mouth. That's not what perpetrators are supposed to look like. They saw themselves as victims and felt like victims, and that's how I saw them as well. And I also began to see myself as their victim. I now know that what they did is also a part of me, but I now handle it differently, and that is the beauty of my life today. (106)

One of the more disturbing interviews is with a young medical student, the son of an SS officer and member of the medical staff at Dachau. The persistence of the past in the present is illustrated by this young man's nearly seamless identification with the Nazi ideology of a father who, not surprisingly, nearly totally ignored him:

The nation, being a living entity, needs doctors. If need be they can also kill, not out of joy in killing but out of necessity. It's part of the job. Just as a doctor can save the life of a patient by removing an appendix he can save the body politic by excising big tumors. The extinction of life also forms the basis of the survival of others. This is where personal conviction comes in. My father serves as a model in this respect. (127)

Yet another way in which Nazi ideology may persist in the second generation is, perhaps paradoxically, through extreme cases of identification with the victims; here the Jewish survivors are expropriated once more, only now not their property or citizenship but the struggles and memories of their survivorship. In the words of the twenty-nine-year-old son of a former SA and SS officer:

There's all that talk about you Jews being the victims of the war. But for those of you who survived, the suffering ended with Hitler's death. But for us, the children of the Nazis, it didn't end. When their world collapsed in ruins and ashes, the heroes of the Third Reich staked out another battleground—the family. (138)

And further:

The Jews now are better off than anybody else. They're being pampered, just like the blacks. Only we, the children of the Nazis, are ignored and overlooked. (145)

One of the few interviews that inspire any genuine hope is with a university professor whose father, a former SS officer, had denounced his own Communist stepfather during the war. That step-father, the interviewee's grandfather, came to represent a positive source of identification, an alternative legacy to the paternal totem: "Grandpa . . . has remained my example and my positive German model. And I stress 'German.' I was spared the fate of many of my generation of having hate drive a wedge between me and the older generation. I loved that old man, and he remains a symbol for me, proof that that 'other' Germany has always existed as well" (158).

Finally, Sichrovsky offers insights into the third generation's experience of awakening into a still traumatically burdened symbolic order. Stefanie, nineteen years old, is the granddaughter of a former high Nazi official executed immediately after 1945 for war crimes. Following the war, her parents became devout Jehovah's Witnesses, part of their own lifelong effort to redeem the crimes of the grandfather. Disgusted by the meek piety of her parents, Stefanie longs for the erotic power she associates with the sleek black uniform and severe gaze of the grandfather: "I know him from pictures. He really looked great. The black uniform, the boots, what a guy! And that haircut, those eyes. I bet they were all afraid of him. Not like my old man, who's afraid of everything" (30). She relates a curious incident that in many ways may emblematize a typical clash between members of the second and third generations:

> We once had a history teacher. Long hair, beard, ski sweater, jeans—the works. Boy, did he carry on about everything. For hours he'd talk about the Jews, the Communists, the Gypsies, the Russians—victims, nothing but victims. He acted as if he'd been persecuted, as if the Nazis were still after him. But what was he? He wasn't a Jew or a Gypsy or a Russian. Maybe a Communist. I never believed the things he told us. Who knows whether it really was so bad. (30)

At one point the students in the class began to demand an answer to the question that had apparently preoccupied many of them for some time: Why, if indeed it had been such a horrible period of history, did people cheer and march and yell "Hurra" and "Heil"?

> We wanted to know what things had really been like. It was like a dam had burst. Always that business about criminals and crimes, always us, the Germans. The whole class was yelling and screaming. It was all idiocy, the things he was telling us, one of us said. We'd seen the pictures. The laughing kids, the glowing faces of the women, the

streets filled with cheering masses. Where did all that enthusiasm come from? (31)

The teacher finally broke down, exchanged insults with his class, and went to the principal, who then delivered a long and no doubt predictable lecture about history, guilt, and shame (this is precisely the sort of address that Philipp Jenninger no doubt wanted to avoid). Stefanie's response points to the total ineffectualness of such a strategy:

> We were covered with guilt and shame, he told us. Maybe he, not I. I didn't murder anyone, I didn't mistreat anyone, I didn't cheer Hitler. If they believe they'd made mistakes, okay. Let them put on a crown of thorns and cry and cry. I'm sick and tired of it. Enough that we Germans are always the bad ones, that we have constantly to be reminded of it. What does that mean—*we* started the war, *we* gassed the Jews, *we* devastated Russia. It sure as hell wasn't me. (32)

And further, expressing sentiments quite close to Hans Jürgen Syberberg's notion of the *"freudlose Gesellschaft"* (joyless society):

> Do you think that back then they were as frustrated as they try to tell us? I'd like to feel as proud as they did then. Head high and belief in the future. Even if things fell apart, but until they did it must have been quite something. I'd like to feel that good. . . . We were somebody. (37)

Stefanie's dilemma, as she herself sees it, comes down to the total absence of any viable resources of identification:

> Do I have any particular ideal? How do you mean that? Can you name anyone here in Germany that I can admire? Who are our models? Yesterday's old Nazis? Or the new Greens? Or people like my parents who are wasting their lives in fear? Who do you think are the models for people in my age group? There's nothing. Nobody. . . . We're the last of the Mohicans. (38)

A rather different experience is related in another interview in which the discovery by the third generation of the traces of the Holocaust within the otherwise normal domesticity of the present, forces the second generation into a more direct and sustained labor of mourning regarding the material and symbolic inheritance left by

43

the generation of the (grand)fathers. Susanne, born in 1944, relates how her son, Dieter, born in 1966, became involved in a project at school in which a group of students researched the effects of the Holocaust on their own community. They examined archives, wrote to Jewish communities, and attempted to reach Holocaust survivors from their town. In the course of these efforts, Dieter made the remarkable discovery that the house in which he had grown up had belonged to a Jewish family until 1941, when the members of the family were deported to Auschwitz. After a long period of tension between Dieter and his parents, he finally reads to his mother from the documents his group had uncovered: "Here, here it says, 'Here lived Martha Kolleg, age 2, Anna Kolleg, age 6, Ferdi Kolleg, age 12, Harry Kolleg, age 42, and Susanne Kolleg, age 38. Arrested on November 10, 1941, deported on November 12, 1941. Offical date of death of the children and mother, January 14, 1944. Father officially missing. Place of death: Auschwitz" (76–77). And as Dieter further relates to his mother: "Your dear father moved into this house with your dear mother the day after they were taken away" (76). Dieter's grandfather, as it turns out, had also for a time been assigned to duty in Auschwitz.

Though she hadn't known about the peculiar genealogy of the material legacy she inhabited, Susanne had known that her father had worked in Auschwitz. But she had never developed her own independent curiosity about this period of history and her father's particular place in it. The key to her lack of curiosity, indeed to what must be regarded as the substantial psychic numbness she had developed regarding this history, would seem to lie in the way her father had related these matters to her. Her father had indeed tried to initiate her into the facts of the past; he had even taken her, at the age of sixteen, on a kind of *Bildungsreise* (educational journey) to Auschwitz. But in none of these efforts did her father reveal any signs of an emotional involvement in the events, any indication that he had experienced contrition, shame, or mourning, anything resembling an *affective* memory to accompany the memory of facts and events:

> In retrospect, the terrifying thing about him was his objectivity. His reports and descriptions, his careful recapitulation of events. I never saw him shed a tear, never heard him break off in the middle, halt, unable to continue talking. Only these monotonous litanies, almost as though he were reading from a script. (73)

And further:

> He used words like "murderers" and "criminals." He never offered
> excuses and never claimed that the things we read about in the papers
> or books weren't true. But as to guilt, he never considered himself
> guilty. He never, not once, said that he had made a mistake or that he
> had been partner to a crime. He was simply a victim of circumstances.
> And I, I always believed everything he told me. (74)

This was all to change with her own son's research and experience
of rage over his discovery of the ruins covered over by his family's
dwelling. Only with the third generation's grief and outrage over
the effacement of the traces of historical suffering by the comforts of
the *Heimat*—of a concrete historical *Unheimlich* within the *Heimisch*—
did it become possible for the second generation to initiate its own
belated labor of mourning.

What these interviews convey most strongly is a sense of the
enormous task left to the postwar generations to discover viable
totemic resources, to sort out the pieces of a symbolic legacy that
could still be safely integrated. The core dilemma is that the cultural
reservoir has been poisoned, and few totems seem to exist which
would not evoke such traumatic ambivalence that only a global fore-
closure of all symbolic legacies would prevent further contamination. To carry out their labors of self-constitution the second and
third generations face the double bind of needing symbolic resources which, because of the unmanageable degrees of ambivalence such resources arouse, make these labors impossible. It is as if
with every word, every name one took into one's mouth, every totem
one tried to internalize, one spit up ashes: "*Aschen—/Schluckauf.*"[13]
The double bind of having to identify with figures of power one also
at another level needs to disavow—of being faced with a homeopathic cure that may prove to be overly toxic—leads to what the
Mitscherlichs, in 1967, referred to as an "*Identifikationsscheu,*" a resistance to identification with parents and elders, in the second
generation. Such resistance ends up making separation from the
parents a difficult and precarious adventure:

> Psychologically, it was a difficult task for most of the young people to
> detach themselves from parents who had been robbed in this way of
> their moral value, since internalization of these parents—the identi-
> fication with them which usually results from the painful parting with
> these figures from childhood—brought no reinforcement of self-

respect. This is, we believe, why the type of youth most frequently met with today shows what we might call a *reluctance to identify*.[14]

To summarize, then, the postwar generations faced a situation in which one of the few strategies for emotional survival open to them was the assumption of a depressive position. In numerous cases the parents were available to the children only on the condition that the children contribute to the restitution of the parents' damaged selves and thereby enter into complicity with their defense mechanisms and their inability or refusal to mourn. In those cases where the children did manage to break through the rigid silences of the parents, they often faced insuperable ambivalences that made the totemic viability of these parents highly problematic. And the third generation is no less implicated in this chain of negative dependencies. To return to Shakespeare's emblematic mourner manqué, one might say that Hamlet's children too find themselves haunted by the ghosts of the past.

II

The double binds that continue to overdetermine political culture in postwar German society have come to the fore in a public debate among professional historians, philosophers, and journalists which has come to be known as the *"Historiker-Streit"* (historians' debate). The beginning of this debate might be dated with Jürgen Habermas's essay "Eine Art Schadensabwicklung: Die apologetischen Tendenzen in der deutschen Zeitgeschichtsschreibung" (A settling of damages: Apologetic tendencies in German historiography) published July 11, 1986, in the German weekly *Die Zeit*.[15] As the subtitle of that essay indicates, Habermas's concern is a certain revisionist or apologetic tendency in recent German historiography of the fascist period. In the essay Habermas focuses on the work of three historians whom he sees as the main exponents of revisionist historiography: Ernst Nolte, Michael Stürmer, and Andreas Hillgruber.

In an essay published in June 1986 in the *Frankfurter Allgemeine Zeitung*,[16] Nolte had argued for an empathic understanding of the anxieties that ostensibly led Hitler to the barbaric (Nolte's word is *"asiatisch"*) Final Solution. According to Nolte, Hitler had reason to fear that the Russians would subject the Germans to horrific tortures in the event of a westward expansion. Nolte evoked the so-called rat cage, an instrument of torture to which Winston Smith finally succumbs in George Orwell's *1984* and which, according to anti-Bolshevist literature from the twenties, belonged to the Soviet arsenal, as the recurring nightmare that finally led Hitler to the prophylactic measures of Auschwitz:

> Is it not likely that the Nazis and Hitler committed this "Asiatic" deed because they saw themselves and others like them as potential or real victims of an "Asiatic" deed? Didn't the "Gulag" come before Auschwitz? Didn't the "class genocide" of the Bolshevists logically and factually predate the "racial genocide" of the National Socialists? Was it not precisely Hitler's inability to forget the "rat cage" that explains his most secret actions? Did Auschwitz perhaps originate in a past that wouldn't go away?[17]

The missing link in this causal nexus is, of course, the equation Bolshevist equals Jew, an anti-Semitic commonplace from the twenties and thirties.[18] Nolte had elsewhere offered further "evidence" also garnered from fundamentally anti-Semitic nightmare visions of the power of world Jewry, to support this empathic, not to say sympathetic, reading of Hitler's situation. He claims, for example, that Chaim Weizmann's declaration in 1939 that the Jews of the world should ally themselves with England might justify the thesis "that Hitler was allowed to treat the German Jews as prisoners of war and by this means to intern them."[19]

Other aspects of Nolte's argument involve by now familiar comparisons between the National Socialist genocide and other modern examples of mass murder, from the Turkish slaughter of Armenians to Pol Pot's decimation of the Cambodian population. The thought behind such comparisons is, of course, that the Jewish Holocaust needs to be placed in the context of other cataclysmic events of twentieth-century history, all of which may be seen under the general rubric: "reactions to modernity."[20] In defense of such comparisons, Nolte offers yet another familiar analogy, that between Auschwitz and the Allied bombing of civilian populations. Nolte's example demonstrates rather clearly that the entire historians' debate is in many ways a continuation of the controversies surrounding Ronald Reagan's visit to the cemetery at Bitburg:

To be sure, the American President's visit to the military cemetery at Bitburg provoked a very emotional discussion; but the fear of the charge of "settling accounts" [*Aufrechnung*] and a more general fear of making any comparisons at all prevented the simple question from being considered what it would have meant had in 1953 the then chancellor refused to visit the military cemetery at Arlington, justifying this refusal with the argument that men were buried there who had participated in terroristic attacks against the German civilian population.[21]

What finally distinguishes the Shoah from other cases of genocide in the twentieth century is, according to Nolte, the technical detail of the use of gas in the extermination of the Jews.[22]

In the end, however, Nolte's argument for a revisionist reading of the place of the Holocaust in modern European history is based on the notion that previous interpretations have been authored by the victors and are thus inherently biased and in need of rewriting from a German national perspective. He offers a curious thought experiment to dramatize his case:

We need only imagine, for example, what would happen if the Palestine Liberation Organization, assisted by its allies, succeeded in annihilating the State of Israel. Then the historical accounts in the books, lecture halls and schoolrooms of Palestine would doubtless dwell only on the negative traits of Israel; the victory over the racist, oppressive and even Fascist Zionism would become a state-supporting myth. For decades and possibly centuries nobody would dare to trace the moving origins of Zionism to the spirit of resistance against European anti-Semitism, or to describe its extraordinary civilizing achievements before and after the founding of the state, to show its clear differences from Italian fascism.[23]

Although few professional historians have been guilty of the rhetorical excesses manifest in such prose, Nolte is by no means alone with regard to the general philosophical trajectory of his national(ist) reappropriation of German history. One finds, for example, in recent writings by Michael Stürmer an explicit appeal to the historian as the figure in contemporary society who must carry on the work that can no longer be performed by religion, namely the unification and consolidation of the social group. By endowing meaning (*Sinnstiftung*) through an act of historical recollection and interpretation, the historian lays the foundation (*Stiftung*) on which a national identity may be constituted. Only after achieving such a firm national ego, as it were, may the Federal Republic come to occupy its rightful place as the "central unit in the European defensive arch of the Atlantic system."[24] The task of contemporary German historiography is to allow Germany to regain its inner continuity, to come home to itself, so that its Western neighbors may know they have a dependable ally anchored in a firm and unconflicted self-understanding: "For it is here a matter of the German Republic's inner continuity and its dependability in foreign affairs."[25] And like Nolte, Stürmer sees in the performance of this quasi-Homeric task of cultural *Sinnstiftung*—the historian becomes the new bard of the national epos—an antidote to the very disorientation that is seen as having given rise to fascism in the first place. It should be clear that Stürmer's—as well as Nolte's—historiographical therapy is quite different from the homeopathic procedures I have been discussing:

> It is doubtful that the uncertainty first began in 1945. Hitler's rise to power was a function of the crises and catastrophes of a secularized civilization tumbling from rupture to rupture; this was a civilization marked by the loss of orientation and futile searches for security. . . . From 1914 to 1945 the Germans were thrust into the cataracts of modernity to a degree that shattered all traditions, made the unthinkable thinkable, and institutionalized barbarity as political regime. It was for these reasons that Hitler was able to triumph, that he was able to exploit and pervert Prussia and patriotism, the state and the virtues of civil society [*die bürgerlichen Tugenden*].[26]

Finally, what scandalized so many readers of Andreas Hillgruber's *Zweierlei Untergang: Die Zerschlagung des Deutschen Reiches und das Ende des europäischen Judentums* (Two kinds of destruction: The shattering of the German Reich and the end of European Jewry [Berlin: Siedler, 1986]) was Hillgruber's declared identification with the perspective of the defenders of Germany's eastern territories during the period of their collapse, even though these "valiant" efforts to hold back the anticipated reprisals by the Red Army allowed for the machinery of the death camps to continue unabated (Hillgruber distinguishes this *verantwortungsethische* or "ethics of responsibility" perspective from the *gesinnungsethische* or "ethics of conviction" perspective of the conspirators of the twentieth of July).[27] Perhaps even more distressing in Hillgruber's study is the assimilation of these two "national catastrophes" to a single, overarching narrative of the destruction of the *"europäische Mitte"* (European center). As the rather asymmetrical treatment of these two catastrophes indicates—the "shattering of the German Reich" takes up a good two-thirds of the book—in this double plot it is the Germans of the eastern provinces who become the truly tragic protagonists of modern European history.[28]

The gist of Habermas's critique of these trends in the historiography of fascism and the Holocaust is that they attempt to recuperate notions of centrality and modes of national identity no longer feasible in the harrowed cultural matrix of postwar Europe; rather than exploring strategies of coming to terms with a historical experience that changed not just the geopolitical, but also the moral and psychological, landscapes of Europe and the West, these historians place historiography in the service of a "national-historical restoration of a conventional identity."[29]

A "conventional identity" signifies in this context a self-structure still rooted in a specular relation to the particular norms, roles, "contents" of a specific social formation such as family, *Volk,* or nation. A more distanced and critical dialogue with the intensely ambivalent cultural legacy of recent German history is thus for Habermas the sign of a cultural self-identity that has begun to work through the radically transformed conditions of identity formation of post-Holocaust and, I would add, postmodern German society. Habermas condenses these determinants of postwar political culture under the sign of what he calls "postconventional identity":

> If among the younger generations national symbols have lost their formative powers; if naive identifications with one's origins and lineage have given way to a more tentative relationship with history; if discontinuities are felt more strongly and continuities no longer celebrated at all costs . . . to the extent that all this is the case, we are witnessing increasing indications of the advent of a postconventional identity.[30]

One can no doubt imagine a number of different explanations for the eruption of the historians' debate at this particular moment in the history of the Federal Republic. And indeed, as one observer has noted, efforts to explain the debate have generated a minor cottage industry.[31] But I would argue that commentators have hesitated to depart from a narrowly drawn framework of political culture in the Federal Republic and shied away from linking the historians' debate to larger questions concerning the discourses of national identity in postmodern politics and culture more generally. As I have already suggested, I think that Habermas's notion of a postconventional identity points in precisely this direction. And indeed, once Habermas's concept of a postconventional identity is situated within this more broadly drawn postmodern context, the texts of the historians' debate quite rapidly become legible as symptoms of a remarkable repetition compulsion. And in good postmodern fashion, it is a repetition compulsion that reenacts history in the medium of representations, in this case, historiography.[32]

Where the Jews were once blamed for the traumas of modernity, the Holocaust now seems to figure as the irritating signifier of the traumas and disorientations of postmodernity. The conditions under which stable cultural identities may be consolidated have indeed *with* and *since* the Holocaust become radically different; the symbolic order to which a German is subjected, that is, that social space in which he or she first learns to say *"ich"* and *"wir,"* now contains the traces of a horrific violence.[33] But the conventional sites of identity formation have become destabilized, have become more and more *unheimlich*, as it were, for a variety of reasons, some of which derive more directly from other, more global, social, economic, and political displacements. In the present historical moment, which, perhaps for lack of a better word, is called the postmodern, Orient and Occident, masculine and feminine, guest worker and indigenous host, to name just a few of the binary oppositions that figure in the process of cultural identity formation, no longer seem to occupy stable positions. The postmodern self is, as I have suggested, called on to integrate an awareness of multiple forms of otherness, to identify him- or herself across a wide range of unstable and heterogeneous "regionalisms," local knowledges and practices. Furthermore, in the postmodern, the availability of the narratives of European Enlightenment culture as resources of legitimation and orientation, as the projection of a progressive synthesis of this heterogeneity under some teleological master term, has, precisely because of the kinds of transformations taking place, become highly problematical. The Jews, no longer available as the signifier of ruptures and disturbances one would like to banish from the inside (of the self, the family, the city, the *Reich*), are being displaced by the event of their own destruction; the Holocaust now figures as the placeholder for the decenteredness and instability experienced as so painfully chronic in contemporary German society, and it is a *national* historiography to which the task is assigned to reconstitute the center— the *europäische Mitte*—once again, if only in the mode of nostalgic recollection or simulacrum. I am proposing, in other words, that much of the historians' debate may be read as a symptom of an inability or refusal to mourn either the particular and deeply traumatic losses to the cultural resources of Germany, namely, the real and ineluctable fragmentation of the cultural identity which results from Auschwitz, or the more structural losses that result from a global remapping of political, economic, cultural, sexual, and moral power over the last forty years (I would include the division of Germany and the loss of the eastern provinces within this second series of losses). Put somewhat differently, I am arguing that in the texts of the neoconservative historians reviewed by Habermas the subtext of the quest for a renewed and vigorous (virile?) national identity has not just a "cold war"/NATO component—Germany's unbroken self-identity with regard to the struggle against Bolshevism—but a postmodern one as well. A national historiography assumes the task of salvaging—or perhaps more accurately, simulating—sites of identity formation no longer available in a cultural space defined by the double "post" of the post-Holocaust and the postmodern. If it has become difficult, under the burden of this double "post," to say *"wir"* in contemporary German society and to know at all times exactly what that little pronoun signifies, that is, if a certain strangeness, a certain alien presence—call it, with Nolte, the "Asiatic"— has come to haunt the first person plural, splitting it from within, a new national historiography has busied itself with working out strategies of narrating this *Unheimlichkeit* to the margins, of deporting it so to speak. This new historiography thus performs double duty: all the difficulties that have come to complicate the enunciation of the first person plural in contemporary German society are assigned a delimited origin in the Holocaust, which in its turn may then be normalized and marginalized by various techniques of "historicization." Whereas once it was the Jews, now the Shoah itself serves as a screen on which is projected, as something that intervenes from the outside—from Asia—that which ultimately keeps Germans from feeling continuous with themselves.

In this respect the neoconservative moment in the historians' debate may be viewed as symptomatic of a more general group psychological trajectory in the direction of a respecularization of the terms of German national identity. And in this context one wonders whether efforts to construct two new museums of national history, the Haus der Geschichte in Bonn and the Deutsches Historisches Museum in Berlin, may not end up with a house of mirrors, an enclosed space in which Germans may go to see themselves reflected and thereby reinstated in an imaginary plenitude and wholeness.[34]

Habermas's interventions in these controversies are directed precisely against this tendency to return to narcissistic patterns of (group) identity formation, patterns that reinscribe, as I have argued, a refusal or inability to mourn. Habermas has, of course, been criticized by just about every postmodern theorist for his refusal to relinquish his commitment to an Enlightenment faith in rationality and the perfectibility of man, and to Western liberal notions of consensus, in short, to the project of modernity. This is not the place to repeat these debates; I would simply like to suggest that Habermas's rigorous adherence to the notions of the shared life-world and communicative rationality is grounded, at least in part, in an understanding of the process of mourning which is necessary for the working through of the burdens signified by the double "post" of the post-Holocaust and the postmodern.

Mourning requires the availability of a "good-enough environmental provision,"[35] a dependable interpersonal rapport that first provides a space in which the work of mourning can unfold. To reiterate an earlier formulation, mourning without the solidarity of some such interpersonal rapport would signal the advent of madness. By focusing so single-mindedly on the communicative context within which the discontinuities of postconventional identity could be worked through, Habermas has no doubt domesticated these very discontinuities. He has tended to equate these discontinuities with an abstract imperative to think abstractly, in terms of universal norms of justice and reciprocity. One wonders at times whether for Habermas the loss of centrality associated with the imperatives of being a Western-style liberal in a pluralist society is as much loss and decenteredness as a person, or at least a European schooled in an Idealist tradition, should be expected to endure. I would, however, like to suggest that in the context of the historians' debate Habermas's thoughts regarding the pressures placed on German national identity at the present historical moment invite one to see a more radical potential in his notion of a postconventional identity than his postmodern critics have granted, a potential that places him much closer to these critics than one might have imagined possible. For as I have already suggested, in the context of the historians' debate Habermas has deployed the notion of a postconventional identity as a critique of current tendencies to respecularize the terms of national identity, and as an insistence on the necessity of a continued labor of mourning. Insofar as the project of modernity may itself be seen to reinscribe the specular pattern of self-identity, albeit at a very high level of mediation, that is, if at the completion of this project we all end up looking into the mirror of a white, male, Europe-oriented *Weltbürger*, then the imperatives of a postconventional identity will demand that this project too be worked through according to the procedures of *Trauerarbeit*.

III

One might argue that this historians' debate has been simply a more journalistic and crudely ideological manifestation of a more properly scientific controversy that began a year earlier in the community of professional historians. The beginning of that controversy may be dated with the publication in May 1985 of an essay by Martin Broszat, director of the Institut für Zeitgeschichte in Munich, "Plädoyer für eine Historisierung des Nationalsozialismus" (The case for the historicization of National Socialism).[36] Unlike Nolte and Stürmer, Broszat is primarily interested not in the role historians could or should play in helping to consolidate a national self-identity in contemporary German society but, rather, in more properly methodological questions regarding the historiography of fascism and the Holocaust. The fundamental question that concerns Broszat is whether the historian's task vis-à-vis this period of history should be radically different from other historiographical labors. Broszat argues that there can be no fundamental difference between the tasks if the concern is to enrich one's historical understanding of this period rather than to quarantine it behind moral judgments that have long since become a series of taboos: "To distance oneself in this global fashion from the Nazi past is yet another form of repression and institution of taboos." There are a number of ways in which these taboos may be dismantled, Broszat argues, for example, by focusing less on the twelve years of Nazi rule and more on the *longue durée* of historical processes of modernization which begin before fascism and continue into the present:

> Rather than creating a more rigid and global moral blockade around the Hitler era, we need to dislodge reified conceptual and linguistic procedures. We must furthermore allow our vision regarding events and historical individuals to move beyond its confinement in the notion of a unified, tyrannical regime that encompassed every aspect of life. Above all we must develop an approach that will be able to map out the larger space of modern Germany history within which . . . National Socialism played itself out.[37]

The methodology most appropriate to this other, more broadly drawn field of investigation is, according to Broszat, what in German is called *Alltagsgeschichte*, that is, the history of daily life, typically reconstructed using the techniques of oral history. A series of microdescriptions of daily life, the *alltagsgeschichtlich* approach offers the opportunity to witness the imbrications of so-called normal life with that continuous state of emergency that was Nazism, and allows the historian to place this subset of experiences—daily life under fascism—within the larger context of a social history of modernization in the twentieth century. Furthermore, oral history offers the prospect of reinvigorating what Broszat has called the "pleasure in historical narration" (*die Lust am geschichtlichen Erzählen*),[38] a dimension of the historian's trade that has, Broszat claims, for the most part been absent in other historical analyses of the Nazi period because of the taboos under which German historiography of fascism has labored.

Broszat's essay has, as one would imagine, generated a wide range of responses often rehearsing, though in less polemical tonalities, many of the themes I have noted in the historians' debate.[39] But it was in a series of open letters between Broszat and Saul Friedländer that the key positions regarding the possibilities and limits of historical contextualizations of Nazism and the Final Solution were most clearly articulated.[40] It is beyond the scope of the present investigation to comment in any detail on these positions; I will simply indicate what I take to be the core of their disagreement since it bears directly on the issues that will be highlighted in the next chapters.

In the course of their exchange, Broszat and Friedländer disagree profoundly about the primary cultural sites where Nazism may most clearly be seen to have produced its effects, where to locate the "stage" on which this primal scene of German history was really played out. Broszat, who favors the *alltagsgeschichtlich* approach to the historiography of the period,[41] argues that the slow rhythms of daily life in the villages and towns offer a privileged point of access into the essential features of German fascism. Friedländer, who continues to see the politico-ideological dimension of Nazism as central, argues against this shift of focus from, as he puts it, the *Ordensburgen* to Schabbach:[42]

> In my opinion, among the ruling members of the Nazi Party as well as among the followers there was the unqualified sense of performing a truly historical, metahistorical, extraordinary task. We . . . know Himmler's Posen speech of October 1943 in all its details. That is not the banality of evil, that is not, at least with regard to the Jewish question, simply a crude appeal to a group of SS officials; on the contrary, it is the expression of an intoxication, a feeling of being part of an undertaking of superhuman significance. For these reasons I tend to view certain important aspects of the Nazi movement within the category of a "political religion." . . . If we assume this point of view, then we are of course quite a ways from normal life in Schabbach, though not so far from the *Ordensburgen* or the resolve of a number of leaders of the special commandos [*Einsatzkommandos*] to do their duty; nor are we very far from the intoxication that penetrated so deeply and reached so far and that was not simply the product of a *Führer*-myth instituted according to a calculus of means and ends.[43]

Schabbach / the *Ordensburgen*: These two cultural sites mark the two, very different directions taken by Edgar Reitz and Hans Jürgen Syberberg in their cinematic conversations with the German past. In the following chapters I will explore in detail the ways in which these two sites are constituted in and as film, the sorts of interrogations to which they are subjected, and above all the ways in which they are deployed in the service of a work of mourning.

3

Screen Memories Made in Germany: Edgar Reitz's *Heimat* and the Question of Mourning

In the fall of 1984, West German television broadcast what was to be one of the great success stories of its relatively brief history: a sixteen-hour television epic with the teutonically resonant title *Heimat—Eine Chronik in elf Teilen* (Heimat—a chronicle in eleven parts). *Heimat* is an untranslatable word with a rich and much-contested field of significations including "home," "homeland," "native soil," "motherland," "place of origin and belonging," and quite a bit more.[1] After an enthusiastic reception by television audiences,[2] the film went on to an equally warm reception at screenings in Munich and at film festivals in Venice, London, and the United States (the U.S. debut was at the 1985 New Directors/New Films festival cosponsored by the Museum of Modern Art and the Film Society of Lincoln Center). It has since been screened under varying auspices, including cable television, the Public Theater in New York City, Goethe institutes across the country, and most recently by various public television stations. The film was produced and directed by Edgar Reitz; the original script, which differs significantly from the final film version and which has been published separately, was co-authored by Reitz and Peter Steinbach.[3]

Born on November 1, 1932, in the Hunsrück region in the western part of Germany, Reitz belongs to the generation that initiated what has, for better or worse, come to be known as the New German Cinema. One of the signatories of the 1962 Oberhausen Manifesto, the document marking the symbolic death of *"Papas Kino,"* and with Alexander Kluge and several other colleagues cofounder of the Institut für Filmgestaltung in Ulm, Reitz went on to become one of the leading theoreticians, teachers, and practitioners of the new cinematic Sturm und Drang generation. After making some fifty industrial films and several highly acclaimed experimental short films (two of these shorts were inspired by compositional procedures of Schönberg, Berg, and Webern, a legacy that reappears in *Heimat* in the form of Hermann's modernist musical compositions[4]), Reitz served as director of photography for Kluge's first feature, *Abschied von Gestern* (Yesterday girl; 1966), the film often considered to be the inaugural work of the New German Cinema. Reitz made his own first feature, *Mahlzeiten* (Mealtimes) the same year. Here, as in his subsequent films, *Heimat* in particular, Reitz demonstrates a commitment to revealing the workings of history, power, and socioeconomic forces in the sensuous details of daily life, intimate relationships, the face, the body.[5]

Several feature, documentary, and television films later, Reitz made a film whose theme relates directly to those concerns that lead him to make *Heimat*. Produced in 1973 and co-authored with Alexander Kluge, *Die Reise nach Wien* (The trip to Vienna) presents the story of two young women from the Hunsrück who, bored and lonely—it is 1943 and their husbands are in the army—take a trip to Vienna, where they hope to find the charm of dashing officers and the worldly atmosphere of metropolis. The trip ends in disenchantment; they are swindled out of their money and find only moribund forms of the dreams they had sought. At home, after overcoming further near disasters—one of the women is in danger of being arrested by Nazi authorities for failing to report the slaughter of a pig—the two women experience the end of the war and the arrival of the new era: the Americans come to town. Essential to the aesthetic of the film is the local intentionality, the attention to the "microstructure on which the superstructure of history unwinds."[6] As Ingrid Scheib-Rothbart and Ruth McCormick have noted: "The film shows the connection between private life and the National Socialist system from the perspective of Toni and Marga. It does not attempt to make a value judgment of National Socialism, but to direct attention to the biographical factors which, in reality, carried the system."[7]

In 1974 Reitz collaborated with Kluge once again, producing the film *In Gefahr und größter Not bringt der Mittelweg den Tod* (In danger and great need the middle road leads to death). Several years later he made a fine, though often neglected, film dealing with the disorientations of the first postwar months, *Stunde Null* (Zero hour; 1977), and contributed to the remarkable collaborative film project dealing with terrorism and the reactions of the German state in the late seventies, *Deutschland im Herbst* (Germany in autumn; 1978).[8] In 1978 Reitz made a highly ambitious but both critically and commercially unsuccessful film, *Der Schneider von Ulm* (The tailor from Ulm). Shattered by this last failure, Reitz retreated to the island of Sylt and even considered giving up filmmaking altogether. During this winter sojourn near the North Sea Reitz began to compose a series of autobiographical sketches tracing out his own path to filmmaking. These notes included fragments of stories that Reitz later developed into a draft of a novel. These novelistic fragments provided the foundation for the screenplay of *Heimat*.[9]

I

Heimat—Eine Chronik in elf Teilen traces the historical metamorphoses of a small rural community, the fictive village of Schabbach, located in the Hunsrück, a small, chilly section of Rhineland-Palatinate near the confluence of the Mosel and the Rhine. The destinies of various villagers, primarily the members of one family, the Simons, are presented more or less chronologically across three generations, from 1919 to 1982. Located initially on the outermost margins of the great movements of history writ large—History as a series of great deeds and decisions emanating from the economic and political centers of the European nation-states—the village offers the opportunity to bear witness to the slower rhythms of history from below. Here life is organized primarily around the concrete temporal rhythms of agriculture, the labor of handcrafts, the preparation and consumption of family and communal meals (nearly every significant exchange between characters is accompanied by eating, and there is a great deal of discussion about food and regional specialties in particular), and the larger generational cycles of birth, marriage, child rearing, old age, and death.

At least in the initial episodes and at various strategic moments, the world in the film is dominated by what Mikhail Bakhtin has called *"folkloric time"* or, more precisely, its idyllic reinscription. Time, in the world of the idyll, is intimately bound to space:

> an organic fastening-down, a grafting of life and its events to a place, to a familiar territory with all its nooks and crannies, its familiar mountains, valleys, fields, rivers and forests, and one's home. Idyllic life and its events are inseparable from this concrete, spatial corner of the world where the fathers and grandfathers lived and where one's children and their children will live. This little spatial world is limited and sufficient unto itself, not linked in any intrinsic way with other places, with the rest of the world.[10]

In the world of the agricultural idyll in particular, the role of labor is primary, for labor in the rural setting "transforms all the events of everyday life, stripping them of that private petty character obtaining when man is nothing but a consumer; what happens rather is that they are turned into essential life *events*."[11]

The opening sequence of the film introduces the audience in subtle, yet dramatic, fashion into this world still organized by idyllic matrices. Paul Simon approaches his native village, returning home from a French prisoner-of-war camp after the "Great War"; moving quickly, finally running through the streets of his native Schabbach, he is noticed along the way by Maria who, anticipating the course of her future relationship with him, can hold him only briefly in the ephemeral reflection of her window. Reitz and Steinbach underscore the element of foreshadowing in the scene by noting in the screenplay that Maria observes Paul "without looking directly at him," and that his reflection appears "in the rippled distortion of the pane of glass," as if Paul were already aboard the ship for America.[12] Arriving home, Paul hears his father working in the smithy adjacent to the Simon house. He instinctively drops his knapsack and silently—mutely—joins his father in the work at hand. Only after the task is completed and he is greeted by his mother does the father utter a "God be praised!" As Thomas Elsaesser has described this scene, "the harmony of the two men's movements sets a rhythm of gesture as aesthetically pleasing as it is evocative of a certain stage of the family as a productive unit."[13]

Paul's reunion with the idyllic matrix is further underscored by the sudden shift from black and white to color the moment he looks through the window of his father's smithy. Though in this sequence the shift to color bears the weight of a narrative signification, shifts in the film from the otherwise all-pervasive black and white, which seems most appropriate to a chronicle of the first half of the century, to color do not appear systematic. Anton Kaes has described these shifts as interruptions of the documentary, prosaic-epic tone of black and white by moments of a lyrical, even hallucinatory subjectivity. According to Kaes, such moments may function as alienation effects that heighten the viewer's awareness of the artificial-artful construction of the image on the screen.[14] Not unlike an intrusion of the primary processes into the order of the secondary processes, these moments may indeed draw attention to the film image *as* image and so fulfill that function that the Russian formalists saw as the poetic function par excellence, namely the removal of objects from the automatism of perception. As Victor Shklovsky has said:

> Habituation devours works, clothes, furniture, one's wife, and the fear of war. "If the whole complex lives of many people go on unconsciously, then such lives are as if they had never been." And art exists that one may recover the sensation of life; it exists to make one feel things, to make the stone *stony*. The purpose of art is to impart the sensation of things as they are perceived and not as they are known. The technique of art is to make objects "unfamiliar," to make forms difficult, to increase the difficulty and length of perception because the process of perception is an aesthetic end in itself and must be prolonged.[15]

Of course these moments of lyrical color may serve precisely the opposite function, namely to constitute objects as *familiar*, that is, to mark that always ideologically inflected selection undertaken by a subject of what is to be allowed and what is not to be allowed into the intimate sphere of interiorizing recollection (*Er-innerung*). Thus Timothy Garton Ash has criticized precisely this aspect of *Heimat*. According to Ash, the message of Reitz's color filters is just this: "'Remember, remember, this is a film about what Germans remember. Some things they remember in full color. Some in sepia. Others they prefer to forget. Memory is selective. Memory is partial. Memory is amoral.'"[16] These issues, so central to any reading and evaluation of the film, will resurface later in the discussion.

To return now to Paul's reunion with his family, the most significant aspect of the scene is the way in which the cataclysmic events of World War I and the scars they may have left behind are organically reabsorbed into the rhythms of the everyday. This apparent power of the idyllic matrix called Heimat to digest shards of traumata shall prove to be a rather ambiguous blessing. The world into which Paul is reabsorbed—unsuccessfully, as it turns out—the world Reitz wants to portray, especially in the early episodes of the film, is the auratic world evoked by Walter Benjamin in his famous essay on Nikolai Leskov, "The Storyteller." In this world the "ability to exchange experiences" is still intact. It is the space of oral tradition, the space of storytellers: "Experience which is passed on from mouth to mouth is the source from which all storytellers have drawn."[17] Reitz's affinity with the world of Benjamin's storyteller finds an echo in the methodology employed in the research and preparation of the film, which in fact involved a kind of informal oral history project in which Reitz (not unlike his two most famous nineteenth-century precursors, the Brothers Grimm) collected stories and general ethnographic information from villagers in the Hunsrück region. That is, even though Reitz had already composed the draft of his novel before going to the Hunsrück, the actual screenplay was written over the course of a nearly two-year sojourn in the region during which Reitz and Steinbach lived among the villagers, participated in a variety of labors from tending farm animals to helping with the harvest, took their meals with members of the community, joined in festival celebrations, drank with locals at their *Stammtische*, and whenever possible, engaged them in informal conversation. As Reitz has said, "I had become one of them without even being fully aware of it."[18] In good anthropological fashion, Reitz and Steinbach strove to develop a foundation of trust on which the villagers would spontaneously volunteer information and stories about life and labor in the community, past and present, without having to be formally and systematically interviewed. These "Stories from the Hunsrück Villages" were subsequently edited in a documentary of the same name in 1981 as a sort of *Heimat*-in-progress.[19]

Essential to the world of oral tradition as characterized by Benjamin is an "orientation toward practical interests" which he finds in writers like Leskov, Gotthelf, Nodier, and Hebel:

All this points to the nature of every real story. It contains, openly or covertly, something useful. The usefulness may, in one case, consist of a moral; in another, in some practical advice; in a third, in a proverb or maxim. In every case the storyteller is a man who has counsel for his readers. But if today "having counsel" is beginning to have an old-fashioned ring, this is because the communicability of experience is decreasing. In consequence we have no counsel either for ourselves or for others. After all, counsel is less an answer to a question than a proposal concerning the continuation of a story which is just unfolding. To seek this counsel one would first have to be able to tell the story. . . . Counsel woven into the fabric of real life is wisdom. The art of storytelling is reaching its end because the epic side of truth, wisdom, is dying out.[20]

This vision of storytelling as the capacity to transmit experience orally and to give counsel much in the way a master might pass skills on to an apprentice, as well as the notion that this capacity is in a state of decline, dominates the consciousness behind *Heimat*. These themes are enacted graphically in the sequence in which Anton is confused and in need of counsel in the face of the lucrative offer by a multinational corporation to buy out his factory. On Martha's suggestion he seeks out his father and heads for Baden-Baden, where Paul is helping Hermann to process the prerecorded sections of his first musical composition to be performed on radio. Paul, who in the later episodes of the film figures as little more than an emblem of all the corruption and alienation associated with the American way of life, the irrevocable homelessness of the *Weggeher*—this is Reitz's neologism for those who go away, who leave the Heimat— has clearly lost that "epic dimension of truth" and is unable to counsel his son appropriately. Anton, who in his lens factory imagines himself to have maintained the best of the premodern mode of production symbolized by his grandfather, seeks in his father the counsel of one who would still speak the language of such a tradition. Instead he faces the caricature of an aging American businessman in Bermuda shorts and Hawaiian shirt who can no longer understand the autochthonous language of storytellers unless, as Paul's later endowment of a *Heimatmuseum* indicates, it is cast as simulacrum, as "hyperreal."[21] In Baden-Baden, Anton also finds the figure of a young German artist, his younger half-brother Hermann, who is busy alienating (*verfremden*) and reassembling prerecorded frag-

The *Weggeher* attempts his return to the Heimat. From *Heimat*, a film by Edgar Reitz, courtesy of the filmmaker

ments of natural sounds—the song of a nightingale, for example—into a patchwork of musical *écriture*. The gist of this sequence is Anton's painful discovery that the father as elder, wise ancestor, storyteller, is no longer available. This same discovery is enacted rather more indirectly at the formal level of Hermann's composition: the voice of nature is recuperated sentimentally, as dissonant text.

Another important aspect of the idyllic matrix as the space of authentic, narratable experience is the central role death plays in such a world. The displacement of history as a series of grand world-historical events by the slower, more "organic" rhythms of everyday existence entails a heightened awareness of the equal subordination of all to the ravages of time and death. Each swing of the pendulum—or rather each intertitle announcing a new year—recalls the arm of the reaper, who actually makes a brief appearance in the film as the ghostly railroad worker who oversees Otto Wohlleben's death. In Benjamin's terms, experience, as represented in the text of the authentic storyteller, is always referred back to a base line of natural history (*Naturgeschichte*)[22]: "Death is the sanction of everything that the storyteller can tell. He has borrowed his authority from death. In other words, it is natural history to which his stories refer back."[23] The force of natural history, as it is invoked here by Benjamin and evoked repeatedly in *Heimat*, is seen in its capacity to assimilate the irregular ups and downs, the fitful accelerations and decelerations of political history as well as what in Western societies is generally called progress, to the regular rhythm of life and death, growth and decay. The gaze of the storyteller, says Benjamin, does not "stray from the dial in front of which there moves the procession of creatures of which, depending on circumstances, Death is either the leader or the last wretched straggler."[24] In *Heimat* this effect is achieved by the fairly steady stream of deaths which accompanies life within the village, eroding, furrowing, and marking the social landscape as a space of mortality. Furthermore, all deaths, whether of small children suffering from diptheria, young men in the war, or elders in the gentle peace of their beds, are treated as natural phenomena and ultimately as the same: as a piece of fate. The general attitude toward death is neatly encapsulated or miniaturized as a kind of proverb in Paul's childhood words, recalled by his mother, during a near-fatal bout with diptheria: "'Now I've turned seven and have to die.'" And indeed, in the village of Schabbach there seems to be little rage against death, only fear, sadness, and finally pious resignation. The one case in which there is open rage is treated parodically, when the official speaker delivers his rabble-rousing revenge speech at the unveiling of the war memorial in 1922. That the speaker has come from the outside and that he continues to link the death of the fallen sons of Schabbach to the inorganic rhythms of European political history, underscores just how alien—and, translated into the codes of the film, inauthentic—his view of death is from the more *naturgeschichtlich* point of view of the Schabbacher.

What ultimately threatens the authentic mode of death and dying turn out to be the same forces that have eaten into the capacity to give counsel. The corrosion of wisdom is equiprimordial with the loss of the capacity, and entitlement, to have one's own death. This connection comes as no surprise since, as Benjamin insists, "not only man's knowledge or wisdom, but above all his real life [*sein gelebtes Leben*]—and this is the stuff that stories are made of—first assumes transmissible form at the moment of death."[25]

The way one dies in the modern age is a central theme of Rilke's remarkable novel, *The Notebooks of Malte Laurids Brigge*. Reitz's evocation of the premodern and its demise shows his affinity with the sensibility of this highly ambivalent modernist text. Rilke describes, for example, the modern procedures for dying:

> Now they are dying in 559 beds. Factory-like, of course. Where production is so enormous an individual death is not so nicely carried out; but then that doesn't matter. It is quantity that counts. Who cares anything today for a finely-finished death? No one. Even the rich, who could after all afford this luxury of dying in full detail, are beginning to be careless and indifferent; the wish to have a death of one's own is growing ever rarer. A while yet, and it will be just as rare as a life of one's own.[26]

Or as Benjamin puts it:

> In the course of the nineteenth century bourgeois society has, by means of hygienic and social, private and public institutions, realized a secondary effect which may have been its subconscious main purpose: to make it possible for people to avoid the sight of the dying. . . . Today people live in rooms that have never been touched by death.[27]

This, as Reitz recognizes, is a condition that sterilizes existence, leaving no traces of *gelebtes Leben*, of exemplary experience that could become the stuff of stories. It is clearly one of the goals of *Heimat* to desterilize the spaces of daily life, to place its audience in rooms, as it were, in which death and the dying have dwelled.[28]

II

In Reitz's attention to death as an expression of natural history, and the consciousness that the rhythms of this other temporality are in danger of being absorbed by the temporality of so-called progress and technology—a theme central to all of Heidegger's postwar writings—the fundamentally elegiac orientation of the film comes into focus. What *Heimat* seems to be mourning is the passing of a world in which mourning was still possible. The film links the capacity to mourn to one's relationship to all forms of separation and, in a central way, one's relationship to objects of daily use. Contemporary Western society represents for Reitz a world in which people have learned to separate painlessly from everything, where what has been lost leaves no scars, no traces, in the psyches and physiognomies of the survivors. This is a world "in which one separates from everything. Where one can separate from parts of one's life and parts of one's soul, one's family, one's experience; wherever we look we find these seemingly painless separations."[29]

In an essay on Chris Marker's film *Sans Soleil*, Reitz articulates the central elements of the elegiac consciousness behind *Heimat*. Among other things, Marker's film documents non-Western rituals of separation and mourning: "He . . . tells of ceremonies of parting in which people take leave from objects no longer needed with a dignity that is ever more foreign to us."[30] This ritualization of separation, the performance of formal *Trauerspiele* for objects of daily use—brushes, needles, dolls, abacuses—is so important, according to Reitz, for it is in one's relationship to the things of the everyday world that one develops the capacity to feel and mourn all other forms of loss. Mourning is understood here as that process whereby an object that was a part of our ongoing lives is ritually guided into the past tense of our lives. For each object the passage from the living moment into the flickering shadow world of memory requires, in other words, something on the order of a funerary ritual or elegiac procedure lest the spirits of the revenant, vampiric object haunt us eternally from that space of the unmourned, the unconscious. And finally, Reitz has claimed, in the age of consumer capitalism, that is, in the *Wegwerfgesellschaft* (throwaway society) the last available site where such rituals may be performed is cinema:

> If I part in an unworthy manner from visible things, if I avoid the anguish of separation, then the wall that separates life from death will become thicker and thicker; history will march forward, blocking off its memory as one might stop one's ears. Without knowing it, consumer society [*die Wegwerfgesellschaft*] is surrounding itself with the ghosts of all the things it has used and tossed away—and which will have their revenge on us. Film can be a medium and a means of reconciliation.

And indeed, film turns out to be remarkably well suited to be the site of the symbolic procedures of funerary ritual because film is, according to Reitz, an inherently elegiac medium. I would like to quote at length from Reitz's remarks on the elegiac dimensions of film, since they resonate so deeply with the concerns of my study:

> The camera transforms everything it films into a thing of the past. Anyone who films thereby takes leave from the things before the lens. . . . The camera is our memory. Whenever we create a montage of film material, assemble it anew into cinematic sequences of image and sound, we're performing memory-work [*Erinnerungsarbeit*]. And that is . . . not the opposite of forgetting; rather we reassemble the fragments of memory in new ways [*wir setzen die Bruchstücke des Gedächtnisses neu zusammen*]. Whenever we tell stories or represent "history" in our feature films, we are remembering in this manner: the temporal continuum has been ruptured. We never recuperate the past. Rather we part, in a definitive sense, from things, but with a dignity and grace that is lacking when we simply forget them.

And further:

> When people and things pass out of reach of our sensory perception, when they go away, die, or we go away, or time takes them from us, we experience pain. This pain is born of the hopelessness of ever being able to truly make things our own, of being able to love them, use or possess them. Even eating, the most intensive form of appropriation, is a modality of leave-taking. But in parting from things, they

pass over into our memory, become integrated into the spatio-temporal relation to which we too belong. In taking leave, in this passage from a sensuous relation to a relation of memory, we discover the origin of the legends and stories, of the images that live on independently of any particular human being, like the wound that exists without a body. When one looks closely, film always has something to do with parting. Film concerns itself with things and people that disappear from our sensory perception, with this pain that every good frame reproduces and produces. . . . Parting is the great theme of every film.[31]

These reflections seem more applicable to still photography than to motion pictures in which the "reality effect"—the illusion of full presence and participation in a living moment—is often quite powerful. Perhaps for this very reason Reitz frequently lets his camera linger on a scene, a landscape, an object, a face, a pair of hands, freezing the incessant forward movement of the film into the (melancholic) equipoise of a still photograph. Beneath each of these stills one can easily imagine a caption: "Katharina, the day Paul returned from the war"; "Women spinning linen in the Wiegands' parlor"; "The day the Americans arrived." This procedure becomes quite self-conscious during the picnic scene at the Baldenau ruins in the first episode of the film at which the members of the various Schabbach clans, arranged for a group portrait, are seen through the lens of Eduard's camera. For a few moments the viewer seems no longer to be watching a film but, rather, to be viewing an old photograph. Reitz repeats this procedure several times throughout the film, even when a scene does not include a photographer: characters simply look into the camera as if they were posing for a photograph. The viewer has the uncanny sensation of being asked to snap a picture (one thinks, for example, of Maria and Anton posing in front of Lucie and Eduard's villa, Christmas 1935). Starting with part 2, Reitz reiterates this photography effect quite systematically at the beginning of each episode. Before the epic action picks up, the viewer is shown Glasisch-Karl's hands as he sorts through stacks of photographs ostensibly taken at earlier moments in the chronicle; he pulls out particular photos, offers brief commentaries, and refreshes the viewer's memory. Kaes has suggested that these photographs, as representations of representations, ironize the documentary fiction of the film and, furthermore, serve as instruction to the audience as

Picnic amid the Baldenau ruins. From *Heimat*, a film by Edgar Reitz, courtesy of the filmmaker

to the proper posture vis-à-vis the film images it is witnessing. The memory-work Glasisch performs with these photographs thereby offers a model of the sort of activity required of the viewer with regard to the film.[32] In this sense, Glasisch-Karl and the viewer engage in an activity not unlike the memory-work of the filmmaker himself which is, as Reitz has said, a labor of re-collection: "we reassemble the fragments of memory in new ways."

But surely the most important aspect of these photo album sequences is the way they underscore the elegiac or funerary dimension of the still photograph:

> Photography is an elegiac art, a twilight art. Most subjects photographed are, just by virtue of being photographed, touched with pathos. . . . All photographs are *memento mori*. To take a photograph is to participate in another person's (or thing's) mortality, vulnerability, mutability. Precisely by slicing out this moment and freezing it, all photographs testify to time's relentless melt.[33]

Or as John Berger who, like Reitz, has situated his own artistic and essayistic practice in a direct, working relationship to European rural life, has more recently described the photographic moment:

> Every photograph presents us with two messages: a message concerning the event photographed and another concerning a shock of discontinuity. Between the moment recorded and the present moment of looking at the photograph, there is an abyss. We are so used to photography that we no longer consciously register the second of these twin messages—except in special circumstances: when for example, the person photographed was familiar to us and is now far away or dead. In such circumstances the photograph is more traumatic than most memories or mementos because it seems to confirm, prophetically, the later discontinuity created by the absence or death.[34]

The rhythms of Reitz's camera work—his choice of what to film, for how long, from what distance and angle, with what filter, and so on—seem to be in large part dedicated to bringing the viewer to a place where he or she can consciously and safely register this second message.

Reitz contends that farmers have,[35] or at least at one time had, no need of photographs or film images because their world is populated by artifacts bearing the scars and traces of the passage of time, legible as signifiers of human mortality. According to Reitz, such traces provide the concrete, material base of all storytelling: "Farmers don't need films. They live amidst the concrete testimonies, the mnemonic tokens of their stories [den realen Beweisstücken ihrer Geschichten]." It is only postmoderns who need film images in order to retain the capacity to experience the movement of time and thereby maintain a deep relationship to their own finitude:

> A long time ago, we were all farmers. For most of us, the memory of this earlier existence has vanished. We mobile citizens of vague, indeterminate places need for our stories new, transportable kinds of testimonies and mnemonic tokens. And film images—or other sorts of images—that we can take with us are just that sort of thing. . . . A film can follow us to all parts of the world and replace our lost village.[36]

In these reflections are motifs I discussed earlier in relation to contemporary discourses of bereavement. Film, much like the signifier in poststructuralist critical practice, becomes here a kind of fetishized elegiac token that is commissioned, as it were, with the task of restoring to viewers a deep existential vocation as mourners in an age when people are, so the story goes, quickly losing touch with the symbolic procedures constitutive of their survivorship. Film invites viewers to overcome a chronic inability to mourn precisely by becoming sensitized to the experience of *chronos*, that is, the passing of time and the losses and separations that belong to their being-in-time. The danger here is that such existential pathos easily spills over into sentimentality and kitsch. As Sontag has said: "As the fascination that photographs exercise is a reminder of death, it is also an invitation to sentimentality. Photographs turn the past into an object of tender regard, scrambling moral distinctions and disarming historical judgments by the generalized pathos of looking at time past."[37] And indeed, over the course of these fifteen and one-half hours of film one comes to suspect that Reitz's interest in and procedures of restoring to members of his audience their deep, mortal awareness of the passing of time and therewith a certain capacity to mourn, may have costs at the level of moral distinctions and historical judgments which may prove to be exorbitant.

III

A good place to begin an examination of such costs is Reitz's essay "Unabhängiger Film nach Holocaust?" (Independent film after *Holocaust?*), a polemic that grew out of the debate surrounding the 1979 telecast of the American miniseries *Holocaust* on German television. It is well known that this film became a major cultural and political event in the Federal Republic. *Holocaust*, which had been roundly attacked in its land of origin for trivializing horror and commercializing historical suffering,[38] became, in the land of origin of the Holocaust, a site at which a nation seemed to begin to engage in the deep emotional labor of mourning. A sentimental work of popular culture had apparently achieved what political documentaries and works of a more avant-garde aesthetic had failed to do. Whether this was in fact the case is not my present concern.[39] Of interest here are the categories Reitz deploys in his evaluation of the film and its effects on the capacities of Germans to remember and come to terms with their pasts. Reitz's position vis-à-vis *Holocaust* becomes all the more important when one recalls that he conceived of *Heimat* to a large extent as a response—or better: as a German antidote—to that American television film.

In his essay on *Holocaust*, Reitz lays out several oppositions that distinguish his own film aesthetic, and therewith an authentic mode of recollection, from the commercial aesthetic of the American culture industry and its inauthentic mnemonic procedures. First, Reitz defines an opposition between what he calls thinking in categories (*Schubladendenken*) and working on memories:

> If we are to come to terms with the Third Reich and the crimes committed in our country, it has to be by the same means we use every day to take stock of the world we live in. We are suffering from a hopeless lack of meaningfully structured and aesthetically mediated experience. The result of this is that our reflexes atrophy, that we no longer detect the scent of evil, no longer spot the Neo-Nazi in his small gestures, that we no longer feel in our bones the anguish of our fellows, that something like real compassion no longer emerges spontaneously in the context of simple human contact. . . . One should put an end to thinking in categories [*Schubladendenken*] even where this terrible part of our history is concerned. As far as possible, we must work on our *memories*. This way, films, literary products, images come into being that enlighten our senses and restore our reflexes.[40]

Schubladendenken is understood as that mode of thinking which levels out the rough surfaces of individual experience, memory, personality, for the sake of a preformed image of universal and homogeneous—and thus predictable—types. Thinking in categories is thus diametrically opposed to the aesthetic of *Heimat*, which entails a vigilant attentiveness to the unique, regional inflections of human behavior. And indeed, Reitz sees *Schubladendenken* as an expression of the very forces that destroy all that is unique and "local" in human existence, namely those deeply resonant layers of experience which attach themselves to one's particular *Lebensraum* and which resist universalizing objectification.[41] In a word, thinking in categories becomes a mark of complicity in the corruption of Heimat and therewith the loss of those aspects of authentic experience enumerated above: the capacity to give counsel; a deep sense of the passing of time and of human finitude; the capacity to tell stories. *Holocaust*, as the embodiment of *Schubladendenken* in the realm of aesthetics, thus comes to represent for Reitz as well as for a number of other German filmmakers (including Hans Jürgen Syberberg), a key moment in the destruction of what is regional, local, individual, and unique in German culture and history, or perhaps more accurately: the capacity of Germans to cathect their regional cultures and histories.

By a peculiar displacement, then, the postwar generation is able to recuperate a moral posture unattained by the elders: the German filmmaker Reitz becomes a kind of Resistance fighter, only in the realm of images and representations, that is, against not the Holocaust but, rather, *Holocaust* and its producers, the Americans. And indeed, Reitz sees this as a struggle against *"der eigentliche Terror"* (the real terror) of the century: American aesthetics. Germans have, Reitz claims, abandoned their unique, regionally inflected experiences and memories because they have been morally terrorized by a television series. The work of resistance therefore must lie in the salvaging of local experience, local history, local memories:

> There are thousands of stories among our people that are worth being filmed, that are based on irritatingly detailed experiences which apparently do not contribute to judging or explaining history, but whose sum total would actually fill this gap. We mustn't let ourselves be prevented from taking our personal lives seriously. . . . Authors all over

the world are trying to take possession of their own history and there-with of the history of the group to which they belong. But they often find that their own history is torn out of their hands. The most serious act of expropriation occurs when a person is deprived of his or her own history. With Holocaust, the Americans have taken away our history.[42]

Reitz's position reflects a tendency alluded to earlier among artists and intellectuals in the seventies and eighties to privilege the local and regional dimensions of cultural and political life in the interest of subverting the hegemony of dominant cultural forms and norms. The dominant culture is understood as what pollutes, dilutes, or colonizes in some way the small local environments with which people most intimately and immediately identify.[43] The phenome-non of the Green Party in Germany is thus only the most visible political manifestation of a more widespread return to the local, which has included, among other things, a revival of interest in regional dialects, folk music, and folklore in general.[44] This power-ful anticentrist ideology is at the heart of Reitz's polemic against *Holocaust*. And here it might bear reiteration that according to Reitz's own rather existentialist version of this "new regionalism," it is only by way of such a local intentionality that a deep relationship to one's finitude—and a capacity to mourn—may be nurtured.

In his polemic against the American culture industry as embodied by *Holocaust*, Reitz introduces another binary opposition that further distinguishes his own approach from the "terror" of the Hollywood film aesthetic. The terms of this opposition are experience (*Erlebnis*) and judgment (*Urteil*). This opposition warrants particular attention, since it introduces the reader to the ways in which Reitz tends to work out his own deep ambivalences about a number of the themes and concerns that become so central to *Heimat*: the family, moderni-ty, art, capitalism, history:

The difference between a scene that rings true and one fabricated by commercial scriptwriters, as in *Holocaust*, is similar to that between "experience" and "judgment." Judgments about events can be circu-lated separately, manipulated, pushed across desks, bought and sold. Experiences, on the other hand, are tied to human beings and their faculty of memory, they become false or falsified when living details [*lebendige Details*] are replaced in an effort to eliminate subjectivity and uniqueness.[45]

The attentive reader will no doubt hear strong resonances with similar binary oppositions—*Schubladendenken*—that have quite often in German cultural history been deployed to identify what is essentially *German* in the European cultural sphere. One thinks, for example, of Luther's distinction between the *Geist* and the *Buchstabe* of biblical script, of the Sturm und Drang opposition between courtly French decadence and earthy German authenticity, or of Thomas Mann's reinscription of this opposition in the first year of World War I as bloodless French and English *Zivilisation* versus an anything but anemic German *Kultur.*[46]

These oppositions, as Jacques Derrida and others have demonstrated in recent years, are emblematic of a certain way of thinking about and imagining difference which has dominated much of Western thought since the Greeks and which recent critical theory has been intent on challenging. The pair "experience/judgment" reiterates an opposition that in a number of different contexts, including those from the German cultural tradition cited above, may be described as one between the voice and writing. Experience, Reitz insists, is "tied to human beings and their faculty of memory," whereas judgments have come untethered from their living source— from their bloodline, as it were—and thus they exhibit, like written, material signifiers, a certain promiscuity, an easy availability to citation; they can, like all texts, be "circulated separately," they can, in the absence of their author, be "manipulated . . . bought and sold."

Derrida in particular has explored the ideological import of such oppositions in ways relevant to my analysis of *Heimat* as well as to broader postmodern questions regarding the representation of difference and marginality. In the present context his analysis of the peculiar fate of the word *pharmakon* in the writings of Plato is especially interesting.[47] Pharmakon in Greek exhibits a polysemy similar to that explored by Freud in his 1910 paper, "The Antithetical Meaning of Primal Words," a continuation of explorations begun in the *Interpretation of Dreams.* The word can signify both medicine as well as poison; it displays the ambi-valence of a philter that can be both beneficent and maleficent. The pharmakon exhibits, in other words, precisely that ambiguity that makes all homeopathy possible. Furthermore, as Derrida demonstrates, there are numerous passages in the text of Plato in which this peculiar *Gift*—the German word for poison is related etymologically to the English "gift"—comes to be associated with writing, with language that has given itself over to the exteriority of written texts, material signifiers that may fall prey to the opinion mongering of sophists. Perhaps even more significant, such written texts seem to have, at least in the context of the *Phaedrus*, the power to seduce one away from home. In the frame story of the dialogue, Phaedrus lures Socrates out of the city to the banks of the Ilissus, where he has promised to read to Socrates from a written text, a speech by Lysias, that he has brought along:

> Operating through seduction, the *pharmakon* makes one stray from one's general, natural, habitual paths and laws. Here, it takes Socrates out of his proper place and off his customary track. The latter had always kept him inside the city. The leaves of writing act as a *pharmakon* to push or attract out of the city the one who never wanted to get out, even at the end, to escape the hemlock. They take him out of himself and draw him onto a path that is properly an *exodus*.

The seductiveness of the pharmakon is underlined by the myth associated with the site chosen for the dialogue, the riverbank where the virgin Orithyia was carried off by Boreus while she was playing with Pharmacia. Mere opinions or judgments, texts that by virtue of their exteriority to an animating voice can be bought and sold, as ghostwriters might sell speeches or Hollywood scriptwriters their textual commodities, can have the power of leading the innocent astray: of making one homeless. The voice of experience, on the other hand, still tied to its living source, is uncorruptible: "The Socratic word does not wander, stays at home, is closely watched: within autochthony, within the city, within the law, under the surveillance of its mother tongue."[48]

In the various significations associated with the pharmakon are elements of the character system that structures the social landscape and most of the important narrative displacements within *Heimat*. The narrative and characterological economy of the film has its sources in a long and powerful tradition in German literature and cinema, from quietist autobiographical writings, to eighteenth-century domestic tragedy, to various *Bildungsromane* of the eighteenth and nineteenth centuries, to the provincial stories and novellas of authors like Jeremias Gotthelf, to the so-called *Heimatfilm* (and one of its major variants, the *Bergfilm*, or alpine film) cited by Reitz in his own work (recall the scene in which various Schabbacher view

Carl Froelich's 1938 film *Heimat* in a movie theater in Simmern).[49] Each of these genres features something on the order of a catastrophe of seduction, of loss of innocence and purity, the violent insinuation of a corrupting and fragmenting distance into a world otherwise informed by a wholesome intimacy, often followed by a recuperation of that intimacy. Quite often the fall into alienation is precipitated by a parasitic intrusion from the outside and alien into the closed familiar world of Heimat, whether defined as the (non-)space of a pietist *schöne Seele* (beautiful soul) in monological communion with itself, the intimate sphere of the bourgeois family, the space of village life, or extended to the borderlines of the *Reich*. In each case the opening up of a realm of separateness and alterity which introduces the possibilities of misprision, dissimulation, intrigue, and betrayal—as well as play and playfulness—is transformed into an identifiable, delimited event brought about by a guilty party coming from the outside, a foreign agent as it were. As Derrida notes, the semantic field of pharmakon includes pharmakos, a word signifying, among other things, the scapegoat, that figure periodically and ritually expelled from the city in order to reconstitute the pure space of communal experience: "The city's body *proper* thus reconstitutes its unity, closes around the security of its inner courts, gives back to itself the word that links it with itself within the confines of the agora, by violently excluding from its territory the representative of an external threat or aggression. That representative represents the otherness of the evil that comes to affect or infect the inside by unpredictably breaking into it."[50]

Of course at one level of the film's discourse, Reitz portrays quite graphically and critically this ritual of expulsion at work in the idyllic matrices of Schabbach, by showing how both Appolonia and Klärchen are purged from the community. Both women are perceived as dangerous because they come from the outside and threaten to seduce the men of the village away from their Heimat. Both Paul and Hermann in fact become *Weggeher* after "contamination" by these women. Also interesting is the fact that each woman is homeless and has the status either of nomad/gypsy or refugee, and that each seeks little more than acceptance from and membership within the community; neither of these women chooses her status as wandering alien. At other narrative levels, however, the film seems to reenact its own rituals of purification and expulsion, its own ways of seeking out scapegoats for the losses that come to scar the communal tissue of Heimat. How one understands these rituals within the film as a whole is a crucial question, since an answer to it will inform an evaluation of the successes of the film as a performance of mourning. Mourning, as noted earlier, implies the refusal to reconstitute a damaged narcissism by assigning guilt to a pharmakos. On the contrary, the homeopathy of mourning always breaks or tropes the path home across the detour of the pharmakon. Is the elegiac story Reitz tells of the loss of the spaces in which losses could still be experienced organized as a performance of *Trauerarbeit*, or is this labor undermined by a renewed search for scapegoats?

These scapegoats, as one might imagine, will exhibit the trappings of the judgment pole of the opposition discussed above; they will embody, among other things, a certain mobility and promiscuity, an alienation from the living voice of experience. The most obvious example of such a figure is, of course, "the American": Paul Simon. That the American will come to stand in as the representative of the floating exteriority of judgment comes as no suprise since the opposition experience/judgment was cast in the context of Reitz's polemic against the American television film *Holocaust*. One of the great dangers of that film is its threat to the capacity of Germans to know, at all times, what is really their own voice, thus preparing the way for "the deepest loss, the loss of one's own language."[51]

Paul Simon returns to Schabbach as the wealthy American. He and his adopted country are repeatedly associated with chronic homelessness, an infantile belief that dollars can buy anything and everything, emotional frigidity—he tries to regain entrance into Maria's heart and bed by telling her that his feet are cold—and ultimately a deep sadness about having to live "in that cold land," as Katherina refers to America. Reitz himself says of Paul: "He has become a real American, in the way he behaves, in his attitudes, even in his ability to express himself. . . . He is a man without a home ("ein Heimatloser"!), without roots, a sentimental globetrotter."[52] " 'American aesthetics' is the 'real terror,' " and Paul represents that terror in the way he tries to buy his way back into Schabbach, displacing the rich, regional inflections of Hunsrücker Platt with the hollow jingle of American coins and *Schubladen*-phrases of American English, the language of "international competition,"[53] as well as in the role he plays as the patron of Hermann's (German)

music. That in the end the American, America, and American aesthetics can come to stand for the "real terror" and for the "deepest
loss" in a film about Germany in the period of history which includes the years of the Third Reich and the Holocaust must raise
questions about how the consciousness behind the film has organized the tasks of mourning that one would imagine need to be
addressed and worked through in this German requiem. This issue
becomes even more vexing in light of this further elucidation on
Reitz's part concerning the "real terror" of the twentieth century:

> America is the foremost example of the development of this new, this
> second culture in our world, the culture of emigrants, of those who
> left home [der Weggegangenen]. Their basic principle is individualism,
> one's feeling of self-worth. [This is] a new society of human beings
> who have no commodity to offer except themselves and thus engage
> in a life-and-death competition. Whatever these many individuals
> bring forth in terms of abilities, inventions, products (including agri-
> cultural products) becomes the exclusive object of commerce, a com-
> merce which demands ever new, ever more spectacular offers and
> which relates everything with everything else through the shared
> vernacular of trade. . . . Thus arises an internationally communicable
> culture of emigrants. The Jews, since time immemorial "people who
> go away" [Weggeher], fit well into this American culture, a culture that
> that only seeks to expand and to compete in all areas, whose very own
> language is competition.[54]

By a peculiar chain of associations the Jews once more come to
occupy the position of scapegoat, here shared with the Americans
and America, in what turns out to be the deepest strand in the
narrative of loss that *Heimat* relates.

IV

Heimat is a story of loss: the disappearance of a world in which experiences of loss and separation are ritualized and thereby integrated, as
a series of visible, legible traces, into the living fabric of the everyday.
It is the world of those premodern artifacts celebrated and mourned
in Rilke's *Duino Elegies* and his novel *Malte*. According to Reitz,
consumer capitalism in its most radical (that is, American) form—
America signifying here, once again, the culture of the *Weggeher*—is

the *Wegwerfgesellschaft*, which in turn represents the final disappearance of the world of human experience in which *naturgeschichtlich* rhythms are still palpable in the timeworn textures of objects of daily use. And indeed, Reitz sees the Holocaust itself as an epiphenomenon of this deeper story of loss. Auschwitz is, in this view, "the most extreme example of the *Wegwerfgesellschaft* the world has ever known, the *Wegwerfgesellschaft* magnified to monstrous proportions: human beings become refuse."[55] Attention to the various strands and subterranean associations of this elegiac master narrative brings a stunning irony into focus. The Jews, as the archaic embodiment of the ethic of the *Weggeher*, come to signify the forces that ultimately rent the fabric of the idyll.[56] But the tropological slippages of Reitz's discourse suggest something more radical still. Since Auschwitz is itself only a surface manifestation of the deeper historical processes governing the *Weggeher/Wegwerfgesellschaft*, the Jews figure, according to Reitz's logic, as a metonymy for the very forces that lead to their destruction. Auschwitz thereby becomes the site not only of the literal destruction of European Jewry but also, at a metaphysical level, of a sort of Jewish self-destructiveness as well: the Holocaust as the closure of the Jewish dialectic of the Enlightenment.[57]

Quite interestingly, in a recent book by an American Jewish author of Reitz's generation, Frederic Morton makes claims about the Jews and about the history of the Judeo-Christian tradition more generally, which in many ways echo those of Reitz.[58] Morton is especially interesting in the present context because he was himself violently transformed into a *Weggeher* when he was forced into exile from his Viennese Heimat in 1939.[59] The fundamental thesis of this remarkable volume is that the entire history of Western civilization is structured as an ongoing falling away from the capacity to dwell within small, familiar spaces of local collectivities. The archaic form of such a collectivity was, according to Morton, the Paleolithic hunting community; this was the primordial site where, to use Reitz's Hunsrücker word, *Geheischnis* was truly experienced for the first and perhaps for the last time: "The Savage was noble all right, in the early, forgotten meaning of the word: *nobilis*, meaning well-known to everyone else in his horizon. Every Paleolithic hunter was well-known to everyone else in his horizon. All his fellow villagers were well-known to him. Compared with today's world, his was a coziness of familiar eyes."[60] Contemporary civilization, dominated as it is by an all-pervasive metaphysic of instrumental reason—Morton's name for this metaphysic is "the Factory," a term that resonates strongly with Heidegger's *Gestell*[61]—stands at the most extreme distance from such a world: "We are all ignoble. . . . We are waiting for some nearness to happen. . . . We're all frozen into separate, stranded selves." The fall from the nidus of "your-face–my-face concord" may be dated, in Morton's narrative, with the invention of the plow, that is, with the shift from hunting to agricultural societies. In agriculture humans experience for the first time a new mode of temporality which introduces new kinds of anxiety and psychic stress: working now for a satisfaction deferred to some indeterminate future. Time, and the law of succession of time, becomes the "chronic" condition of agricultural society:

> For the hunters, the chasing of the deer was as exciting as the eating of it together. Both acts composed the same communal arc, the same collective joy. But with the plow, the first bisection of life was invent-ed: monotonous effort here—mere gorging way over there. . . . It was in agriculture that the instincts of the Factory were bred. The hunters lived, lunged, consummated in the gregarious instant. The plower sweated in lone postponement; he heaved and strained for an abstraction, for the crop that is not yet.[62]

It is also, Morton continues, with the rise of agricultural societies, that a new form of ritual worship comes on the scene. As hunting is displaced by agriculture, so the sacrificial meal, celebrated as an act of communion with the deity, is displaced by the sacrifice in the sense of tribute:

> The plower had to push and push and push the plow blade through furrow after furrow after furrow. He would not bend his back to wearisome rote unless driven by an exacting king, by a rigorous god-head. The plower made his offerings to a Deity Who was too peremp-tory to permit inferiors at His table. This God ate alone and He ate every shred. The plower, a fearful, resentful, sinful toiler, submitted his grain to appease a wrathful, jealous all-consuming God. And, of course, his God accepted nothing but a *holocaust*—that which is *wholly burned*—nothing but the sort of drastic homage that finishes entirely in ashes. There was no holocaust, no real war, no large-scale system-atic slaughter until the plower's anger and fear.

It was, finally, the Hebrews (whose name, as Morton mentions, means "the ones from the other shore of the river") who came to internalize and systematize this agricultural Factory metaphysic, who became, in other words, chronic Cainites dedicated/condemned to a fate of ceaseless striving and transcendence, compelled always to move beyond the equipoise of local habitations. And as a result of the suffering that comes with such a remorseless existence, the God of the Hebrews introduced into Western civilization yet another new phenomenon, the Sabbath: "His gift unyoked the Hebrews for one day from the compulsions ruling their week. Before the Hebrews, no other people had a Sabbath. No other people needed one."[63]

The rest of Morton's book traces the vicissitudes of the Factory metaphysic as it comes to absorb ever greater spaces of human existence—in the modern period, including even the Sabbath—and as it comes to dominate and organize the epochal movements of Western history. Included in this history of the Factory are the imperial strivings of Ancient Rome, the rise of Christianity, the triumphs of Renaissance spirit, the French Revolution, the conquests of nineteenth-century imperialism and twentieth-century fascism, and finally the emergence of a postcolonial, postmodern media society. In this contemporary phase, the space and time of local habitation have been finally reduced to a hyperreal simulation; the kairos, in which the ecclesia or "local assembly" once gathered in authentic communion, has become the prime time of network television. This is, of course, a thoroughgoing monist vision of history according to which every event and every instance of human behavior is intelligible only insofar as it signifies a moment either of complicity with or resistance to the dialectic of the Factory as it plows under and swallows up all forms of the local: those small places where a human gaze was met and returned by familiar eyes.

Both Morton's vision of the history of the West and Reitz's microcosmic version of that history as it is played out in the fictive village of Schabbach between 1919 and 1982 share a familiar narrative strategy: an allegorical doubling of an autobiographical narrative of loss. Morton's forced expulsion from his Austrian homeland in 1939, his journey west toward New York, and the alienation that informs the life of an artist are doubled in the elegiac plot that begins with Abraham's covenant with God six thousand years ago in Mesopotamia— "'Get thee out of thy kindred and from thy father's house'"[64]—and ends in the diaspora that is postmodern society where, Morton claims, the "local" can be recuperated only as simulacrum. *Heimat* exhibits a similar, if somewhat more complex, deployment of double plots.

V

The film as a whole centers on two archetypal plots, one female, one male. The first narrative unit is articulated by the life of Maria who, when she dies, "has grown as old as our century,"[65] and is the primary carrier of the positive values of Heimat and the slower rhythms of folkloric time. The male narrative is organized essentially as a *Bildungsroman* and is enacted in two variants, the story of Paul and the story of Hermann, the latter representing that subgenre of the *Bildungsroman* exemplified by the ontogenetic (as opposed to the phylogenetic) narrative of Morton's double plot, the *Künstlerroman* (artist's novel). In each variant the protagonist experiences a traumatic alienation or expatriation from the idyll which prepares the way for entrance into a more abstract symbolic order that might, in good Hegelian fashion, be called "civil society."[66] And in both variants, the catastrophe of alienation from the idyllic matrix is enacted as an estrangement from Maria, bringing with it an enormous burden of guilt. The story of this estrangement is then doubled at the quasimythic level of the story of the destruction of Heimat under the pressures of modernity. The association of these estrangements from Maria/Heimat with the more general disintegration of the idyll is especially strong in Paul's case. At the beginning of the film, Paul is associated with the new technologies—radio and electronics— which eventually seduce Schabbach out of its protective insularity at the margins of historical process. When this disintegration becomes most accelerated, Paul's association with forces of corruption has become all-encompassing; it invades his national identity, and he becomes other, alien, "the American." The story of young men abandoning their home/wife/mother/mother tongue is doubled, in other words, at the level of mythically conceived historical processes that rend the fabric of communal life in Schabbach. At this second narrative level the introduction of technologies of mechanical reproduction, communication, and transportation lead, ultimately, to an inability to experience Heimat except as its own hyperreal projection, emblematized by Ernst's commerce in simulacra and Paul's transformation of the Simon house into a museum/mausoleum.[67] Given the supplementary association of a corrosive modernization with Americanization in the later episodes of the film, this doubling creates the illusion of a magical causation whereby one of the double plots seems to be called forth by the other. This illusion makes the pain of leaving home—the mournful assumption of an identity mediated by symbolic codes and the laws of substitution—seem *caused* by a seduction from the West, from the other shore. "America" thereby becomes the signifier not so much of this or that concrete transformation of social relations but of the evil of having to enter into social relations beyond the immediacy of the idyllic matrix at all, that is, the evil of mediation.

Each level of the double plot is informed by that powerful habit of the imagination which I will call, following James Clifford, the "salvage paradigm," itself a variant of what Raymond Williams has analyzed as "pastoral narrative." According to this all-too-familiar narrative form, a "relatively recent period of authenticity is repeatedly followed by a deluge of corruption, transformation, modernization. . . . A 'good country' is perpetually ruined and lamented by each successive period, producing an unbroken chain of losses leading back ultimately to . . . Eden."[68] Eden, of course, is the name of that place where man has still been spared the poisons of the pharmakon.

This paradigm has had powerful consequences in the theory and practice of ethnography. Typically the Western ethnographer arrives at his or her non-Western site just before this exemplar of authentic local habitation is destroyed by the forces of history and modernity:

> In a salvage/pastoral setup most non-western peoples are marginal to the advancing world system. Authenticity in culture or art exists just prior to the present—but not so distant or eroded as to make collection or salvage impossible. Marginal, non-western groups constantly (as the saying goes) enter the modern world. And whether this entry is celebrated or lamented, the price is always this: local, distinctive paths through modernity vanish. These historicities are swept up in a destiny dominated by the capitalist west and by various technologically advanced socialisms. What's *different* about peoples seen to be moving out of "tradition" into "the modern world" remains tied to inherited structures that either resist or yield to the new but cannot *produce* it.[69]

Whether it is Morton's Paleolithic hunting band before the invention of the plow or the village of Schabbach just prior to the onslaught of the American century—fascism appears in the film more or less as the first wave of this larger, more destructive and all-encompassing flood of modernity and postmodernity—the ethnographic present of the local habitation is denied an internal historical dynamic and is circumscribed and fetishized as virginal, natural preserve. Both Morton and Reitz fall short when it comes to the development of a more complex vision of an authentic regional culture as, to use Clifford's suggestive formulation, a "hybrid, creative activity in a local present-becoming-future."[70] The salvage paradigm underlying the double plot that organizes the fate of Schabbach and its citizens has no place for a hybrid condition in which the life of the individual and the life of the village as a whole would be "implicated by an interconnected world cultural system without necessarily being swamped by it." What is absent from *Heimat* is a vision in which "local structures produce *histories* rather than simply yielding to *History*."[71]

In summary, narratives organized according to the salvage paradigm attempt to freeze that fantasized moment just prior to the mournful entrance into the symbolic order and seek to assign blame for this catastrophic intrusion of alterity which, even for the (dialect-) speaking subjects of authentic regional cultures, has in a sense always already happened. The salvage paradigm, as it figures in *Heimat*, distributes the poles of ambivalence associated with entrance into that symbolic order known as the modern (and, finally, the postmodern) in such a way that the pain of loss which comes with this passage may be represented as a delimited moment of contamination, as an identifiable evil: as pharmakos.

At the same time, the film offers a great deal of material to undermine this master narrative and the fantasy that fuels its construction, namely that one could assign blame for the disintegration of Heimat to a quasi-demonic agency that comes from "the other shore" and that could, perhaps, be purged from the system called "home" (recall Nolte's references to the "Asiatic").[72] I have already alluded to the presence of such resistant material in my discussion of the first sequence of the film. There Paul has returned home from the war and internment in a prisoner-of-war camp and is reabsorbed into the rhythms of the idyllic matrices of labor and family. What is significant in this scene is the implication that such a reabsorption, insisting as it does on the repression of whatever traumata Paul may have brought back from the war and the camp, will lead to a potentially dangerous splitting of the self. This splitting leads to the formation of what Jameson calls, a "political unconscious" into which the remainders, the "structural irritants"[73] that cannot be acknowledged and integrated into the communal fabric, must be exiled. A form of exile thus begins *within* the borderlines of Heimat. The disposition of such irritants is especially significant given Reitz's insistence that his film, unlike American films, portrays the "irritatingly detailed experiences" of everyday existence.

Yet another, quite obvious irritant, or remainder, is the figure of Glasisch-Karl, whose scars from the war, a skin disease caused by exposure to mustard gas, contribute to making him an outsider in his own village. His alienation is graphically reenacted on numerous occasions when he is systematically excluded from family and communal photographs; only after much insistence on his part is he grudgingly awarded entry into the frame. Glasisch's position as a sort of village idiot evidently also has something to do with the question of his lineage. At the beginning of the final episode, Glasisch annotates the family tree of the three families central to the film. Only then does the audience become aware that he is Marie-Goot's son. Glasisch however insists, in the tone of an aside whispered in secret to the audience, that Mäthes-Pat, Marie-Goot's husband, was not his father. Glasisch's marginality is thus to a large degree a result of a dynamic intrinsic to the psychosocial economy of the village. Interestingly, Glasisch is the only villager who seems to understand Hermann's musical composition *"Bindungen"* (Connections). Hermann, of course, is Schabbach's other bastard. Furthermore, aside from Maria, Glasisch is the only other Schabbacher who has enough curiosity to ask Paul why he left home. Glasisch's curiosity about Paul, as well as the tone of voice in which he makes his query, suggests that he is perhaps hoping to learn something about himself in this exchange, secretly expecting a moment of anamnesis. Add to this the simple fact that both he and Paul are war veterans and that both men were at one time in love with Maria, and a deeper affinity between these figures seems implicit. Both men seem isolated by traumata they experienced during the war. Such traumata are graphically present in Glasisch's case. In Paul's case the traces of traumatization are evoked in part by the appearance, in the first episode of the film, of the ghost of the fallen soldier and friend Helmut Legrand. One suspects that neither Paul nor Glasisch discusses his war experiences and the ways he continues to be haunted by them, because the social structures and codes of interpersonal discourse of the Heimat provide no space in which these experiences could be named and integrated. Paul's isolation is further emphasized during the scene of the unveiling of the war memorial. In the midst of the ceremony, a lone mourner clutching a private monument for the loss of three sons marches alone and sings his own, unofficial lament. Eric Rentschler's remarks on this scene emphasize its elements of disturbance and resistance:

> The subjective response stands at odds with the public demonstration, suggesting a dissonance between the ritual act of remembrance and the actual fact of human suffering, a disparity between the perspective of a mythic community and that of an estranged individual, an antinomy between the organizational structures of public life and the lived realities of single persons. This is an outside perspective, one introduced by the gaze of Paul, an individual who throughout the sequence looks at the village with a growing discontent, and will later leave for America. The baker offers a moment of discord, a resistance to the codified containment of emotion; he, like Paul, has to go "outside" Schabbach to satisfy his sense of lack.[74]

The lack, in other words, already dwells within the idyll.[75] And indeed, the lack would appear to consist, at least in part, of an inability to acknowledge and accommodate occasions of mourning which transcend the horizons of local experience. But once more, according to the master narrative that organizes the film as a whole, to leave the circle of the local to make up for this lack is an act of betrayal which ultimately destroys everything of human value and which can never be made good again. One senses here Reitz's own deep ambivalences and feelings of guilt: an unresolved oscillation between feelings of repulsion toward and longing for the idyll of his film/memory: "The Hunsrück is still the home I abandoned. . . . I find in myself a fear of closeness and at the same time a longing for closeness."[76]

Other examples of irritants in the film are the various allusions to brutality and violence which punctuate the film like a series of demonic parapraxes tripping the mother tongue as it tries to stick close to its Hunsrücker Platt—the dialect spoken in heaven, as a local verse would have it. Among these slips of the mother tongue are the case of Hänschen, the boy whose left eye was poked out by a sibling at the dinner table, the brutal rhyme the village children sing to taunt the sexton, the dead woman found naked in the forest and the later discovery of her clothes—a strangely staggered return of the repressed—young Hermann's discovery of a severed finger during a Sunday stroll after the war, and of course the treatment, discussed earlier, suffered by Appolonia and Klärchen.

Once again, it is not that Reitz omits complexity or ambivalence from his portrayal of the idyll called Schabbach but, rather, that these ambivalences and inner tensions which are indeed shown to exist within the local, in part through the sheer excess of visual and anecdotal material, are strategically divided up and assigned to particular characters and distributed across the narrative axis of the film. The result of this process is the creation of a very powerful illusion, namely that all this complexity intervenes from the outside in the manner of a contamination. The narrative figuration of experience and bereavement in the film orbits around the fantasy of a realm of cultural purity and authenticity, a place where the autochthonic voice of experience has not yet been harrowed by the (American? Jewish? modern? postmodern?) plow of history.

VI

This tension between the excess of visual and anecdotal material—the film's tendency toward microdescription—on the one hand, and the vigilant narrative figuration of experience on the other, derives largely from the hybrid process of the film's production. As noted earlier, Reitz had already conceived the basic narrative structure of *Heimat* before beginning his two-year sojourn in the Hunsrück, during which time he and Peter Steinbach then composed a working draft of the screenplay. In addition, Reitz wrote this novel fragment—Reitz has always referred to *Heimat* as a *Filmroman* (film novel) rather than as a television miniseries—in the context of his own, very personal labor of coming to terms with his identity as a filmmaker after the failure of *Der Schneider von Ulm*. The novel fragment of *Heimat* was thus largely autobiographical, part of Reitz's efforts to map out and comprehend his own path from the idyllic matrix to the life of an artist in the metropolis.[77] The *Künstlerroman* framework was thus already in place before the oral history phase of the production began. The controversies surrounding this mode of historiography were articulated in the discussion of the debate between Friedländer and Broszat regarding the possibilities of historicizing the Shoah. And as noted there, *Heimat* has actually come to figure as an emblem for this *alltagsgeschichtlich* approach to the writing of history.

Alltagsgeschichte, or the history of the everyday, has for the most part been understood as a form of history written from below. Attention to the oral testimonies of those nonruling groups and classes that have heretofore been excluded from or represented in only distorted ways in the written record, and attention to documents previously neglected—diaries, family Bibles, photo albums—may bring to light new forms and aspects of subjectivity as a carrier and index of historical processes, and even newly conceived subjects of history. The imperial Book of History is democratically scattered, as it were, into the heterogeneous, populist text of multiple histories and their uneven, staggered temporalities. The work of decentering and decentralization that characterizes this approach to history is thus congruent with that more general tendency in political, aesthetic, and academic culture in the seventies and eighties to privilege the local and regional dimensions of human experience and to relinquish the totalizing claims of a single, univocal narrative of history. Here one might recall Eduard's response to Lucie's fantasies about the Simon "estate" as they approach Schabbach: " 'You know, in our language, in Hunsrücker Platt, words like "estate" just don't mean the same thing. . . . Those big words that name big things don't have any place in our world.' "[78] I suggest, however, that in *Heimat* Reitz falls prey to certain methodological pitfalls of oral history without sufficiently deploying the more exciting and progressive aspects of that practice; that he depends both too little and too much on the testimonies of his "informants." Reitz's particular application of these procedures in fact ends up working against the critical, counter-hegemonic potential of this turn to local knowledge and experience.

Writing about the narratological consequences of the shift from more traditional modes of historiography to oral history, Alessandro Portelli notes that the latter mode of historiography implies a transformation of the narrator's function analogous to the unsettling of that function in the modern novel. No longer an omniscient story-teller unproblematically free of the trappings and perspective of any particular subject position, the modern narrator—Portelli's example is Marlow in *Lord Jim*—becomes much more dependent on informants for the telling of his or her tale. And as Portelli argues, "The same thing happens to the historian working with oral sources: on entering the story and explicitly declaring control over it, he or she must on that very account allow the sources to enter the tale with their autonomous discourse. Thus, oral history is told from a multitude of 'circumscribed points of view'."[79] In *Heimat* Reitz never really makes use of this subversive potential of oral history methodology; rather than allow a variety of autonomous sources to enter the tale and assert their heterogeneous discourses, Reitz vigilantly enlists all voices in the service of a preconceived narrative itinerary.[80]

At the same time, the particular way in which Reitz prefigures Schabbach's course through the Weimar Republic, fascism, the occupation, the economic miracle, and its final entrance into a postmodern society of the hyperreal, reinscribes other, more ambiguous aspects of oral history methodology. One thinks here, for example, of the ways in which the film seeks to reproduce the experiential horizon of knowledge—and lack of knowledge—so often registered in the oral testimony of people speaking about their daily routines. What oral history quite often salvages is experience untainted by the rigors of judgment. As Kaes notes, in *Heimat* nearly all major historical events—changes of government, the end of the war, the currency reform, the formation of the two German states—"are not directly registered since they have not affected the cyclical patterns of village life in any immediate or palpable way."[81] The complicity of the film's narrative discourse with certain structural blind spots of the oral historian's methods may best be observed in that aspect of the film which has aroused the sharpest criticism: the representation of Jews and the Holocaust. As Gertrud Koch, one the most outspoken critics of the film, has said:

> The problem with that kind of experiential narrative is that experience itself necessarily works with fade-outs. The concept of Oral History, after all, was the attempt to show how history can be reconstructed in terms of individual consciousness. . . . I think that the fade-outs operative in *Heimat* are not at all original. In fact, the film reproduces the standard ellipses concerning the extermination of the Jews. . . . Whenever real horror would have to be thematized, the film resorts to these fade-out strategies which are analogous to the defense mechanisms of experience and as such elude critical reflection.[82]

What must be kept in mind here is not only the film's use of anecdotal material cited from within the experiential and mnemonic horizon of people who would have little motivation to remember Jews or the Holocaust but also the ways in which the elegiac master narrative of the film assigns a subordinate and marginal position to the Holocaust. Before addressing this latter phenomenon, I want to discuss the fade-outs Koch mentions.

The scene that is most emblematic of the activity of repression—the labor of absorbing textual irritants into the voice of experience—comes in the first episode. It is 1923; Eduard and Pauline make an afternoon excursion to Simmern, the largest town near Schabbach. Pauline wanders off alone and finds herself looking at the window display of the town watchmaker and jeweler. Suddenly a group of young men run up behind her—including Eduard, armed as usual with camera and tripod—and begin throwing rocks at the window of the apartment above the watchmaker's shop where, as the film later discloses, a Jew—in this case also branded as a separatist—resides. They are chased off by police but the shards of fallen glass have cut Pauline's hand. Robert Kröber, the watchmaker, signals her to come into the shop where he cleans her wound, thereby initiating the love story of Pauline and Robert. Later on in the film—it is 1933—the audience hears that the now-married Pauline and Robert are buying the Jew's apartment. As Robert remarks, "The house belongs to him and now he wants to sell it. . . . The Jews don't have it so easy anymore."[83]

This small *Kristallnacht* sequence shows how the shards of the Jew's shattered existence—he is never seen in the flesh—are immediately absorbed into a sentimental story of courtship and matrimony, that is, into experience. It is, of course, the filmmaker who is exposing this mechanism, who is depicting how experience forms and constructs itself around such blind spots. One wonders, however, whether the filmmaker is not in the end complicitous with such mechanisms, that is, whether Reitz is not content to absorb the shards of suffering of the other into so many anecdotes of love and family in the provinces. One way in which this complicity becomes manifest is the remarkable lack of curiosity shown by almost every character in the film about cases of historical suffering that become visible at various moments in the film. By historical suffering I mean precisely that suffering that disrupts, in a radical way, the normal rhythms of the kitchen and the blacksmith's workshop as well as the larger organic rhythms of birth and natural death: the disruption of the voice of *Naturgeschichte* by the text of an *Un-Naturgeschichte*, the most radical example being, of course, the Holocaust.

One of the most striking examples is Lotti's—and everyone else's—total lack of curiosity about her father, Fritz Schirmer, who was a Communist and has been taken to a concentration camp. There is actually some confusion in the film regarding Fritz's fate, since there is a scene set in 1943 in which Ursel, Lotti's younger sister, born in 1936, refers to her father as a soldier on the Eastern Front. Fritz, as the Schirmer's family tree reveals, died in 1937, in Dachau we may presume. That Lotti has not forgotten her father is suggested by the way she cuts off her sister when she begins to talk about him to Pieritz. And yet the audience never hears a word about him from Lotti herself who was, after all, already nine years old when her father was taken. Another, more striking example is the apparent lack of curiosity on anyone's part concerning the fate of Otto Wohlleben's mother who was, as he himself reveals, a Jew. She is in fact mentioned only in the context of Otto's allusion to his own career difficulties. As a so-called *Mischling*, the child of a mixed marriage, not professing the Jewish faith—Reitz refers to Otto as "the poor, propertyless half-Jew who could be kept at home and tamed"[84]—Otto was himself in no immediate danger. It is nonetheless quite uncanny that no one in the film asks about Frau Wohlleben's fate before, during, or after the war. Implicated in this strange sin of omission is also, of course, Frau Wohlleben's (illegitimate) grandson, Hermann. Hermann's silence is especially significant since he is, after all, a rather thinly veiled autobiographical portrait of the filmmaker-artist as a young man.[85]

In this context the composition of the one scene in which the Final Solution is even mentioned becomes all the more interesting. Episode 6, "The Home Front," shows a party at Eduard and Lucie's villa in Rhaunen. In the course of the evening, which takes on a comic undertone through Lucie's exaggerated performance as cultivated hostess, Wilfried whispers news of the extermination camps to two officers: "'The Final Solution is being carried out radically and without mercy. I really shouldn't be telling you any of this—between you and me, we know what's what. Up the chimneys, every last one of them.'" A few seconds later the camera pans across the room and follows Lucie to Eduard who has been sitting alone the entire evening blinking his left eye. When Lucie inquires about this peculiar behavior, Eduard reveals the object of his preoccupation: "'I . . . can't . . . stop thinking of little Hans, the basket weaver's boy. That he might still be alive today if only I hadn't taught him that.'"[86] Eduard had of course fostered Hänschen's talents as a sharpshooter, thus accelerating the progress of the boy's short-lived military career. The effect of this sequence, whether intentional or not, is the creation of a symmetry: all victims of the war are equal, whether German soldiers killed in battle or Jews murdered in Auschwitz. The symmetry is further underscored by the fact that it was originally through young Hänschen's eyes that a concentration camp was first seen earlier in the film. But to speak here of a symmetry may actually be too generous, since the Jewish victims remain invisible and Hänschen is a figure toward whom the audience has come to feel quite affectionate (recall in this context the asymmetrical symmetry of Hillgruber's study).[87]

Reitz has defended the marginalization of the fate of the Jews in *Heimat* with several different arguments. On a very pragmatic (or "documentary") level, he notes that the Hunsrück had a relatively small Jewish population and that the average village resident would have lacked concrete experiences with and memories of Jews.[88] It is not, in other words, that oral history fails methodologically in this regard but rather that there is a real paucity of lived experience to be remembered. And indeed, in *Heimat*, Jews never actually enter the frame but are present rather in three different modes of absence: as fantasy (when the naked woman is found dead in the forest in the first episode of the film, one of the villagers wonders if she might be a Jew); as cliché (one thinks of Eduard's remark that the new National Socialist agrarian reforms will cleanse the local economy of "Jews and profiteers"); or absent cause (aside from Robert and Pauline's buy-out of their Jewish landlord and Otto's career difficulties, Eduard and Lucie finance their villa through Bielstein, a Jewish banker from Mainz). The invisibility of Jews in *Heimat* is especially interesting with regard to the figure of Eduard Simon who is clearly—and admittedly—Reitz's favorite character in the film.[89]

Given the overwhelmingly sympathetic portrayal of Eduard, it comes as no great surprise that after holding forth to Schabbach farmers about getting rid of the Jewish influence on the local economy and later arguing with Lucie against her plan to borrow money from a Jewish banker, it is Eduard who, still only partially able to read the writing on the wall, finally defends Bielstein's financial claims: "'And as for Bielstein's death, should something terrible happen to him, my hands will have been clean. Besides, debts are debts, no matter who one owes the money to.'" At this point Eduard gives voice to the photographer/collector's melancholic sensibility that pervades the film as a whole, here as a kind of a prayer: "'Now is the exact moment when time should stand still. . . . When everything we've accomplished should remain just as it is. The new road, this completely new life—it should all remain just as it is for everyone and for all times. And we should stop wanting to have *more*. And everyone should remain healthy, everyone we know. And Bielstein too, with his bank in Mainz.'" But as Martina, who has just arrived from Berlin, immediately reminds him, "'of course then you've got your debts again.'"[90]

In this scene it is Eduard who claims the sympathy of the audience as the hapless pawn of forces beyond his control, as the passive victim of the blind and anonymous law of time itself. Absent from this portrayal of Eduard are indications of a more active participation in this cruel "anonymity" of *chronos*. One has to wonder about the day-to-day decisions Eduard, as the mayor of a small town in which there was in fact a small Jewish population, would have had to have made with regard to the administration of the National Socialist *Judenpolitik*. What of the Aryanization of Jewish businesses and farms? What of the administration of the racial laws? What of the organization of deportations? For the mayor of a town the size of Rhaunen, it would have been a matter of reading the writing not just on the wall but also on the documents that crossed one's desk each day.[91]

These reflections concerning the construction of the character Eduard already lead beyond Reitz's documentary argument, that is, that the Hunsrücker had little contact with Jews and would thus have little "irritatingly detailed experience"[92] to remember, to the far more interesting question of the place of the Jews within the narrative and characterological economy of the film as a work of fiction. "The question of the Jews and National Socialism," Reitz has said, "is a topic about which so much has been said, and had I ventured onto this terrain, the story would have immediately taken a different turn."[93] Or as Reitz has said in another context regarding Hermann's lack of curiosity regarding the other history buried within his paternal legacy, to have portrayed such curiosity would have "overburdened the narrative" and would have furthermore made the character of Hermann less believable by turning him into an ideal moral figure.[94]

As Reitz makes abundantly clear in his essay on the television film *Holocaust*, he is primarily interested in storytelling and not moralizing. According to Reitz, the audience must be offered chances to recognize themselves in concrete situations rather than easy opportunities to engage in complacent identifications with superior moral positions (here one is again reminded of Philipp Jenninger's ostensible reasons for delivering his ill-fated *Kristallnacht* speech). Reitz furthermore insists that his narrative film aesthetic is not without a moral and political dimension, one which seems to derive from a certain homeopathic procedure. Precisely by inducing small doses of loss, separation, and disorientation, Reitz claims to sensitize his audience to the ways in which individuals and entire populations become numb to the experience of loss. And according to Reitz, psychic numbness of this kind is one of the main sources of violence in history:

> My hope is that secondary experiences produced by viewing a film will leave behind traces in us. It is alchemy as method. It's my hope that in the relationship spectator-film something like an icy surface will form on which one loses one's footing; where for a time one has the feeling that the film is speaking my language—that it's me up there on the screen—and suddenly one slips and falls and thinks, that's not me anymore, or now I've lost my bearings. These small slips seem to me to constitute a genuine experience. . . . It doesn't have to lead to the question, "What happened to Uncle Fritz from Bochum?" But then there is the little daughter, and there are memories, and we identify with her, and all of a sudden we sense his absence. . . . Let's take a different example. You have an apartment [*Wohnung*]. In this apartment you have all the things you've accumulated, all the things that have meant something to you in your life. . . . Amidst these things there is a vase. You've never touched it or taken note of it. One day it is no longer there and then, perhaps, you feel its absence. As long as it is there it never concerns you. I'm trying to achieve something similar. Precisely this feeling. That one has the sense that something is not quite right in one's apartment. And if I see my whole life as an apartment, then that is more or less the idea.[95]

So Reitz returns once again to the central elegiac thrust of the film, which achieves its final and fullest articulation through the figure of

Hermann who in his musical finale—a kind of Hunsrücker Requiem—very clearly takes on the role of arch-mourner in and for the Heimat.

VII

The "deepest loss," Reitz insists, is that of the mother tongue. Although dialect is used throughout *Heimat*, Hunsrücker Platt is explicitly reflected on and thematized only three times in the course of the film, each time in a context associated with loss, death, or bereavement. In the first episode, the ghost of Helmut Legrand recites the verse about his native dialect ending with the line, "In Heaven they all speak Hunsrücker Platt"; in the last episode—"The Feast of the Living and the Dead"—Hermann and an old Schabbacher have a conversation in the cemetery about their mother tongue (it is shortly after Maria's death), during which Hermann admits that he can no longer speak it properly; and finally, in his requiem culminating the feast of the living and the dead, Hermann makes use of fragments of his native dialect, including the dialect words for various berries and, importantly, the word *Geheischnis*. That word signifies "shelter and trust, a relationship to a very special, select group of people who occupy an important place in one's life, more than friendship, less than love, something indispensable."[96] This deepest loss of the native dialect stands in, metonymically, for the loss of a formerly intact rural culture as a whole.[97]

Hermann's musical resumé of the *Trauerarbeit* that the film enacts recapitulates this irrevocable loss of Heimat by way of various traditional elegiac procedures. In the composition the mourner returns to the Mother Earth, to Heimat in a quasi-mythological sense—Hermann records the piece in a womblike cavern beneath Schabbach—in order to reenact a separation from and loss of this symbolic union with the idyll. This loss is symbolized by the distortion and fragmentation of the words of the mother tongue. By choosing the dialect words for berries as the words to fragment, Hermann reiterates Milton's plucking of berries, itself a reinscription of traditional topoi of pastoral elegy, in his "Lycidas":

> Yet once more, O ye Laurels, and once more,
> Ye Myrtles brown, with ivy never sere,

> I come to pluck your berries harsh and crude,
> And with forced fingers rude
> Shatter your leaves before the mellowing year.[98]

The piece recapitulates the painful displacement from the organic nature and pure voice of *Muttersprache* to the inorganic symbolic order of the *Vaterlandssprache*. This displacement is further emphasized by Hermann's location above ground while his music is being sung in the cavern below. The crushed fruits of the elegy bear the traces of this symbolically castrative passage but also maintain a now more mediated—a more "troped"—connection to what has been lost. Like Apollo's construction of the laurel wreath out of the traces of Daphne, the lost object of desire, or Pan's construction of pipes out of the reeds marking the absence of Syrinx, Hermann's music is a "sign not only of his lost love but also of his very pursuit—a consoling sign that carries in itself the reminder of the loss on which it has been founded." Hermann's representation of his entry into the symbolic order of High German and musical notation, a realm that for him has been associated with homelessness and errancy, thus "invites us to watch the emergence of this arbitrariness and disjunctiveness as an event and to reintegrate the sign with the passionate story of its derivation."[99]

The stranded objects of the lost idyll—in this case words—have been reinscribed within a new symbolic whole, a work of elegiac art. Such a reinscription stands in marked contrast to that other mode of recuperating stranded objects, Ernst's *Entrümpelungsgeschäft* (he hauls away old pieces of furniture and farmhouses, restores them, and sells them as antiques). Here too there is a rude plucking out of the organic materials of the idyll. These auratic objects, that is, "objects not severed from the labor that produced them, objects indissolubly linked with this labor and the experience of everyday idyllic life,"[100] are transformed into simulacra of what they once were. Removing a door or half-timber beam from its original use and setting, and selling it to an urban restaurant—spraying it first with a chemical designed to evoke "the scent of 1865"—in order to re-create a rustic, peasant atmosphere instead effaces all signs of loss and creates the illusion that the objects of one's nostalgia are always immediately available. The simulacrum may thus be understood as the paradox of an elegiac token in which the traces of bereavement, rather than causing anguish, are savored as the true commodity. The simulacrum satisfies, in near perfect fashion, one's narcissistic fantasy that losses are never necessary or irrevocable, that everything can be retrieved, even that which was never there to be lost in the first place. The simulacrum is aura made to order (regardless of whether made in Hollywood or made in Germany).[101]

However, in both Hermann's and Ernst's modes of recuperating auratic objects, the same deep nostalgia—in the latter case narcissistically flattered; in the former, chastised, "castrated," disrupted—is at work. It is a nostalgia for a particular relation to time, a nostalgia for that passage of time which inscribes itself on artifacts, objects of everyday use, even including the words used in daily discourse. It is a nostalgia for *traces* of past generations and thus, indirectly, of one's own mortality, as well as for the capacity to register and creatively transform these traces which scar the things that populate daily existence. They are the traces of time's slower, organic rhythms, the temporality of *Naturgeschichte*. In a world primarily organized according to a *naturgeschichtlich* mode of temporality, mortality is the force that gives poignancy and beauty to all things, from the lines marking a human face, to the worn leather of a pair of boots, to the wood of a threshhold imprinted with the footsteps of generations.[102] In such a world, death does not cease to be tragic or painful; it is, however, seen as having a place within the life cycles organizing existence and so can be mourned according to the conventions of the funerary discourse that corresponds to this organic world, namely those of pastoral elegy. Hermann's requiem, as well as the film as a whole, are meta-elegies: elegies for the disappearance of the world of pastoral elegy. But as I have been arguing, this dominant elegiac discourse prefigures the narrative field in such a way that the filmmaker must make a very careful selection of the artifacts, words, significant dates, traces, and scars that will have a place in the story. In his attempt to evoke and to grieve for the passing of a world of *Naturgeschichte* Reitz excludes a great many traces of that *Un-Naturgeschichte* called the Holocaust. As Terry Eagleton has written of traces:

> For just as the psychoanalytic subject is able to designate itself as a homogeneous entity over time only by repressing the traces of its unconscious desires, so the auratic object, whether it be cultural ar-

tefact or state apparatus, continually rewrites its own history to expel the traces of its ruptured, heterogeneous past. The political task of "liberating" an object, then, takes the form of opening up its unconscious—detecting within it those chips of heterogeneity that it has been unable quite to dissolve.[103]

By focusing primarily on the task of unearthing the traces of idyllic time beneath the layers of Americana that have fallen on the good German earth like so much deadly snow, Reitz circumvents other no doubt more complex and difficult archeological tasks. It is not that the trace-work accomplished by Reitz is apolitical; *Heimat* shares in a contemporary political and cultural discourse that has attempted to resist the destruction of local environments and traditions by industrial, postindustrial, and military expansion. Reitz's own rather more existentialist version of this new regionalism—to lose the local is to lose a deep relationship with death—however, impoverishes the web of historical traces which scars the tissue of the Heimat. Reitz thins out the textual layers of his palimpsest, removes, much as Robert removes the glass splinters in Pauline's hand, precisely those orders of heterogeneity that would endanger the salvage work of his most privileged category: experience. Reitz distributes his ambivalences vis-à-vis the idyllic matrix according to the schema of a *Bildungsroman* that in turn figures the disruption of the clear voice of experience (that always says what it means and means what it says) as a seduction from "the other shore of the river." The film thereby entangles itself in what Miriam Hansen has called the "double bind of 'mourning work' and 'rehabilitation.'" That is, the narrative strategies I have identified entail a "slippage from coming to terms with the past, in the sense of 'working through,' to a discourse of denial which strives to restore the damaged collective narcissism by eliminating from consciousness the very events that jeopardized the possibility of national identification in the first place."[104]

After viewing *Heimat* one has the peculiar feeling that the real, and in essence only, obstacle blocking the capacity of Germans today to feel continuous with their past, that is, to inherit a cultural legacy from their elders, is the so-called terror of American aesthetics, a metonymy for the ravages of capitalism suffered by Germany in the last hundred years. Capitalism is not blameless in the losses recounted by the film; yet Reitz's existentialist antimodernism comes uncomfortably close to becoming an instance of apologetic ideology when it is deployed in the service of effacing the traces of other strands of recent history. The representation of fascism, or of the connections between fascism and capitalism, or of the relation of both to the cultural sphere cannot and should not have to absorb the tasks of mourning and working through of guilt resulting from that other cultural legacy, the Holocaust. Mourning the destruction of Schabbach cannot replace or displace the *Trauerarbeit* created by Auschwitz. Or vice versa. The fatal error is to place these tasks in competition with one another, to imagine, as Reitz seems to, that *Heimat* must overcome *Holocaust*, a concrete reenactment, perhaps, of a more generally conceived agon in which experience must overcome judgment and the voice must overcome writing. The text of history that has, to use Celan's word, "written asunder" the voice of experience—even in those places where it speaks Hunsrücker Platt—is a complex one and most certainly includes those events that Reitz would like to keep outside the boundaries of his pastoral elegy.

The most important question facing the current generation of Germans may be just this: How can they undo this false competition which, as Hansen suggests, is an immobilizing double bind? By what feat of the elegiac imagination can something like a German identity be restored and sustained across—rather than around—the fissures of guilt and violence that score German history in this century? How, in other words, can something like a German self be restored without excluding the chips of heterogeneity which litter the path into the symbolic order like so many shards of glass, and to achieve this without searching for a pharmakos, without blaming the victims for their broken windows? And how much chastisement needs to be enacted, how much decentering by the pharmakon of recent history can be undergone, before the self and its voice are shattered into so many bits and pieces of schizophrenic discourse? Is there a safe homeopathic procedure left that would allow for the mourning work that needs to be accomplished? Or would every dose of the negative, every immersion into this destructive element be irrevocable? And who, after all, would administer the philter? If, as Lacan and others have suggested, all mourning must pass through the instance of the paternal signifier, be performed, at some level, in the Name-of-the-Father, how might this be done when it is the fathers who have littered the path with so many dangerous splinters and shards?[105] How can one trust the medicine given by these fathers? One of the successes of *Heimat* is that it illustrates, if only by a variety of strategies of denial and exclusion, just how difficult this complex of issues truly is; that is, just how tempting the *path home* is—though this Heimat may be little more than a screen memory—in the face of *homeopathic* cures that seem to promise only more suffering.[106]

4

Allegories of Grieving: The Films of Hans Jürgen Syberberg

No contemporary German artist has been associated more consistently with the tasks of mourning than the filmmaker Hans Jürgen Syberberg. There is no major essay on Syberberg that does not at some point invoke the term *Trauerarbeit* as the key to the metapsychological underpinnings of Syberberg's film aesthetics, as metaphor for the aesthetic and intellectual labor to which Syberberg invites his audience with each new film.[1] This by now nearly automatic association of Syberberg's oeuvre with the tasks and procedures of collective mourning has been to a large extent the achievement of Syberberg himself. In his copious essayistic work, which includes long commentaries on and defenses of his own films, Syberberg has quite often used the word *Trauerarbeit* (along with other related terms) to describe the moral and psychological dimensions of his work.[2] Indeed, at least one of the sources of Syberberg's isolation from his colleagues in the New German Cinema, as well as from the cultural scene generally, has been his insistence that he alone among German artists has been willing to take on the postwar burdens of mourning and repairing the damage to their nation's bereft cultural identity.

What makes Syberberg's work in general, and *Hitler, ein Film aus Deutschland* (Hitler, a film from Germany),[3] in particular, so important in the present context is that Syberberg's meditations on and cinematic performances of *Trauerarbeit* always situate the particulars of the postwar German tasks of (and impediments to) mourning in relation to other, more properly postmodern phenomena and considerations. Syberberg's attempt to operate at multiple levels of moral engagement and conceptualization in his films and writings warrants particular attention. Shifts from one level of discourse or analysis to another, for example, from discussion of the uniqueness of the Holocaust and the particular tasks of mourning it has left in its wake to meditations on the universality of what made it possible, are always strategic and significant. As Edgar Reitz's *Heimat* demonstrates, such shifts, which may take the form of double plots, may reproduce patterns of thinking which are content simply to displace burdens of guilt and mourning, and allow one to rewrite one's position as that of the true victim without such a move necessarily signifying an act of solidarity or empathy with other more recognizable victims. One's own despair and losses become the central catastrophe, flooding out empathy for all others.[4]

An example of such a problematic leap from one level of analysis to another is Syberberg's rhetorically charged remark concerning the screening of *Holocaust* on German television: "America now has its own reparations to pay [*hat einiges wiedergutzumachen*] after this *Holocaust* from Hollywood in the German media."[5] Such a claim suggests that for the maker of *Hitler, A Film from Germany*, the real violence of recent history has occurred not so much in the Holocaust as in the *Holocausts*, and thus that souls sensitive to Hollywood's cheap games with history and experience are the real victims of the twentieth century.[6] The point behind such outrageous and deeply offensive rhetoric is, however, somewhat less outrageous, and one with which Syberberg, in often brilliant and compelling ways, forces viewers and readers to contend, namely that the psychological mechanisms that lead to the construction of places like Auschwitz are akin to those that continue to be deployed by what has come, since Adorno and Horkheimer, to be referred to as the culture industry.[7] A corollary to this thesis is the claim that the psychological mechanisms of identity formation which helped to guarantee Hitler's success in Germany in the thirties and forties and, as Adorno and the Mitscherlichs have suggested, continue to inhibit the work of mourning in post-Hitler Germany, are of the same order as those that, to an even greater extent today, organize postmodern psyches. These mechanisms, so the argument goes, not only block one's capacities to carry out the work of mourning but, what is more, so numb one's sensibilities that one is incapable of knowing any longer what human loss feels like. Syberberg aims to inscribe the so-called inability to mourn endemic to postwar Germany within a larger history of Western culture, understood as a series of shifts and transformations of the sites of identity formation. According to Syberberg, this history enters its modern stage in the European nineteenth century and continues into the present of postmodernity, though now centered, like a shifting meteorological turbulence, not in Europe but in America, whose capital city turns out to be, in this particular narrative, Hollywood. Syberberg's films, beginning with his *Ludwig—Requiem für einen jungfräulichen König* (Ludwig—Requiem for a virgin king) in 1972 and culminating in *Hitler* in 1977 (and, to a certain extent, continuing with his next two films, *Parsifal* in 1982 and *Die Nacht* (The night) in 1984), attempt to follow and to decipher the course of this migratory world-historical force that describes, in Syberberg's dark vision, the story of the end of the Occident. Before introducing the reader to the "eye of the storm,"[8] I want to step back and briefly map out the trajectory of Syberberg's concerns prior to the vast project that was to occupy him for over a decade.

I

Though primarily known in the United States for his seven-hour opus *Our Hitler* (Syberberg premiered the film in England rather than Germany after feeling snubbed by the German press in Cannes where parts of the film were first shown), Syberberg has been a consistently prolific artist over the course of some thirty years of filmmaking. His career as a filmmaker began in the early 1950s in Rostock, where as a seventeen-year-old high school student he made his first 8-mm documentaries, of political demonstrations and sports events primarily, as well as several film versions of Chekhov stories.[9] Syberberg's most significant cinematic endeavor during these years was, however, his filming of rehearsals of Brecht's Berlin Ensemble in 1953. This footage, which includes rehearsals of *Mother Courage, The Mother, Puntila,* and Goethe's *Urfaust,* was incorporated seventeen years later into an autobiographical documentary, *Nach*

meinem letzten Umzug . . . (After my last departure . . .). An equally
important consequence of this first commission was that it brought
the young Syberberg to Berlin, where in the western part of the city
he was to have his first contact with French cinema (Syberberg re-
members having seen, for example, *Orphée, Les enfants du paradis,*
and *La belle et la bête*).[10]

After leaving East Germany in 1953, he eventually settled in
Munich, where he studied literature and art history and attended
lectures by Hans Sedlmayr. Sedlmayr's notion of the "loss of the
center" in Western culture has remained a significant influence on
Syberberg's thought about art and society throughout his career.[11] In
1962 he completed a dissertation on mythic elements in the dramas
of Friedrich Dürrenmatt. As Syberberg later claimed, what interested him even in this early piece of work, completed some ten
years before his first decidedly mythopoetic film, were the "archetypal, primal foundations" of events and individuals: "According to
the title of my dissertation, it had something to do with Dürrenmatt,
but it was really a study of the Sisyphus myth."[12]

After finishing his studies, Syberberg went on to work for Bavarian television, where in the next several years he produced, directed, shot, and edited 185 films on local cultural and topical
themes and events ranging in length from three to thirty minutes.[13]
Between 1965 and 1972, the year he began the series of films that
make up the body of his mature work, Syberberg made eight major
films: two documentaries on the grand old man of German theater,
Fritz Kortner (*Fritz Kortner probt Kabale und Liebe* [Fritz Kortner rehearses Schiller's Love and Intrigue, 1965]; *Fritz Kortner spricht Mono-
loge für eine Schallplatte* [Fritz Kortner speaks monologues for a record, 1966]); a documentary on Romy Schneider (*Romy: Anatomie eines
Gesichts* [Romy: Anatomy of a face, 1965]) which, after disagree-
ments with Schneider and her representatives concerning his portrayal of her in the film, was distributed in a much shortened version
without Syberberg's name; a documentary about the eccentric Bavarian aristocratic family Pocci (*Die Grafen Pocci* [The Counts Pocci,
1967]); a documentary about the German pornography industry
(*Sex-Business made in Pasing*, 1969); the autobiographical documentary mentioned earlier; and finally, two feature films, each based on
a literary text: *Scarabea—Wieviel Erde braucht der Mensch?* (Scarabea—

How much earth does a man need?, 1968), based on a story by Tolstoy, and *San Domingo* (1970), based on Kleist's novella *Die Ver-lobung in San Domingo* (The betrothal in San Domingo).

Already in these early works the themes that would come to oc-cupy Syberberg's cinematic imagination over the course of his next series of films, beginning with *Ludwig*, take on recognizable con-tours (these themes become visible not only in the films themselves but also in the circumstances of their production, distribution, and reception). One thinks, for example, of Syberberg's determination to work against the voyeurism characteristic of so much television doc-umentary filmmaking which seeks out the sensational in the public and private lives of cultural figures. Another theme is expressed in Syberberg's outspoken commitment to serving the subject of his film rather than trying to appropriate it by means of tendentious voice-over and montage. Most important, however, Syberberg conceives his documentary style in terms that prefigure what would come to be identified as the aesthetic scandal of his later films, namely the marriage of Wagnerian and Brechtian aesthetic techniques. The term Syberberg uses to characterize that syncretic style, or more precisely, the consciousness appropriate to the making and reception of these films, is an oxymoron that belongs to a long tradition of such for-mulations in the history of German letters (one thinks, above all, of the *intellektuelle Anschauung* [intellectual intuition] of German Ideal ism): *aufklärerische Trance*, or "enlightening trance."[14]

This early and not yet explicitly articulated combination of Brecht and Wagner, that is, of an aesthetics of enlightenment and an aes-thetics of trance, is underwritten so to speak by yet a third major cultural figure. Between the historical and theoretical poles of Syber-berg's oxymoronic aesthetic system—between Wagner and Brecht—stands, as mediating third term, Freud. What Syberberg means by "enlightening trance" is, as it turns out, quite close to what hap-pens, by way of the transference, in the psychoanalytic session:

And now something remarkable happens, similar, perhaps, to what occurs in psychoanalysis. . . . A sensitive, reciprocal relationship is formed between the partners, each maintaining the utmost distance and mental clarity. Earlier eras would speak of hypnosis or occult procedures, today we think perhaps of drug trips. . . . The maker of such a documentary film must be able to serve, in the old-fashioned sense, almost monk-like.[15]

And perhaps Syberberg's famous transformation of Clausewitz's remark about war and politics may also be understood in the context of this analogy to psychoanalysis: neither film nor psychoanalysis is simply a mimetic retelling or reproduction of life but, rather, a "continuation of life with other means."[16]

From the beginning, Syberberg has understood and defended the aesthetic principles guiding his documentary production in strongly polemical terms (one can easily get the impression that Syberberg is incapable of a nonpolemical thought[17]); he deploys these films expressly as interventions against the modus operandi of the culture and consciousness industry (he makes a more frontal assault on patterns of voyeurism in film production in the documentary on the pornography industry). Almost from the start Syberberg engages in what later becomes a long history of struggles for economic and moral support from the very system of cultural production which his own work attempts to undermine (as already indicated, the Romy Schneider film was an early defeat in this agon). The terms in which Syberberg casts this struggle are, from the first, moral, theological, existential, even cosmological. Syberberg inscribes his own position and struggle within the German cultural scene—a scene that of course includes an entire system of film subsidies and supports—in a highly charged allegorical discourse. This is, perhaps, what distinguishes Syberberg from any number of other filmmakers in the Federal Republic who see themselves caught in the same economic and aesthetic double binds as Syberberg. Syberberg's own career, or at least the way he has, with an increasingly compulsive energy, documented and plotted it, enacts, in other words, what eventually becomes the subject of all his later films: struggles of light against darkness, quests for redemption from degeneration and corruption.[18]

Syberberg's powerful affinity to allegory as a privileged symbolic mode is also apparent quite early in his career in the way he thinks of the subjects of his documentaries. His cinematic gaze transforms its subjects into microcosms, richly textured emblems crossed by a nexus of multiple historical and, as will become clearer in the later feature films, mythical and archetypal texts: "Here it is a matter of representing a macrocosm within a microcosm. In order to represent an epoch or any other important events, it can be more productive if one focuses with clarity and precision on a person, a house, a journey, a street, or place, as long as the particular object and/or theme is well chosen, i.e. if it is the center of a field of tensions."[19]

Perhaps the most interesting film among the early documentaries is the 1967 film about the Bavarian aristocratic family Pocci, whose most famous scion, Franz, created the Kasperl figure for the Munich puppet stage in the mid-nineteenth century. As Berman has noted, the film's division into chapters and Syberberg's use of montage anticipate much of what was to come with *Ludwig* and after. More important, however, the film places in the foreground the sixty-three-year-old Count Konrad, whose eccentric antimodernism reflects the sort of utopian impulses inherent in the "great refusals" that would become the thematic core of all of Syberberg's major works.[20] As Syberberg says of Pocci's refusal to turn over his land to developers: "Taken seriously, these Pocci-sentences would be a revolution. A revolution in our action, thought, and spiritual life: no longer to buy and sell everything, no longer to be in constant pursuit of goals, for once not to 'modernize' until there's nothing left . . . but rather . . . to tolerate riddles, mysteries in image and sound . . . always mindful of ancient myths, wisdom, and calamity."[21] Also significant in this context is Syberberg's citation of Adalbert Stifter's *sanftes Gesetz* (gentle law) as the key to the sensibility behind this film:

> Regarding the intention and pretension of the maker of such films, I might recall Stifter's "gentle law"; Stifter, not unlike the Chinese philosophers, recognizes the great laws of life in the rhythms of the winds and the growth of grain and the composure of a tranquil death and sees volcanoes, revolutions, and the hunger for vengeance as the loud but in the end smaller, transitory events of the world and represents them as such.[22]

Syberberg's first feature film, *Scarabea*, relocates Tolstoy's tale of a pact with the devil to the Sardinian coast where a German tourist is confronted with the fatal hubris of his dreams of possession. Not so much deconstructing as disemboweling the German's rapacious greed, Syberberg confronts him, in what he has called a "surreal fairy tale," with the archaic sensuousness of heat, blood, sand, sexuality, and death.[23] The film also contains a parody of the genre that for Syberberg most clearly represents Hollywood's colonization and trivialization of romance and its inherent utopian impulses: the Western. In its opposition to Hollywood's corrosive influence on the utopian imagination, the film assumes the qualities of, as Russell Berman has put it, a "battlefield of the opposing forces of civilization and myth."[24] The tourist returns in both *Ludwig* and *Hitler* as a quasi-demonic figure embodying civilization's most recent and, according to Syberberg, most destructive and insidious mode of colonization: the commodification of entire ways of life.

Syberberg's second feature film, *San Domingo*, an experiment in German neorealism made by and large with amateur actors, is interesting not only as an adaptation of Kleist but also as a first step in a typically Syberbergian probe into the psychic roots of terrorism in recent German history (the film transports the action of the novella to the Munich youth underground). The film ends with a quotation from Eldridge Cleaver containing the warning "'to watch out and not to forget or underestimate or scorn these youths, or there will be catastrophes of vast proportions, revolutions or anarchy in which they'll smash everything to pieces.'"[25] But despite the presence of so many seminal motifs, themes, formal techniques, narrative strategies, and compositional principles that are more fully developed in later works, *San Domingo* marks the end of one creative period for Syberberg; a distinct new period of creativity follows: "After this film [*San Domingo*] there remained only the possibility of a radical new beginning."[26]

II

With *Ludwig* in 1972, Syberberg sets out on a vast epic journey through the prehistory of modernity in the European nineteenth century, modernity's explosive culmination in German fascism, and finally into what for Syberberg is clearly the most horrible episode of all, the more recent ruins of postmodernity's "joyless society." It is a journey that passes through landscapes that are not so much historical as mythic and psychic. Whatever political, juridical, or even military struggles Syberberg portrays or alludes to in his films, they are immediately endowed with the form and value of allegorical battles and quests played out between forces and polarities that, according to Syberberg and his particular form of Freudianism, occupy the deep psychological and ideological core of real historical events. From the very beginning of the cycle, Syberberg engages in a dramaturgy of a metaphysically conceived political unconscious.

Syberberg's vision of European history and of what has become, in the age of multinational capitalism, a somewhat perverse mode of universal history, resembles Benjamin's "caption" to his famous emblem of history, Paul Klee's *Angelus Novus*, to which I have already alluded:

A Klee painting named "Angelus Novus" shows an angel looking as though he is about to move away from something he is fixedly contemplating. His eyes are staring, his mouth is open, his wings are spread. This is how one pictures the angel of history. His face is turned toward the past. Where we perceive a chain of events, he sees one single catastrophe which keeps piling wreckage upon wreckage and hurls it in front of his feet. The angel would like to stay, awaken the dead, and make whole what has been smashed. But a storm is blowing from Paradise; it has got caught in his wings with such violence that the angel can no longer close them. This storm irresistibly propels him into the future to which his back is turned, while the pile of debris before him grows skyward. This storm is what we call progress.[27]

Beginning with *Ludwig*, Syberberg freezes the movement of this universal catastrophe at strategic junctures in his films in order to gather and interpret the shards and stranded objects strewn about its attendant funereal landscape; he awakens the dead and records their wild monologues as they tell, each in their own eccentric rhythm, how they tried to walk against the wind or, rather, whom they eventually found to blame and make pay for their suffering. In Syberberg's view, every act of resistance to the storm of history, no matter how pathetic, misguided, or violent, embodies a profoundly utopian impulse. Syberberg also points to the ways that these various responses to history may have, knowingly or unknowingly, made use of the very force they were trying to resist, thereby helping only to feed the storm, entering into complicity with it, sacrificing more and more human habitation to its dominion. In the context of this vision, Syberberg begins to address the historical occasions of mourning which culminate in the Holocaust but which begin, according to Syberberg's epic tale, much earlier, perhaps even at the very start of the "singular catastrophe" that Benjamin names. The narrative argument that weaves together the films of Syberberg's cycle links the resources and tasks of mourning to the fate of the utopian imagination in modern European history. According to Syberberg, the capacity to mourn remains intact only to the extent that one is, like Benjamin's angel, still capable of looking backward toward paradise and, in works of art, able to gather the ruins left in the wake of the storm and decipher the dialects of the dead.

As with Reitz, one must pay careful attention to the question of just which fragments are gathered and which are not, just whose monologues are recorded and whose are not, and finally, whether these selections in the end in fact serve or undermine the purposes of mourning. Syberberg's vision of history as a single apocalyptic *grand récit* may itself become a kind of alibi, so thoroughly universalizing all catastrophes that their contours blur, leaving nothing in particular to mourn. Ultimately one must ask if Syberberg's descent into the thanatotic landscape of European history is performed in the service of a homeopathic cure or, rather, if it is an act of a deeply melancholic mind no longer interested in the stories and faces of the living.

In *Ludwig*, the economic, political, and ideological fields of force which shaped the late nineteenth century in Germany are presented in a series of nearly thirty tableauxlike episodes, each organized by means of a rich iconography of props, back projections, and musical and textual citation.[28] The episodes are concentrated in and around the court of the mad Bavarian King Ludwig II. The Wittelsbach princes are preparing to depose—by way of a staged suicide—their decadent monarch who has financially drained the court with his extravagant support for Wagner and the construction of a series of pseudo-medieval castles. Waiting in the wings of this historical scene as constructed by Syberberg is the mad king's ideological other: Bismarck and his visions of unification and modernization under Prussian hegemony.[29] As a result of Syberberg's overtly allegorical style, both Ludwig and Bismarck figure more as particular positions within a larger array of available possibilities of thought, action, and ideology than as unique individuals whose behavior might otherwise interest the viewer voyeuristically.

Ludwig's position is of special importance to Syberberg. It is that of the ultimately helpless visionary whose madness it was to oppose the forces of industrialization and modernization with the erotic and thanatotic phantasmagoria supplied by Wagner's operas. Syberberg underscores Ludwig's Wagnerian mythomania by coordinating the progression of the film with that of Wagner's *Ring des Nibelungen*: the film begins with the opening of *Rheingold* and ends with *Götterdämmerung*. "The myth of the Nibelungen thus supplies the framework."[30] What interests Syberberg about the fate of Ludwig and his relationship to Wagner is not only the ambiguous glory of Ludwig's imaginary solutions to real contradictions but also the two strands of Ludwig's legacy and how they affect the political unconscious of Germany over the next hundred years. This legacy is presented in two dream sequences—a nightmare and a waking dream or vision—in the course of the film.

In the first nightmare sequence, Ludwig has a vision of Hitler and Ernst Röhm (Röhm is played by the same actor, Peter Kern, who in an earlier scene played Ludwig's hairdresser Hoppe) dancing a Bavarian folk dance surrounded by the Wittelsbach princes, the Prussian crown prince, and Kaiser Wilhelm against a back projection from *Tannhäuser*, the Venus grotto as Ludwig had re-created it in his castle at Linderhof. Thomas Elsaesser has decoded this tableau vivant in light of Syberberg's overall allegorical project:

> Prussia's colonization of Bavaria as the price of unification has driven underground and inward another dream of unification and identity, that of German Romanticism and Idealist Humanism. In the process of repression it has turned the utopia into a no less fervent death-wish, a longing for extinction and redemption that announces itself in the affinity of Wagner's music and Ludwig's architectural follies. And one day—in the person of an Austro-Bavarian bureaucrat's son—it will avenge and redeem that fantasy of an expansionist and at the same time self-destructive inwardness, by undertaking a most ruthless decolonization in the name of autarchy and self-determination.[31]

In the second vision, Ludwig stares into the camera, behind him a back projection of one of his castles, apparently in flames, filled with American tourists clicking cameras as their tour guide leads them through the original Disneyland; the sound track plays an allusion to the earlier nightmare sequence: cries of *"Sieg Heil"* and march music. The sequence suggests the coming absorption of Ludwig's nineteenth-century mythomania by the forces of a mass culture and its industries of fantasy production. Syberberg uses the sequence to link the two ways that a mass, popular culture—for Syberberg this is another way of saying democracy—will appropriate and debase what might be called the utopian libido still available to Ludwig. These two forms of debased utopianism are fascism, already alluded to in Ludwig's nightmare, and what for Syberberg is ultimately the more powerful and sinister form, commodity fetishism. Syberberg sees both fascism and consumer capitalism (especially its mechanisms of commodification) as using utopian libido to fuel the machines that ultimately destroy all objects to which such libido had previously attached itself. In the second of the visions, Ludwig's Wagnerian aestheticism, deployed as a sort of anaesthesia to freeze the movement of history—the catastrophe, as Benjamin has said, that things just go on—is itself absorbed into an even more powerful machinery of desire in which the oppositional traces and resonances of Ludwig's madness have been expunged, converted into tourist attractions: "Ludwig's life and activities, i.e. what makes him significant as a protagonist of an aesthetic revolt that included a rejection of centralization, capitalism and the erosion of regional autonomy, have been eliminated in the legend of the mad and fantastic king. With this, he disappears from history and enters into the realm of spectacle and voyeurism."[32]

It is important, however, to note the ways in which Ludwig is presented as being complicitous with the forces that would ultimately become parasitic on the trilogy of ecstasies at the core of his utopianism: *Sehnsucht, Heimweh, Wahnsinn* (longing, homesickness, madness).[33] Syberberg casts Ludwig in the role of a sort of aristocratic flaneur who was able, if only as caricature, "to salvage the imaginary on the very brink of its being swallowed up by the symbolic, wresting a last gleam of aura from faces about to dissolve into difference and anonymity."[34] Such salvage work is possible only by means of a retreat to fantastic and regressive utopias constructed as so many specular exchanges of self with mythic self-images, anarchistic Wagnerian sabbaths wrested—Syberberg's privileged term for such an act is *abtrotzen*—from the storm of progress. These artificial paradises are little more than a series of ephemeral snatches of narcissistic compensation in the midst of social relations otherwise experienced as one long narcissistic injury. These sabbaths are thus themselves incipient commodities. The kitsch Gothic of Neuschwanstein is, in other words, no more original or authentic than Disneyland's re-creation; it too comes into being as simulacrum and proto-commodity, it too is assigned a position by economic and political forces beyond its ken or control: the shifting storms of industrialization, capitalism, and colonization, blowing from the (Prussian) north. In this sense, to quote Elsaesser, Ludwig's life is a "parable of the origins of the commodity-form."[35]

In Syberberg's view, however, another important aspect of Ludwig's utopian mythomania remains (aside from the oppositional import already noted) which distinguishes his artificial paradises from what they became under the gaze of the tourist. "The commodity," Eagleton says,

> is a death's head that, unlike the skull of the *Trauerspiel*, has ceased to know itself as such. In the presence of fashion, that supreme cult of the commodity, we are in the presence of death—of a hectic repetition that gets precisely nowhere, a flashing of mirror upon mirror that believes that by thus arresting history it can avoid death, but in this orgy of matter succeeds only in being drawn more inexorably into its grasp. What is reflected in the mirror of the commodity is the absence of death in a double sense: its erasure, but also its sinister blankness.[36]

Ludwig's phantasmagoria have not yet reached this stage in the life of the commodity. Indeed, he seems to represent for Syberberg Thanatos's last semiconscious gasp before being thoroughly assimilated into the lethal numbness of commodity fetishism. For Syberberg, the Wagnerian pathos of death is preferable to the short circuiting of the death drive in the eternal recurrence of the *petit mort* of commodity consumption.[37]

Syberberg understands his own cinematic system, which he refers to as "requiem," as an interruption of the circuit of cheap satisfactions supplied by the commodity. His films attempt to reanimate what he sees as deeper, more authentic desires, which he in turn circumscribes by the names *Sehnsucht*, *Heimweh*, and *Wahnsinn*. Syberberg attempts to revitalize this utopian libido in the context of a new, properly filmic sublime:

> The requiem circumscribes the secret landscapes of our most cherished spiritual property. Bloch said it too, "Home, the place where no one has ever been," the destinations of all human migra-

tions, where the paradises and utopias, the Golden Ages, the famous El Dorado of the wish-landscapes of our legends and fairy tales are preserved as the deep desires of entire peoples in the art of dream and fantasy, realized time and again in our works of art: artificial paradises, constructed by artifice, there to be seen and heard, and why not also through the art of film? . . . And that doesn't mean simply modish melodrama, why not high masses, for example, as ceremonies of life, of world, and of art. But for that laws are needed, laws one must make for oneself.[38]

III

It is now possible to formulate, in a preliminary way, a fundamental dilemma in Syberberg's film aesthetics—one is tempted to say his anthropology—as it begins to take shape at the outset of his epic cycle. This dilemma arises out of an apparent inability to conceive of human desire except in cosmological, theological, or otherwise grandiose metaphysical terms. This is, of course, the reason why he is first and foremost a maker of allegorical rather than mimetic art. There is, in Syberberg's conception of art, a kind of contempt for the local, for anything less or smaller than questions of totality and eternity in human affairs. One begins to suspect, even as early as *Ludwig*, that in Syberberg's world there is really only one sort of pain, one sort of suffering worthy of the viewer's, or at least the artist's attention, and that is the pain of the first and deepest narcissistic injury: separation from one's maternal origins, from the primal matrix.

This conception of the human dilemma also contains a paternal component, namely the "father hunger" that for Freud stands at the origin of the religious imagination. In Syberberg's film cosmos, however, the father figures less as paternal law or as a source of oedipal chastisement—the "no" that as totem may also empower—than as fellow-sufferer (*Mit-leidender*) who shares the deep longing for return to origins, that is, for the peace of extinction. Perhaps this is why Syberberg is consistently drawn to the narrative mode that most powerfully embodies the conception of existence as a sort of chronic narcissistic injury unhealable by the work of mourning: the romance. It is thus quite interesting to note that when, after completing *Hitler*, Syberberg decided that he wanted to make a comedy, he chose, of all things, *Parsifal*. Jameson's remarks on the different generic signals emitted by comedy and romance are most enlightening in this context:

> The materials of comedy . . . are not the ethical oppositions and magical forces of its generic opposite, but rather those of the Oedipal situation, with its tyrannical fathers, its rebellious younger generation, and its renewal of the social order by marriage and sexual fulfillment. Comedy is active and articulates the play of desire and of the obstacles to it, whereas romance develops . . . under the sign of destiny and providence, and takes as its outer horizon the transformation of a whole world, ultimately sealed by those revelations of which the enigmatic Grail is itself the emblem. Comedy is social in its ultimate perspective, whereas romance remains metaphysical; and the wish-fulfillments of comedy may be identified as those of the genital stage, whereas romance would seem to betray older, more archaic fantasy material and to reenact the oral stage, its anxieties (the baleful spell of the intruding father-magician-villain) and its appeasement (the providential vision), reawakening the more passive and symbiotic relationship of infant to mother.

And as Jameson then adds, the archaic fantasy material that one may detect in these generic forms "can never be imagined as emerging in any pure state, but must always pass through a determinate social and historical situation, in which it is both universalized and reappropriated by 'adult' ideology."[39] Given that the psychological foundations of the procedures of mourning are laid, in significant ways, in the course of the oedipal drama and its "comedic" resolution, the deployment of the romance paradigm may seem paradoxical in the context of a body of work that appears dedicated to tasks of mourning. And indeed, how Syberberg finally works through the potential hazards of this paradox will determine the success or failure of his film cycle as a performance of *Trauerarbeit*.

IV

A companion film to Ludwig's requiem, *Theodor Hierneis oder, Wie man ehem. Hofkoch wird* (How one becomes a former royal cook, 1972), develops more fully the legacy evoked in Ludwig's second vision, his transformation into a commodity. The film is based on the memoirs of an apprentice cook in Ludwig's court and is presented as a ninety-minute guided tour of Ludwig's various residences, which either appear as back projections or are described without being seen. Walter Sedlmayr plays the role of cook/tour guide Hierneis.

In some respects, this is one of Syberberg's more Brechtian productions.[40] For example, the artificial lake in Ludwig's elaborate pleasure garden on the roof of his Munich residence—this particular artificial paradise appears in all three major films of this cycle—regularly leaks into the cook's quarters below, so that Hierneis has to take an umbrella to bed, "proof that all artificial paradises have a concrete base."[41]

The life of Ludwig's court is mediated in large measure by long lists of elaborate menus and the details of food preparation for a master who could eat only certain foods and cuts of meat because of rotted teeth. But perhaps more significant than details of the court—and this comes across in the film's title—is Hierneis's savvy exploitation of his apprenticeship in the kitchens of the king to establish himself as a successful caterer in, of all places, Berlin. (Hierneis not only used his former association with Ludwig but, having witnessed the machinations leading to Ludwig's so-called suicide, was also able to blackmail the Wittelsbach family.) In effect, Hierneis commodifies the past, his own and that of the king. The commodity thereby absorbs all histories, from below and from above, into its law. The detailed descriptions of foods and recipes—documents of Ludwig's gastronomical Wagnerianism—turn out to be a sort of tease on Hierneis's part; Ludwig's exoticisms in the archaic realm of the palate also become the grist for the mills of voyeurism: "A cruel mockery of the existence of a . . . Golden Age, the tragi-comical failure of man—at the top and at the bottom—in the face of his most exquisite possibilities. The one pays nobly with his life, the other with his soul, as one used to say."[42]

v

Syberberg's next film, *Karl May* (1974), follows the figurative and literal trials of the famous turn-of-the-century Saxon author of adventure and travel stories as he struggled against the machinations of publishers and speculators trying to cash in on his huge popular success in less than honorable ways. The author who gave generations of (for the most part male) Germans—including figures as diverse as Hitler and Ernst Bloch, Einstein and Hesse—their first passionate reading experience turned out not to be who he claimed to be and who his readers desperately wanted him to be.[43] May wrote his tales of life amid the American Indians and various tribes of the Orient in the first person, as Old Shatterhand and Kara Ben Nemsi, respectively; he also claimed to have actually made the various journeys he relates in those tales, though he in fact never left Central Europe and rarely left his native Saxony. In the self-transfiguration effected by a fictitious autobiography, May also managed to attain a doctoral degree. Furthermore, the author whose writings gave voice to the popular fantasy of the noble and honorable Christian German turned out to have a few skeletons in the closet: he had been thrown out of a teacher's training academy for theft and had authored pornographic juvenilia. May's legal struggles interest Syberberg insofar as they offer a paradigm for a labor of transfiguration at work at all levels of May's life and literary production. In each case the labor takes the form of an impassioned quest for renewal—Mahler's *Resurrection* Symphony provides the musical backdrop for the film—in the paradises of one's own making:

> One can search for one's paradises by traveling to the sites of one's fantasy; this was Karl May's way. And one will no doubt fail, as May did when everything fell apart for him. One can search for them in human love and the recognition of one's accomplishments; the figural and textual arguments of the film showed this to be hard work. And one can search for them in self-overcoming, in the struggle against oneself, along the path into one's inner self, into the soul and the unconscious, as church and psychologists would say. And in this respect Karl May went far and paid for his triumph with his death.[44]

May's own particular *manie de perfection* lends him the pathos of a Faust character, but one whose striving takes place within a very particular historical constellation that overdetermines the goals and strategies of his quest. It is quite important for Syberberg that Karl May's particular search for paradise takes place at precisely that historical moment when psychoanalysis was becoming a science, when a mass popular culture was beginning to emerge in a form that could become a new market and industry proper, and finally, when film was being introduced as a new medium for the exploration of fantasy, if at first only as carnival sideshow. Framing these emerging cultural practices and tendencies and entering into their very constitution was, as Syberberg takes great pains to illustrate, the epoch of European colonialism.

The film opens with a conversation between May and a dedicated friend and admirer, both wearing the garb of white colonialists and set against a back projection of Ludwig's pleasure garden, suggesting the Far East. Their conversation revolves around the core of May's work: the creation of images of paradise (*Abbilder des Paradieses*) and the danger of neglecting such work. Later May appears in his villa in Saxony—Villa Shatterhand—surrounded by an assortment of colonial knicknacks including, among other trophies, a stuffed lion.[45] In another sequence, fairly early in the film, Emma and Klara—May's first and second wives—wander through a small provincial fairground that includes among its attractions *das lebende Bild*, a miniature cinema or *Guckkasten* in which Syberberg installs a brief homage to Georges Méliès, whose early illusionist filmic landscapes are cited again in *Hitler* and *Parsifal*. And finally, as if to condense in one metaphor the secret conspiracy between film, psychoanalysis, colonialism, and May's struggle to preserve his mythic self-image against the attacks of his enemies, May utters the portentous words, "'the soul is a vast land to which we flee.'"

This collusion of cultural practices is presented according to a familiar logic. Just as in *Ludwig*, where Bismarck and his realpolitik of Prussianization doubled Ludwig's search for artificial paradises, colonialism provides the makings of one strand of a double plot in which the above-mentioned cultural tendencies collectively form the other strand. Such a double plot structure suggests, of course, that the journeys described in each strand stand in parallel to one another, that their subjects are fueled by the same hungers, desires, and compulsions. As was the case in *Ludwig*, each quest is enacted as a sort of spiritual analgesic for what Syberberg sees as the deepest and most authentic of all human pains: nostalgia. The exotic landscapes of the East and the American West (whether colonized in fact or merely visited in the imagination), the psychic terrain as explored and mythologized by Freud, the flickering projections of light on white screens, and the fictions and myths that one creates out of the fragmented materials of one's own life, all become ciphers for a singular, primal yearning. What makes one expression of such long-ing more acceptable than another, one true, another false, appears to be the presence or absence of self-reflexivity as well as the degree of complicity any particular enactment of this primal yearning might exhibit with the forces that destroy the object of desire. In good Blochian—and Reitzian—fashion, Syberberg understands this yearning essentially as homesickness.

Home, for Syberberg, is first and foremost that place, to para-phrase Bloch's contemporary Walter Benjamin, where one finds the aura constituted by eyes that return a gaze. In this context May's blindness from birth until the age of four takes on nearly metaphysi-cal significance. May's search for paradise lost begins in the absence of a matrix of mirroring, a rather literal narcissistic injury the trauma of which May was able to survive only thanks to the empathic sup-port of a grandmother. This "psychological oxygen" (Heinz Kohut's phrase) provided by the grandmother included rituals of storytell-ing. Syberberg, the master of cinematic overdetermination, has May relate the story of his blindness and his grandmother's narrative nurturance as he drops artificial snowflakes from a cocoa tin— emblazoned with the image of a smiling white child—on a scale model of his native village. In this scene May praises the life and power of the inner world (" 'the most beautiful deeds . . . have al-ways been born of this inner realm' "), an imaginative space that only a few years later a poet from Prague would name *Weltin-nenraum*. The sequence thus groups together a series of metonymies for the various strands of the double plot alluded to above and unites them into one emblematic scene of primal homesickness: colonialism (and its ideological dissimulation in the innocent face of the child on the cocoa tin); film (the illusionist special effects of the miniature village); the new science/mythology of the inner world of the psyche. The scene as a whole may be viewed as an exercise in the iconography of the political unconscious in the age of European colonialism, a "typical panorama of the soul of a European people at the beginning of the proletarian age of the masses."[46]

In this scene Syberberg has May utter the ominous warning: " 'Woe, if the false one comes.' " As it happened, this wrong or false messiah was a man who during World War I experienced, if only briefly, the trauma of blindness. Syberberg further develops May's prophetic allusion by having Hitler, who was himself a great fan of May's, attend May's last public reading in 1912 in Vienna. Hitler walks through the men's shelter in the Meldemannstraße where he pronounces the words, "'whenever the weapons needed for freedom are missing, the will must take their place.'"

The ambiguous position of May's utopianism in German cultural and political history is further underscored in the sound track. In the final sequence of the film—May's death and transfiguration—May is laid out behind the Villa Shatterhand on a table of stone before a full-sized tepee; beside him his second wife Klara, herself dressed as squaw-in-mourning, sits silently; snow blows in through the broken glass roof of this Indian burial site transplanted to a Saxon hothouse like a rare tropical orchid. In the background is a musical citation from Liszt: the *Siegesfanfare* that was used in the Third Reich to accompany radio announcements of German military victories.[47]

That the utopian libido, which has clearly emerged as a kind of primal nostalgia, is in essence a yearning for a space of specular mutuality, a place where eyes return a gaze, is further underscored by Syberberg in a way that also adds more iconographic substance to his argument for the link between this yearning and fascism. Nearly all the major roles in the film are played by actors and actresses from the UFA-studios of the thirties and forties. This self-conscious inscription of German film history into the visual text of his own work seems to be not only a gesture toward undoing the repression of the history of the Third Reich, which includes the films it produced, but also, as Berman has suggested, "a visual quotation implying a hidden affinity between May's fantasies and the aura of film stars."[48] The absence of a space where eyes return a gaze initiates, according to the film's allegorical argument, all those quests for and conquests of new territories of auratic experience, new searches for the gaze that would finally authenticate one's worth and reality. The movie star and the charismatic leader are for Syberberg the two distinctly modern figures that have come to embody such a gaze. And as the title of his magnum opus suggests, these two forms come together in Hitler.[49]

VI

This notion of home as a place abounding with auratic gazes needs to be pondered more carefully. As is well known, the great theorist of the auratic gaze and its disintegration in the modern period was Walter Benjamin. Much of his thinking about the gaze and aura was worked out in the context of his studies of Paris as the capital of the nineteenth century and of Baudelaire in particular as the modern poet par excellence. Benjamin's important essay, "Art in the Age of Mechanical Reproduction," also belongs within this general context of concerns and explorations.

For Benjamin, Baudelaire is so remarkable a poet precisely because he placed at the center of his work the shock of moving amid urban crowds, the first public sphere in which one is systematically trained not to return the gaze of the other: "What is involved here is that the expectation roused by the look of the human eye is not fulfilled. Baudelaire describes eyes of which one is inclined to say that they have lost their ability to look."[50] The shock of the chronic inhumanity of such eyes stands in contrast, as *spleen* to *idéal*, to the notion of *correspondances* which signifies in Baudelaire a quasi-mystical familiarity and intimacy with the other even as it recedes into a distance that can never be overcome. In the sonnet "*Correspondances*," such intimacy is explicitly evoked as auratic gaze:

> La Nature est un temple où de vivants piliers
> Laissent parfois sortir de confuses paroles;
> L'homme y passe à travers des forêts de symboles
> Qui l'observent avec des regards familiers.
>
> (Nature is a temple of living pillars
> where often words emerge, confused and dim;
> and man goes through this forest, with familiar
> eyes of symbols always watching him.[51])

For Benjamin, the world of such gazes is shaped by the social practices associated with premodern communal life and modes of production. Above all it is a world organized by the temporal rhythms of rituals and ceremonies which provide continuity with the past, including, of course, the ritual of storytelling. Modernity, on the other hand, is seen to be organized according to the pure rationality of clock time, suggesting in turn yet another sense of the chronic inhumanity of the modern metropolis: this is a world in which, to use terms suggested by Frank Kermode, *chronos* has thoroughly displaced *kairos*.[52] As Benjamin says, "The *idéal* supplies the power of remembrance; the *spleen* musters the multitude of the seconds against it." What makes Baudelaire the preeminent modern poet is his apparent capacity to resist the seductions of regressive nostalgias for premodern experience (what Benjamin calls *Erfahrung*); rather he becomes the first great lyricist of modern experience (what Benjamin calls *Erlebnis*): "The poet who failed to found a family endowed the word *familier* with overtones pervaded by promise and renunciation. He has lost himself to the spell of eyes which do not return his glance and submits to their sway without illusions."[53] The field of force of such dead gazes becomes, by a slight but significant displacement, that of the commodity, the pure surface of which, as Eagleton has put it, "combines the allure of the mythically untouchable madonna with the instant availability of the mythical whore."[54] Aura—or rather its various simulacra—becomes available for a price.

Against this backdrop, both Ludwig and Karl May represent distinctly antimodernist sensibilities in their lack of this peculiarly Baudelairean equanimity vis-à-vis the shocks of modernity. Syberberg, however, is intent on demonstrating how these two figures attempt to recover their premodern homelands by means of the image machinery of at least an incipient modernity, that is, as simulacra constructed out of the materials and according to the laws of the social formation from which they were attempting to escape. Both figures are seen as producers of commoditylike fantasies anticipating the most elaborate fantasy machine ever constructed, the cinema. It is thus no accident that the final scene of *Karl May* made one critic think of John Ford's *Cheyenne Autumn*.[55] The ritual, auratic space of the campfire, this minimal unit of your-face–my-face communion, is recuperated in *Karl May* as special effect and simulacrum.[56]

The thought behind this system of hidden conspiracies of ideas and discursive practices runs something like this: The need for a communal structure in which one may find eyes that return one's gaze is universal and transhistorical; there are social formations, however, that impose a double bind on one's attempts to satisfy this human need. A particular social formation may require for its own continued reproduction social practices and behaviors that in turn make the satisfaction of this need increasingly difficult and even impossible. To assume one's position within such a symbolic order is to live a contradiction. The social order requires one to participate in the destabilization of the very communal structures that alone would provide a setting in which eyes could return a gaze. As relief from the pressures of such an intolerable double bind, society must provide alternative satisfactions that at least allow one to remember or to imagine what a vital human gaze must have been like. These satisfactions are provided by the culture industry, which in turn participates in creating the very instabilities that called forth its machinery of simulacra and compensations. Indeed, all of the cultural tendencies and practices discussed thus far participate in this double bind structure: by making the other the same, colonialism destroys what it needs for its continued existence; the clinical intimacy of psychoanalysis reproduces in a certain sense the very social isolation it is intent on healing; fascism secures the gaze of the other only to the extent that it enslaves it or turns it into a corpse.[57] Syberberg's fundamental claim in all of this, a claim first made by Bloch in the thirties and one that has been newly theorized by Jameson, is that one must learn to read the utopian subtext in all of these cultural practices and tendencies, no matter how destructive or self-destructive their machinery might be. One must, in other words, learn to recognize and even celebrate the deep core or libidinal fuel of these apparatuses: the need for eyes that return a gaze.

As I argue in chapter 1, much recent critical theory has tended to respond to these and indeed all attempts to recuperate the space of a human gaze with a categorical disavowal of the narcissistic needs associated with the gaze. This position tends to equate the desire for eyes that return a gaze with violence, ideology, and everything that is destructive about Western patriarchal culture. But is such a position not itself entangled in a network of rather questionable binary oppositions: infantile narcissism/lucid melancholy; the oblivion of eternal sleep/perpetual insomnia; merging with the matrix/becoming hopelessly stranded from any matrix; paradisiacal intoxication/traumatic sobriety?[58] Given such a vision, one feels compelled to choose between a caricature of Biedermeier harmoniousness and a caricature of Nietzschean modernity. The choice appears to be to regress, as Eagleton has formulated this double bind, to an imaginary past or to "remain disconsolately marooned in the symbolic order." But as Eagleton has also suggested, there remains a third strategy available to members of a social order in which the gaze, understood as the emblem of premodern intersubjectivity, has been traumatically occulted: "This is to re-channel desire from both past and present to the future: to detect in the decline of the aura the form of new social and libidinal relations, realizable by revolutionary practice."[59]

Another way of dismantling these oppositions, one that lightens the eschatological burden of Eagleton's discourse, is to return to the terms of the discussion of the labor of mourning. Mourning, as its structures and rhythms first emerge in the work/play of constituting the self, is in essence a ritual of de-auratization. The self emerges out of the ruins of the primitive auratic symbiosis with the mother. But this can happen only if the process is empathically witnessed by the mother's gaze or that of some other significant person. Otherwise mourning cannot take place and the thereby dangerously depleted and unstable self will permanently hunger not for the gaze that bears witness to one's grief over the necessary local spoilings of the auratic gaze but for the archaic aura of prelapsarian eyes, eyes that offered themselves before the need to mourn and to become a self became necessary (though perhaps not possible). A hunger of this kind is the beginning of secondary or pathological narcissism. Much recent critical theory erroneously sees all gazes as embodying the same primitive narcissistic greed. But what the self needs in order to mourn and assume its selfhood—a process that is, to a certain extent, reenacted with every experience of trauma or loss—is not the perfect, auratic gaze at all—this would be experienced as a blinding hallucination—but, to paraphrase Winnicott, the *good-enough gaze*, which enjoys its own chastened form of aura deriving from the solidarity of the empathic witness. Under the good-enough gaze of the empathic witness the self may take leave of its more archaic hankerings for the full hallucinatory gaze that sees nothing because there are, in a sense, not yet any separate objects to be seen. Mourning, and the use mourning makes of transitional objects, may thus be understood as a paradoxical ritual of auratic de-auratization. Without the intermediate area of such a ritual there will be no *transition* but, rather, only a mad *oscillation* between the individually intolerable terms of a double bind.[60]

What is dangerous, then, about modernity is not that it signifies the disintegration of a world in which all gazes were spontaneously and magically focused on one another—such perfect specular reciprocity is really more a dystopian than utopian prospect—but, rather, that it destabilizes the good-enough communal structures that are required for the constitution of human selfhood as well as for the performance of labors of mourning in adult life. In this context Jameson's critique of existentialism takes on a special resonance:

> The point is . . . less the "truth" of the philosophical description—our condemnation to be free, the discontinuity of time, ultimately even, if one likes, the absurdity of natural or organic life and of being itself—which every modern individual is surely prepared to accept as such: it is rather the situation which suddenly allows the veil to be ripped away from this intolerable ontological bedrock, and imposes it on consciousness as the ultimate lucidity. . . . The real issue is not the propositions of existentialism, but rather their charge of affect: in future societies people will still grow old and die, but the Pascalian wager of Marxism lies elsewhere, namely in the idea that death in a fragmented and individualized society is far more frightening and anxiety-laden than in a genuine community, in which dying is something that happens to the group more intensely than it happens to the individual subject. The hypothesis is that time will be no less structurally empty, or to use the current version, presence will be no less of a structural and ontological illusion, in a future communal social life, but rather that this particular "fundamental revelation of the nothingness of existence" will . . . be of less consequence.[61]

In Syberberg's *Hitler* the question of mourning as a ritual of auratic de-auratization becomes central. Yet before turning to that film, I want to address briefly Syberberg's documentary on Winifred Wagner.

VII

In 1975, while engaged in the research for *Hitler*, Syberberg returned once more to the documentary form of his earlier works. The result, *Winifred Wagner und die Geschichte des Hauses Wahnfried von 1914–1975* (Winifred Wagner and the history of Wahnfried, 1914–1975), was less an interruption than a further preparation for his magnum opus. The film is a five-hour interview with Richard Wagner's daughter-in-law Winifred, née Williams, the woman who directed the Bayreuth Festival from the time of the death of her husband Siegfried Wagner in 1930 to 1945, and whose well-known friendship with Hitler—she is reputed to have supplied Hitler with the paper on which he wrote parts of *Mein Kampf* while in prison—was the subject of a special session at the Nürnberg trials (at this special hearing, Winifred's daughter's book, *Night over Bayreuth*, was used as a major piece of evidence against her).

Before the interview, which was filmed over the course of five days, begins, the camera surveys a courtyard of ruins still remaining from the bombing of Wahnfried, while Syberberg ruminates over the detritus in off-screen commentary, seeking out the possible significances of this historical site. He mentions the names of the ghosts still haunting these fragments: Nietzsche, Ludwig II, Houston Stewart Chamberlain, Hitler; the titles of books: Wagner's *Mein Leben*, Hitler's *Mein Kampf*; black G.I.s dancing on Wagner's grave to jazz in the moonlight. The fitful beginnings of a labor of decipherment are heard: Wagner's cultural revolution as a mythic counterworld to the age of industrialization; the destruction of the German bourgeoisie; the disintegration of aura.

And so, even before Winifred Wagner speaks, the audience is thrust into the midst of a complex network of ideas and legacies which will be its responsibility to reclaim as its own and, if possible, to sort out and make productive. The Wagner estate becomes, under Syberberg's gaze, the emblem of a particularly shocking condition of *thrownness*: whoever wishes to inhabit the symbolic order of postwar Germany cannot, according to Syberberg, avoid passing through the rubble of Wahnfried. *Wahn-fried*—literally respite from delirium—figures in Syberberg's film not so much as the place of peace and respite for which Wagner constructed it but, rather, as that space where the connections between the metaphysical sabbath Wagner longed for and the political literalizations of those longings in Nazism, become legible. Recall the case of the schoolboy in Sichrovsky's anthology of interviews who discovers that the house he had grown up in had been previously inhabited by a Jewish family until their deportation in 1941; the grandfather, who then took possession of the house, had never spoken of the dwelling's special genealogy. The trauma of this boy's awakening to the violent history of his home is not unlike the trauma through which Syberberg wants to lead his audience by way of a peculiar tour through the history of the house of Wahnfried by Wagner's daughter-in-law.

The centerpiece of this marathon interview is made up of sections in which Winifred Wagner recounts the course of her relationship

with Hitler and National Socialism. Most significant here is her refusal to recant anything about her friendship with Hitler. In this
relationship, Wagner insists that she was able to separate the private
from the political:

> "I will never disavow my friendship with him, I couldn't do that. . . .
> You see, I'm capable of totally separating the Hitler I know from all the
> things people blame him for now. . . . And I am sure that if . . . Hitler
> would walk through that door I would be just as happy and delighted
> as ever to see him and have him here, and all the things that point to a
> dark side of the man, I know these things exist but for me they don't
> exist because I don't know this part of him."[62]

Wagner's capacity to make these separations seems a function of
the fundamentally private relationship she maintained with politics
in general. At one point in the film she insists that her connection to
National Socialism was based on her experience of Hitler's personality and, as she characterizes it, its *demonic* aura. To support her
views in this regard she cites an early letter by Houston Stewart
Chamberlain, written to Hitler after his first meeting with him in
October 1923. The aura constituted by Hitler's gaze at that meeting is
seen to be the source of his power:

> "You are destined to achieve great and awesome things, but despite
> the force of your will I do not take you for a man of violence. Accord-
> ing to Goethe, there is a kind of power whose essence it is to shape a
> cosmos. . . . I mean it in this sense of giving form to a cosmos, when I
> place you among the builders and not the destroyers and men of
> violence. Your capacity to soothe me has a great deal to do with your
> eyes and your gestures. Your eyes are, as it were, endowed with
> hands; they take hold of a man and keep him in their firm grip."[63]

What comes across most strongly over these five hours of what is
essentially a monologue on Wagner's part is the rigidity of her character and a nearly grotesque incapacity to feel remorse for her in-
volvements with Hitler and National Socialism, empathy with those
who suffered, or understanding for those who opposed the Nazi
regime.[64] When asked by Wilhelm Furtwängler how she felt about
her treatment by the courts and the public after the war, her response typifies the frozen aspect of a person utterly incapable of
mourning: "'And my answer to him was that when you come right

down to it, it didn't bother me in the least. . . . And then I asked myself why. . . . And I believe it had to do with the fact that I never felt guilty of any kind of misdeed or crime. Had I felt guilty, then I most likely would have been somehow more affected [by these attacks]; but they never seemed to touch me in the slightest way.' "[65]

VIII

Syberberg would apparently agree with the Mitscherlichs' thesis that the rigidity that marks not just a figure like Winifred Wagner but the collective psychological economy of postwar Germany more generally is a result of the country's failure to mourn and heal the wounds opened during the Nazi period. This failure, however, as Syberberg's argument continues, is in turn rooted in (or at least, to use a Heideggerian locution, equiprimordial with) a collective disavowal of the promise of happiness with which the Nazis were able to enthuse the vast majority of the German population. That promise was, as Syberberg's other films demonstrate, a promise directed toward the deep homesickness at the core of the modern subject who must sustain, on a daily basis, the stress of the chronic narcissistic injury of dwelling among eyes that do not return one's gaze. Fascism was, according to Syberberg, a paradoxical attempt to undo these structurally omnipresent shocks by voluntaristically creating a space of immediacy and intimacy, of my-face–your-face communion—the *Volksgemeinschaft*—with the very means that were, at another level, contributing to the dissolution of communal spaces and, furthermore, by finding a pharmakos who could be blamed for occulting the otherwise pure blue gazes of Aryan eyes. According to Syberberg, the global disavowal of the utopian longings at the core of this fascist voluntarism has resulted in a general state of ennui or *Freudlosigkeit*, as Syberberg likes to refer to what he perceives as the emotional deadness of contemporary German society. *Hitler* argues that such joylessness is itself sustained by the same mechanisms—primarily the mass media as an apparatus organizing collective patterns of identity formation—with which German fascism had staged its phantasmagoria, only now deployed without the former claims and presumptions of utopianism. What at times appears to be a nostalgia on Syberberg's part for the dubious monumentalism of Nazi phantasmagoria is thus primarily a function of his vision of contemporary German society as the real dystopia: that place where one has become numb to the pain of no longer believing in utopia. For Syberberg the real catastrophe of modern history is not so much the destruction of the monumental temples of culture but, rather, the forgetting of their ruins or, worse, the transformation of those ruins—the wailing walls of Western history—into so many tourist attractions. The task that Syberberg sets himself in *Hitler* will be not only to recall and to scrutinize Nazism's appeal to the utopian libido in the form of phantasmagoric recuperations of a perfect human gaze but also to recollect and reanimate the deep longings and nostalgias that the contemporary culture and consciousness industries effectively disperse and anaesthetize. In this context, mourning will involve a process of leaving behind contemporary strategies of dispersing utopian libido while at the same time reclaiming that libido as the source of a still viable legacy and indeed, of human creativity as such. The success of this labor will depend, in turn, on Syberberg's ability to reconstitute the intermediate area in its primal sense as a realm of *Trauer-Spiel*, or mourning-play, as a space, in other words, where rituals of de-auratization may be performed under the auratic auspices of art. According to Syberberg, his own compatriots are not even aware that such a space or cultural site is lacking:

> The magical places have either . . . been determined by the ancestors and are to be found only there, and when they have been destroyed a great restlessness ensues, or they must be established anew. If, however, one isn't even aware of having lost this or that it must be newly constituted, then the matter has become disastrous. And that is how I sometimes see the Germans; they no longer have any awareness of this.[66]

It is as just such an auratic de-auratization, finally, that Syberberg seems to understand the combination of irony and pathos in his films as well as the so-called scandal of his efforts to blend Brechtian and Wagnerian aesthetic styles.

Once more, Syberberg casts his argument in a decidedly allegorical mode. This is, after all, a film of ideas—or as Syberberg likes to say, the "music of our ideas"[67]—and allegories, as the most lucid theorist of that symbolic mode has remarked, are precisely monuments to ideas, ideals, ideologies: "They do not mimetically show us the human beings who need these ideals, but they examine the philosophic, theological, or moral premises on which we act, and then they confront us with the perfection of certain ideals, the depravity of others."[68] In the course of its seven hours of running time, this emphatically allegorical film presents an inventory of richly textured representations of the ideas, discourses, and phantasms that made up the German collective psyche in the years prior to, during, and immediately after the Third Reich. These representations are divided among four major parts or chapters ("Hitler, A Film from Germany: From the World Ash Tree to Goethe's Oak in Buchenwald"; "A German Dream"; "The End of a Winter's Tale and the Final Victory of Progress"; "We Children of Hell Remember the Age of the Grail"), which are in turn composed of some twenty-two more or less distinct sequences.

Russell Berman has analyzed the iconographic composition of typical sequences of the film in terms of five formal positions: back projections; the foreground; music; noise on the sound track; the spoken text.[69] The back projections can range from a Méliès moonscape, Gustav Doré's illustrations of the *Divine Comedy*, 8-mm films taken by amateur photographers during the Third Reich, reproductions of significant sites such as the rooms of the Reich chancellory or Hitler's residence in Berchtesgaden, slide reproductions of drawings and paintings by William Blake, Otto Philipp Runge, and Caspar David Friedrich. In the foreground typically are a series of emblematic objects such as fragments from the ruins of Wahnfried, a miniature reproduction of the "Goethe oak" in Buchenwald, the polyhedron and number tablet from Dürer's *Melencolia I*, cardboard cutouts of figures from the early history of cinema, a large assortment of puppets, a model of Edison's film studio (the Black Maria). The music itself becomes an agonistic site in which ideological polarities and affinities represented by strategic musical citations—Wagner, popular music of the period, military music—reproduce the psychomachy enacted at other levels of the film. The miscellaneous noise on the sound track contains radio announcements, news reports from mass rallies, and sounds of battle. The spoken text consists in large part of a series of extended monologues such as the forty-five minutes of personal reminiscences spoken by Hellmut Lange in the role of Hitler's valet Krause or the various monologues performed by André Heller and Harry Baer.

As even this cursory description of the compositional strategies deployed in the film suggests, this work crowds the imagination, forcing the viewer into an exegetical frame of mind. What one sees must be read and deciphered if one is not to feel hopelessly overwhelmed. It is a film that demands not so much criticism as commentary. Every object in the film functions as an ornament in the ancient sense of cosmos, that is, as a marker of a position in a social or cosmological hierarchy or genealogical construction.[70] In this sense, Achilles's shield as described by Homer—perhaps the most important paradigm of allegorical ornament in Western literature—may be the most appropriate analogy for a frame in one of Syberberg's films. Just as in the Baroque when German orthography began to capitalize nouns, everything in Syberberg's film universe is capitalized. The ordering of sequences creates jarring juxtapositions of tonalities, niveaus, discourses, and styles, thus further complicating analysis. A circus barker is followed by a melancholic dialogue with a puppet of Ludwig II; a monologue that details the banalities of Hitler's toiletries and choice of underwear is flanked by various cosmological speculations about origin and end of the universe; and so on.

The iconography of *Hitler* is, as in the earlier works of the cycle, designed to reveal both the modes of address and technologies with which Nazism made its utopian appeal and the history of these techniques—the place they have occupied in various social formations—prior to and after their deployment in the Third Reich. The allegorist's freedom to manipulate freely the citations and emblematic relics that are his raw material allows for the construction of the various genealogies that already inform the earlier films of the cycle (included among the relics are numerous citations from Syberberg's own films). By juxtaposing anachronistically objects and texts within or across the five formal positions of any sequence (or from sequence to sequence), the filmmaker-allegorist may suggest correspondences between otherwise radically dispersed texts, images, and practices. Susan Sontag lists some of the genealogies that are proposed in *Hitler*: "from Romanticism to Hitler, from Wagner to Hitler, from Caligari to Hitler, from kitsch to Hitler"; "from Hitler to pornography, from Hitler to the soulless consumer society of the Federal Republic, from Hitler to the rude coercions of the DDR."[71]

A few examples may illustrate Syberberg's allegorical/genealogical strategies in the film. In one sequence Alfred Edel is seen in the attic of Wahnfried surrounded by mannequins covered with the "cobwebs of the centuries." He recites a bizarre, quasi-psychotic Weberian monologue about charismatic leadership (" 'Ruling is sensual. Ruling is blood. Ruling is self-realization, ruling is feeling, feeling anew, ruling is Eros, an inexhaustible Eros' ") while excerpts are played from the march from *Das Rheingold* interspersed with cries of "*Sieg Heil*" and Goebbels's call to Hitler in the name of the masses, "Führer, command, and we will obey."[72] This sequence is in turn surrounded by two short texts by the Jewish cultural historian Egon Friedell. The texts are spoken as monologues by Peter Moland (in the role of Himmler's private astrologer) and are delivered before projections of Wagner's piano and Benno Arendt's design from the Nazi period for the second act of *Tristan*, respectively. Both Friedell texts situate European history in general, and European rationalism in particular, within a cosmic framework that suggests the extreme hubris and ethnocentrism of the Western rationalist tradition.[73]

In another sequence—the one that delivers the signature icon of the film as a whole—Heinz Schubert appears as Hitler: shrouded in hellish smoke and draped in a Roman tunic, he rises from Wagner's grave (the image is composed after one of Doré's illustrations for Dante's *Inferno*); the floor is strewn with leaves, omnipresent emblems of grief in the film. The sound track plays excerpts from Wagner's early grand opera *Rienzi*. The text Schubert recites, which includes citations from Shakespeare and Thomas Mann, restates, as do so many of the spoken texts in the film, Syberberg's central thesis, namely that Hitler was chosen by the masses freely and democratically to redeem their petty miseries and, more important, to give their lives meaning and substance (here one detects what I earlier alluded to as Syberberg's nostalgia for the Nazi period): " 'And one should consider to how many people I gave something worth being against. And just compare the lives of so many people—listless, empty. I gave them what they put into me, what they wanted to hear, wanted to do, things they were afraid to do.' "[74]

An allusion to his brief episode of blindness in Pasewalk during which he claims to have made his decision to become a politician underscores the mechanism through which Hitler was able to secure his place as the German "black messiah," namely, according to the

"I gave them what they put into me. . . ." From *Hitler, ein Film aus Deutschland*, a film by Hans Jürgen Syberberg, courtesy of the filmmaker

specular logic of narcissistic identifications: the German people with Hitler, and Hitler in turn with a Wagnerian operatic hero, Cola di Rienzi, the last Roman tribune. The absence marked by blindness is redeemed, in other words, by the "cinematic" pleasure of specular identifications. Hitler's identification with Rienzi anticipates the long dialogue in part 3 between Himmler and his Swedish masseur, which reveals Himmler's secret identification with the medieval German prince Heinrich der Löwe.[75] By providing the German masses with a realm of intimacy and participation constituted as a sort of relay of narcissistic identifications, Hitler was able to become the archaic wish fulfillment for an entire population: "'I was and am the end of your most secret wishes, the legend and reality of your dreams.'" And as he then adds: "'So we have to get through. Finally. The final time? Nightmares? Not by a long shot.'"[76]

These last words suggest that the mechanisms of identification and projection which allowed for the collective construction and maintenance of the Hitlerian aura—of the hyperreality of "Hitler"—have survived the flames of the Berlin bunker. Accordingly, the scene that follows Hitler's monologue seems to argue against the assumption that one overcomes "Hitler," that is, Hitler as (cinematic) phantasm, by simply burying and profaning Hitler and what is perceived as Hitlerian. Here Syberberg stages as surrealist "danse macabre"[77] what Winifred Wagner had witnessed with so much horror: Black G.I.s dancing with blond German women around Wagner's now closed grave in front of a projection of Wahnfried in ruins. The sound track consists of the text of Brecht's "Die Zeit muß sich erfüllen, wir Toten wachen auf" (The age must be fulfilled, we dead are waking up), a poem about the dead taking revenge on those who stole their lives. In the context of Syberberg's strategic reinscription, the poem suggests that an unmourned "Hitler"—not Hitler—will remain a vampiric threat to the postwar republic.

Yet another sequence in which Hitler is evoked as messiah-as-auratic-gaze is a remarkable scene shortly before Edel's lunatic discourse on charismatic leadership. André Heller sets the scene as a ritual reenactment of an elite social gathering of 1923; the scene apparently intends to evoke Hitler's aura in order to decathect it within the auratic parameters of play:

Just imagine a gathering of 1923. Why, everything's still here, unchanged to this day. They are enacting the scene, compulsively, by

". . . while the pile of debris before him grows skyward." From *Hitler, ein Film aus Deutschland*, a film by Hans Jürgen Syberberg, courtesy of the filmmaker

way of atoning, in the historical locale, in the manner of an Oberammergau votive offering. The children come, the grandchildren, the children's children, and each one plays his part and they exchange them among themselves, they trade, and we hear the noises of the past, the cars, the voices, the laughter, the waiting, the work, the grief, the catharsis of fear and pity.[78]

The third figure to speak at this social gathering populated for the most part by contemporary mannequins dressed in clothes from the twenties, is Rainer von Artenfels as Goebbels describing the first time he saw and, more important, was seen by Hitler. During the monologue the audience hears a sound-montage of street noise, machine guns, various political and popular songs of the twenties, a brief excerpt from Brecht's *Mahagonny*, and a speech by Hitler at a mass rally. The back projection is the slide of the Venus grotto from *Tannhäuser* which had provided the mythic backdrop to Ludwig's nightmare in the earlier film. Goebbels is heard describing the ecstatic impact of his initial encounter with Hitler:

> "I go, nay, I am driven to the tribune. I stand there for a long time and gaze into the face of this One Man. This is no orator. This is a prophet! Sweat is streaming from his forehead. In this gray, pale face, two glowing eye-stars are fulminating. . . . The man up there gazes at me for an instant. . . . That is an order. From that moment on, I am virtually born again. . . . I am intoxicated. . . . All I now know is that I put my hand into a throbbing male hand. That was an oath for life. And my eyes sank into two great blue stars."

The effect of the relation constituted between Hitler and his audience is the sudden emergence of a magical community, a sort of barroom Grail society suspended within the highly unstable medium of a specular exchange: " 'Around me, all at once, there are no more strangers. They are all my brothers.' "[79]

This scene echoes an earlier episode in which Peter Moland, speaking for a puppet version of Albert Speer in his prisoner's uniform (Speer is the last puppet to appear in this sequence in which one after another puppets of Goebbels, Göring, Himmler, and Eva Braun emerge from their tombs in Hell's antechamber and speak of their fates and achievements), describes a similar barroom encounter with Hitler. Here the narcissism at the core of their hallucinatory exchange is signaled by Speer's confusion about who chose whom and whether the encounter had ever really taken place, as if the entire event had occurred in a sort of dream-time in which all boundaries were blurred: "'Did I choose him or he me? I do not know. It had to come somehow or other. . . . Or was it the way I just described?'"[80] Elsaesser summarizes the argument linking these two scenes:

> Both scenes record how individual alienation and social marginality are overcome and swept away by the spontaneity of a curious reciprocity of recognition, whose agent is Hitler's gaze, his "star-blue eyes." Fascism is here typified as a mutual and mutually sustaining self-confirmation in the public sphere of urban life, outside the family and the usual places of bourgeois (and oedipal) socialization. Instead, the places and occasions are rallies, mass-meetings, beerhalls, street-battles.[81]

Yet another scene in which narcissistic identifications figure in a central, though more complex way, is Peter Kern's tour de force performance as a neo-Nazi who imagines himself to be an incarnation of Hitler's private film projectionist Fritz Ellerkamp. Narcissistic structures function in this scene at several different levels, the most important of which is the fantasized incorporation of Ellerkamp, recalling in turn not only Hitler's identification with Rienzi and Himmler's with Heinrich der Löwe but also an earlier scene in which Peter Kern, dressed in an SA uniform, reenacts the child murderer's monologue of self-defense from Fritz Lang's *M*. The compulsion under which the (Nazi) murderer stands suggests an inability to stabilize the boundaries of a self except by repetitively expelling and destroying those aspects of the self which arouse too much ambivalence.

Another layer of Syberberg's allegorical strategy comes into view in this scene quite dramatically and uncannily. Kern's reenactment of *M* is simply a psychologically more transparent version of a mode of agency informing not only all performances in the film but allegorical action in general. Angus Fletcher has characterized the tendency of allegorical agents to act only within the strictest bounds of a singular obsession as "daemonic agency": "Coming from the term that means 'to divide,' *daemon* implies an endless series of divisions of all important aspects of the world into separate elements for study and control." And further:

> Daemons . . . share this major characteristic of allegorical agents, the fact that they compartmentalize function. If we were to meet an allegorical character in real life, we would say of him that he was obsessed with only one idea, or that he had an absolutely one-track mind, or that his life was patterned according to absolutely rigid habits from which he never allowed himself to vary. It would seem that he was driven by some hidden, private force.

Like the child murderer in *M*, or any number of other figures—or puppets—allowed to speak during the course of the film's seven hours, the allegorical agent is driven by an unknown compulsion: "There is no such thing as satisfaction in this world; daemonic agency implies a *manie de perfection*, an impossible desire to become one with an image of unchanging purity. The agent seeks to become isolated within himself, frozen into an eternally fixed form." The allegorical agent may thus come to resemble a machine: "Constriction of meaning, when it is the limit put upon a personified force or power, causes that personification to act somewhat mechanistically. The perfect allegorical agent is . . . a robot."[82]

As I have suggested with regard to the child murderer/SA-commando, the compulsion that drives the allegorical agent may be a function of a double bind structure, namely being in the impossible position of having to stabilize a self in the absence of a good-enough environmental provision: in a space where eyes do not return a gaze. Caught within the intolerable closure of such a double bind, the subject will be unable to mourn and integrate the losses necessary to becoming a self and will instead engage in repetitive rituals of exorcism and purification, hopeless efforts to cleanse the body of the (homeopathic) impurities—the pharmakon/pharmakos—it needs to become a stable self. The compulsive rituals of the allegorical agent are thus not unlike the elegiac loop discussed earlier: rituals performed again and again in the absence of a space in which genuinely elegiac rituals of mourning could be enacted and brought to some sort of completion.[83]

In the scene that initiated this excursus on demonic agency, another layer of narcissistic identifications comes into view in the content of the "gossip" this neo-Nazi relates. Of particular significance are the anecdotes concerning intimate details of Hitler's private life and childhood which he relates in the voice of Ellerkamp as he leads the audience through the ruins of the Hitler residence on the Obersalzberg. He mentions, for example, that Hitler had the habit of whistling—often out of tune—along with the classical recordings he would regularly listen to; that Hitler was beaten as a child by his father; that he learned from a Karl May story that it was a sign of courage not to reveal one's pain, a lesson that put an end to those beatings; and finally, he mentions a Christmas anecdote: "'Hitler was deeply affected by Christmas. He couldn't look at a Christmas tree. I asked him why he never went to any Christmas parties or gave one himself. He said: "No, my mother died on a Christmas Eve, under the Christmas tree."'"[84] At the end of this anecdote, Kern sings the forbidden first strophe of the German national anthem and finally breaks down in tears. The story recalls another Christmas anecdote told by Hellmut Lange as Hitler's valet Krause in his long monologue at the end of part 2. This sentimental "upstairs/downstairs" tale tells of a Hitler who led his valet arm in arm on a bizarre incognito journey through nocturnal Munich, Christmas Eve 1937. Both anecdotes are punctuated on the sound track by excerpts from a 1942 Christmas radio broadcast in which soldiers from the various European and African fronts all join together in one electronically mediated communal chorus of "Silent Night." At stake in each of these scenes is the constitution of an intimate space of my-face–your-face communality, whether in the sudden fraternity of master and servant who finally meet as two regular guys, the pathological imaginings of a psychotic fan who secures his alter ego by way of delirium, or the immediacy instituted by the magic of the electronic media.[85]

Both Christmas anecdotes bring to mind the gossip one is now more accustomed to hearing about the lives of film and television stars, and it is, of course, no coincidence that Kern's neo-Nazi believes himself to be Hitler's private film projectionist, the man who, as Baer remarks in an earlier monologue, knew Hitler's deepest and most secret wishes.[86] Film, or rather Hitler-as-film, has been the subject of Syberberg's own film all along: *Hitler, ein Film aus Deutschland*. And indeed, Syberberg wants his audience to inhabit consciously, self-reflexively, the particular space in which he stages his surreal *Trauerspiel* of history: the film studio. To this effect, the visual special effects of the initial shots of the film, themselves perhaps film-historical quotations of Hollywood special effects,[87] take viewers through the ether into a kind of mythic, cosmic tear that leads to a glass ball reminiscent of Charles Foster Kane's snowy, glass talisman; that relic represents, as Timothy Corrigan has noted, "the lost world of the child's imaginary, a loss which drives the adult through an endless series of grandiose replacement images."[88] The audience then enters into the glass ball and its magical interior: a miniature replication of Thomas Edison's first film studio, known as the Black Maria, which for Syberberg figures, with typically ominous ambiguity, as the "black studio of our imagination."[89]

Inside the studio the stage is littered with the stranded objects, emblems, cut-outs, and puppets that will become the relics and talismans of the film. The back projection in the interior of the studio reveals the World Ash Tree from Wagner's *Walküre*, suggestive of the title of part 1: "Hitler, A Film from Germany: From the World Ash Tree to Goethe's Oak in Buchenwald." The World Ash Tree in the Black Maria thereby becomes the complex emblem of the quest structuring this entire cinematic allegory. Film, once the promise of light and wisdom, now bears the festering wound of its guilty history (according to the myth, Wotan paid the price of one of his eyes to be able to drink from the fountain of wisdom at the foot of the World Ash Tree Yggdrasil; he also broke off one of its branches to hew a spear). According to this mythic tale of guilt and corruption, cinema, understood as a technology for the production of reality effects, became the literal and figural site of that lethal aestheticization of politics which was German fascism. The guilt or fallenness of cinema derives, then, from its complicity in mechanisms of projection and identification which were deployed by the Nazis to mobilize the population and which have become integral to a postwar society largely grounded in image consumption and spectacle. Those mechanisms are in turn seen to originate in Wagner's own system of phantasmagoric special effects, suggesting an indirect complicity between Wagner and Hitler, Wagner and Buchenwald. This genealogical construction, rather than the fact of Hitler's enthusiasm for Wagner's music, is crucial to Syberberg, just as Hitler's reputation as a cineast, about which much is made in the film, is secondary to Hitler as a quasi-filmic projection of a collective. According to the film's argument, then, Germany can master its fallenness, its entanglement in a mesh of contaminated cultural traditions—this is, once more, the thought that the World Ash Tree already contains the seeds of Goethe's oak in Buchenwald, that Wagner's monumentalism and mythomania prefigure the phantasmagoria of Nazi spectacle—only by entering into the machinery of the cinematic imagination which for Syberberg is the true locus of these poisonous complicities. We defeat Hitler by defeating "Hitler," we overcome fascism by overcoming fascism-as-film; we master the guilt of our history by mastering the guilt of our film history (this is, no doubt, the reason for the long, sarcastic digressions on particular scandals in the history of cinema such as the Soviet persecution of Eisenstein and Hollywood's treatment of von Stroheim). To return to the Wagnerian underpinnings of Syberberg's allegory, one might say that his own film takes on the the role of a kind of cinematic *Notung*, the sword Siegfried used to splinter Wotan's spear.

This process of working through the cinematic imaginary unfolds in two distinct but related ways. First, by leading viewers through the film studio and allowing his actors to *reenact* the kitsch fantasies of the Third Reich, to recall, with carnivalesque irony, the lethal pathos of Nazi ideology, Syberberg effectively displays the inner gears of the most powerful politico-cinematic machinery ever known. Indeed, Syberberg wants us to believe that Hitler himself, consciously or unconsciously, conceived of the Third Reich as just such an apparatus, as one vast cinematic *Gesamtkunstwerk*. By opening to view the guts of this apparatus—the product of which is fascination—Syberberg hopes to demystify (*ent-täuschen*), though not necessarily demythologize, its seductive powers.

More important, however, is that aesthetic strategy that has led critics to link Syberberg's film with the baroque allegorical sensibility as described by Benjamin. For the film studio in *Hitler* is not only the inside of a machine capable of churning out simulacra of auratic gazes and creating its own charismatic star system; it is a field of ruins, akin to the *Schädelstätte* or calvary at the conclusion of Spirit's journey through the history of consciousness in Hegel's *Phenomenology*. And indeed, included among all this mnemonic detritus are also the ruins of German Idealism itself and its dreams of totality: "At the end, the silence of melancholy remains as a new variety and consequence of abortive German idealism."[90] By locating his studio in a sort of posthumous time and space—the owl of Minerva has long departed, perhaps never to return—Syberberg attempts to transform all historical attempts to realize and fulfill mythic longings for power into so many cinematic ruins. In this way, Syberberg clears a space where his audience may reclaim those longings in the mode of a *chastened* remembrance (evidently Syberberg's conception

143

of irony). Thanks to this Syberbergian therapy audiences may develop an immunity against the seductions of any future aestheticizations of politics as well as against cheap Hollywood imitations of full human gazes. In Elsaesser's eloquent words: "For the cinema, when it assumes its affinity and collusion with myth consciously, can represent the anticipatory and utopian memory, but it can only do so by insisting on partiality and division, by suspending any sense of immediacy in the negative dialectic that expresses itself as melancholy, in the requiem and mourning-work of collecting fragments."[91] It is in this sense that viewers can finally read the crumbling blocky letters of "The Grail" seen at the beginning and the end of *Hitler*, as well as identify and understand the fragment of Schiller's/Beethoven's "Ode to Joy" heard toward the end of the film.[92]

In a number of ways the film bears a remarkable resemblance to the structure of Paul Celan's stunning elegiac recantation of elegiac poetry, "Engführung" (Stretto). There, a journey through a petrified landscape—one thinks of Méliès's fissured moonscape cited by Syberberg—is marked by signposts and is organized according to textual strategies related to those of Syberberg's film. The reader moves, by way of the corrupt textuality (the infected *Buchstabe*) of Western history, between a now invisible Bukovina, Celan's birthplace, and Buchenwald. The journey ends at a site of remembrance, where the Jews are recalled who prayed to their God even as they were being gassed. But Celan fragments, much as Syberberg does with the entire Romantic and Idealist tradition, the psalmic call for mercy; it remains, as if obeying an imperative invoked in the poem's first strophe, *auseinandergeschrieben*, written asunder:

> Chöre, damals, die
> Psalmen. Ho, ho-
> sianna.
>
> Also
> stehen noch Tempel. Ein
> Stern
> hat wohl noch Licht.
> Nichts,
> nichts ist verloren.
>
> Ho-
> sianna.

(Choirs, back then, the
psalms. Ho, ho-
sanna.

And so
temples still stand. A
star
may still have light.
Nothing,
nothing is lost.
Ho-
sanna.[93])

For Syberberg, as perhaps briefly for Celan, the only source of hope in a world that threatens to become absorbed, without remainder, into a global system of technologically produced immediacy is to be seen in the capacity to remember and to preserve negative spaces, fissures, traces: to preserve, as it were, the wailing walls of the world and to keep them from becoming so many tourist attractions.[94]

Finally, still another mythic association suggested by Syberberg's project underscores the homeopathic dimension of this cinematic labor of mourning. The spear and the sword of the *Ring* anticipate that other Wagnerian weapon, the spear of Longinus in *Parsifal*. There the homeopathic strategy is cited more or less directly: "Nur eine Waffe taugt:—/Die Wunde schließt/Der Speer nur, der sie schlug [Only one weapon will suffice:—/Only the spear that opened the wound/Can close it now]." For Syberberg, film itself—and film's most important forbear, Wagner—is both the lance and the site of its application, both transitional object and the locus of its deployment. Film is the space in whose aura all misguided pursuits of aura are recollected as ruins, ambiguous monuments to longings for a full and pure human gaze.

IX

At this juncture I would like to place in a more critical light some of the arguments and claims that the film makes, in particular with regard to the work of mourning it ostensibly achieves in and through this cinematic journey into the inner space of the postwar

145

German imagination. Syberberg's black studio of the imagination seems to be a space in which the work of mourning has largely been usurped by a melancholic repetition compulsion, a golemlike allegory machine that can be stopped only by the grace of a deus ex machina; hence Syberberg's apparent inability to end his film. Fletcher has noted that allegories in general "have no inherent 'organic' limit of magnitude" and that the action "will go on as long as a daemonic agent is present, since . . . a daemon never tires or changes his nature." For this reason the narrative organization of an allegory may come to resemble the open-endedness of a mathematical progression.[95]

The ceaselessness of the allegorical action in *Hitler* seems to be primarily a function of the principle of contagion at the core of Syberberg's vision of the fallenness of the German language and imagination, that is, the pollution by Nazism of the utopian imagination. Heller's final monologue of the film provides a brief inventory of some of the things that have been lost to this fallenness (the monologue is addressed to a puppet of Hitler):

> "You took away our sunsets, sunsets by Caspar David Friedrich. You are to blame that we can no longer look at a field of grain without thinking of you. You made old Germany kitschy with your simplifying works and peasant pictures. And you are to blame that we have lost the pride of restaurants [*Stolz der Gasthäuser*], that people are driven into fast-food places for fear they might still love their work and something other than money, the harmlessly harmful, the only thing you left them with, since you occupied everything else and corrupted it with your actions, everything, honor, loyalty, country life, hard work, movies, dignity, Fatherland, pride, faith. . . . The words 'magic' and 'myth' and 'serving' and 'ruling,' 'Führer,' 'authority,' are ruined, are gone, exiled to eternal time."[96]

In such a vision there can be no real place of rest. And indeed, the film is framed by Heine's famous insomniac lament, "Denk ich an Deutschland in der Nacht, dann bin ich um den Schlaf gebracht [I think of Germany in the night/And thereby all my sleep takes flight]." As Fletcher has noted of Spenser, the figures in Syberberg's allegorical world "can never come to rest after a victory; no pause in the action ever is fully realized, and one senses in such a poetry an anxiety to get on to the next challenge, a strong suggestion that the poem is sickened throughout by its own acceptance of the idea of spiritual contagion."[97] Syberberg's strategy is that of a ritual *dispersion* of anxiety by means of a relentless accumulation of visual detail and the sheer verbal spell that is sustained throughout the film. But this waking dream can, finally, be ended only by a science fiction fantasy of a leap beyond, into the "black hole of the future."[98] This strategy is, however, more akin to an exorcism than to the labor of mourning.

The repetition compulsion that is melancholy emerges, as I have suggested, out of the struggle to engage in the labor of mourning in the absence of a supportive social space. Melancholy is a sort of chronic liminality; one becomes, as it were, addicted to the homeopathic drug, uses transitional objects in order to block, rather than to facilitate, transition into a "sobered" space of object relations. One way in which a collective may fail to support the work of mourning is its failure to supply totems, those symbolic figures of power with whom the mourner identifies, thereby anchoring him- or herself within a legacy that allows loss to be survived. Syberberg's film is, however, at least in part precisely an attempt to mourn the loss of such totems. The film thereby becomes an enactment of the double bind named by the equation: the Name-of-the-Father="Hitler." Syberberg's attempt to undo this bind apparently takes the course of searching out, within the legacy that the name "Hitler" has come to overshadow, certain paternal resources that, despite defilement, may still prove viable. Indeed, Ludwig II, Karl May, and Wagner are the totems that Syberberg attempts to salvage from the wreckage of the Name-of-the-Father(land). These choices, however, may in the end imply that Syberberg's concern is less with a labor of mourning than a reinscription of grandiose refusals to mourn: quests for a regressive return to origins, and ultimately for oblivion.

The mourning performed in and by *Hitler* turns out to be primarily about the pollution of a tradition of regressive romance fantasies rather than, for example, the social injuries that called such fantasies forth. What Syberberg finally seems to be lamenting is, to put it somewhat crudely, that Hitler gave the death drive a bad name. Restoring the good name of Thanatos and that of its various German disciples in music, art, philosophy, and even politics, seems to be be Syberberg's paramount intent.[99] So rather than working through and helping to overcome an inability to mourn, Syberberg's film is intended to induce melancholy, that psychological state that, accord-

147

ing to the Mitscherlichs, never emerged in the postwar period because of a ready availability of new narcissistic fixes in the consumer-
ist bacchanalia of the "economic miracle."[100] Syberberg wants to
induce melancholy not so much as a prelude to mourning but rather
as a way of remembering and honoring the deep, "authentic" narcissisms motivating the figures in his canon of Western *exaltés*. He
dismembers romance in culture and politics not in order to remember it under the auspices of the collective sensibility of comedy,
whose pattern of oedipal resolution resembles the work of mourning, but as a last-ditch effort at some sort of personal, if only negative, romance ecstasy. The auratic de-auratization that is the work of
mourning never succeeds in *Hitler* because the intermediate area is,
in a sense, the only habitable space for a Syberberg. As his next two
films demonstrate, that space too becomes ever more constricted,
ever more a place of ascetic resignation.[101] Perhaps for this reason
Syberberg has, since *Hitler*, renounced the term *Trauerarbeit* and
instead insisted on terms he sees as being more compatible with the
changing intentions of his art and cultural criticism. Here the two
most important concepts are *freudlose Gesellschaft* (joyless society)
and *Auslöschung* (extinction, extinguishment, effacement), taken
from the title of Thomas Bernhard's recent novel which Syberberg
reviewed for the Berlin daily, *Die Tageszeitung*.[102]

X

At the end of his brief essay on the Swiss author Robert Walser,
Walter Benjamin distinguishes between the world of myth and the
world of fairy tale as a way of circumscribing the particular qualities
of Walser, his characters, and his delicate prose texts. According to
Benjamin, Walser's world is informed by the peculiar capacity for
pleasure and delight characteristic of people recovering from an
illness—or madness:

> For no one experiences pleasure like one who is convalescing [*niemand
> genießt wie der Genesende*]. His delights are not orgiastic in nature: the
> flow of his renewed blood resonates with the murmur of streams, the
> purer breath from his lips with wind in the tree-tops. The people we
> meet in Walser's texts share this childlike nobility with fairy tale char-
> acters. They too have escaped from the depths of night and madness,
> the madness, namely, of myth.[103]

One suspects that the child wandering among the stranded objects of myth, history, and film history in Syberberg's studio has not been placed on the path of such convalescence but, rather, back into a darkness where dreams of apocalypse may continue; the elegiac loop has, it would seem, been finally literalized in the endless reels of celluloid projected and reprojected in the black studio of the Syberbergian imagination.[104]

Epilogue

In my readings of the two most ambitious attempts in recent years at
a dramaturgy of mourning in film, Edgar Reitz's *Heimat* and Hans
Jürgen Syberberg's *Our Hitler*, I have shown how each work re-
negotiates a cultural identity for Germany at a moment of danger. I
speak here of danger because the present historical moment is generally perceived to be one of great disorientation, even despair—
recall Syberberg's notion of the "joyless society"—and one in which
most people find it difficult to see themselves as participants in
ongoing historical processes and traditions endowed with a legible
meaning. The historians' debate and the controversies surrounding
the construction of two new museums of national history are only
the two most obvious manifestations of this general disorientation
and concomitant desire for a stable national identity based on a
positive and authoritative version of German history. I have argued
that this moment of danger may best be understood as a function of
the enormously complicated task of reconstituting a German cultural identity—of saying "*wir*" in an emphatic sense, as Habermas has
put it—within a cultural space marked off by the double "post" of
the post-Holocaust and the postmodern.[1] Germans must reconstitute a cultural identity out of the recent ruins of the most radical
attempt ever witnessed by humankind to "master" difference, that
is, to find for the disturbing presence of an alien, *unheimlich* element
within the body politic, a Final Solution. To work through this mo-

ment of danger by way of a labor of mourning means to abandon the notion that alterity is something that requires a solution.

Both of the filmmakers I have discussed have taken important steps in this labor of recollecting a cultural identity out of the stranded objects of a poisoned past. Both have recognized that without the intermediate area of play, that symbolic space of ritual and aesthetic experience, there can be no leave-taking and thus no transition toward a more flexible and open (i.e., nonparanoid) cultural identity. Reitz and Syberberg have understood that one does not relinquish patterns of behavior, ideas, or fantasies simply because one is told they are wrong, immoral, or even self-destructive. To relinquish something requires a labor of mourning, and mourning requires a space in which its elegiac procedures can unfold. These two artists have made very significant contributions toward creating such a space in cinema. In some ways, however, the elegiac labor to which the two major works of these filmmakers appear to be dedicated, was undermined by various reinscriptions of discourses of exclusion (the search for a pharmakos, or scapegoat) as well as by nostalgias and narcissisms insufficiently chastened by homeopathic renunciations.

But what would an alternative model for reconstituting a cultural identity look like? One that would not reinscribe the very patterns of thought and feeling that produced the wreckage in the first place? How does one face a past such as this one at a time such as this one and manage to avoid the two extremes: global disavowal of identification with ancestors on the one hand, revision of the past into a less abhorrent version, on the other? How, in other words, does one avoid the maddening binary opposition: schizophrenic dissolution of identity/narcissistic respecularization of identity? In these final pages I would like to make a few remarks about some possible ways out of this bind and other directions that the work of reconstituting a German cultural identity might take.

I

In his famous "Theses on the Philosophy of History," Walter Benjamin characterizes the procedures of a historical materialist appropriation of the past in typically suggestive fashion: "To articulate the past historically does not mean to recognize it 'the way it really was' (Ranke). It means to seize hold of a memory as it flashes up at a moment of danger. Historical materialism wishes to retain that image of the past which unexpectedly appears to man singled out by history at a moment of danger." And further:

> Materialist historiography . . . is based on a constructive principle. Thinking involves not only the flow of thoughts, but their arrest as well. Where thinking suddenly stops in a configuration pregnant with tensions, it gives that configuration a shock, by which it crystallizes into a monad. A historical materialist approaches a historical subject only where he encounters it as a monad. In this structure he recognizes the sign of a Messianic cessation of happening, or put differently, a revolutionary chance in the fight for the oppressed past. He takes cognizance of it in order to blast a specific era out of the homogeneous course of history—blasting a specific life out of the era or a specific work out of the lifework.[2]

What happens when these materialist procedures are applied to the situation of members of the second generation of Germans trying to constitute a viable legacy out of poisoned totemic resources? What is there to blast out, as it were, from the homogeneous course of this history so full of horror? It cannot be simply a matter of transforming the parents into helpless victims, of seeing them as the oppressed who were caught up in the ruthless conspiracies of events and who must now be redeemed. Nor can it be a matter of turning everyone who, say, refused to read the *Völkischer Beobachter* into a crypto-resistance fighter (or even *Resistenz*-fighter).[3] But short of such wish-fulfilling transformations, it might yet be possible to discover in the lives, in the words, in the faces and bodies of the parents traces of another history, another past, that might have been but was not. The "oppressed past" that Benjamin speaks of is, in other words, one that never in fact took place but that nevertheless might become available to future generations. This past would be, as Benjamin suggests, a construction. It would be pieced together out of a different sort of stranded object than, say, the Hunsrücker words for berries or the ruins of Wahnfried. These stranded objects would be composed of symptoms.

Symptoms, as Freud has taught, are traces of another, unconscious reality that haunts one's conscious reality like a revenant being. In the present context, they would be the traces of knowledge denied, of deeds left undone, of eyes averted from pain, of shades drawn, of moments when it might have been possible to ask a question or to resist, but one didn't ask and one didn't resist. These were moments when a chance for solidarity with (or later, mourning for) the victims was offered but was left untouched. For the postwar generations it is, I am suggesting, a matter of seizing those chances now, of constructing an alternative legacy out of the archive of symptoms and parapraxes that bear witness to what could have been but was not. It is a matter of reading the "documents" of the elders the way Benjamin looks at a photograph. That "tiny spark of contingency, of the Here and Now, with which reality has so to speak seared the subject"[4] that Benjamin searches out in the photograph can, I am suggesting, be read as an index of a historical opportunity that was left unrealized but that still remains available as a sort of energy potential that continues to dwell in history. By searching out these signs of a history-that-might-have-been in the documents of their own lineage, the postwar generations can begin to mourn these lost opportunities without disavowing their ancestry. These generations may yet be able to unearth new resources of identification out of the unconscious layers of the history into which they were born.

One might argue that just such a mnemonic procedure forms the methodological core of all of Alexander Kluge's literary, theoretical, and filmic work. His writings and films seem to be single-mindedly dedicated to the labor of discovering residues of resistance and protest, of what Terry Eagleton has called "chips of heterogeneity,"[5] in an otherwise thoroughly administered world. As Andreas Huyssen has put it in his fine essay on Kluge's narrative techniques:

> It is as if modernization speaks itself as a machinery of discourses in whose grids individual subjectivities are simultaneously constituted and imprisoned, even stunted and mutilated. . . . Kluge's stories spin themselves out of the residues of subjectivity, distorted subjectivity, stunted subjectivity, subjectivities which can never be separated from . . . objective determinations . . . but which are nevertheless not identical to them.[6]

Perhaps the best example of a representation of this sort of residual subjectivity is the talking knee in Kluge's *Die Patriotin* (The female patriot; 1979), a film concerned with the excavation of a posi-

153

tive legacy out of an otherwise dismal historical tradition. In the course of the film, a wild monologue is spoken in the voice of the knee of a certain Corporal Wieland who died in Stalingrad on January 29, 1943.[7] Against a backdrop of images of Stalingrad, Wieland's surviving knee declares: "It is time that I clear up a fundamental misunderstanding, namely that we, the dead, were somehow dead. We are full of protest and energy. Who, after all, wants to die? We race through history searching and researching without pause."[8] And as the knee later remarks: "I am not the calf and I am not the thigh, but rather the in-between [*das Dazwischen*]."[9] In a brilliant essay on Kluge's story, "The Aerial Bombing of Halberstadt," David Roberts has identified this nonspace of the in-between as those gaps in history where oppositional energies—those revolutionary chances of which Benjamin spoke—continue to dwell: "If in the general population there seemed to be no trace of a spirit of resistance, this spirit had disappeared into the *lacunae of history*—covered over first by bombs and than by the reconstruction."[10] Though this spirit has been buried, Kluge's work provides an extended argument for its continued availability to those with the proper archeological tools.

Kluge's preoccupation with the lacunae of history is no doubt one of the reasons why his work is so hermetic and why he is consistently drawn to the techniques of montage in his films, stories, and theoretical writings. One cannot directly represent the in-between, those ruptures in history where other histories dwell like invisible veins of ore in stone. As the knee says: "See if you can find an opponent who could hit the in-between right on target."[11] In *Die Patriotin* the knee thus becomes the privileged emblem not so much of a counterhistory of actual resistance (or even *Resistenz*); it stands in rather for other histories that might have been possible and thus continue to be possible, given the right direction and degree of flexion.

Despite these promising aspects, Kluge's work in general and *Die Patriotin* in particular have only limited applicability to the issues I have addressed. Kluge is, after all, interested in working through the entirety of German and indeed world history as the story of constantly accelerating processes of division, abstraction, and reification, in a word, as the history of the progressive Taylorization of all human labor potential culminating in the technology of modern warfare. As *Die Patriotin* demonstrates, within the framework of this particular master narrative, Auschwitz has a peculiar tendency to recede into the background. And indeed, in the course of this remarkable film, which is in part about how a people has labored for eight-hundred years on its wishes and fantasies and whose protagonist, the film's narrator claims, feels solidarity with all the dead of the *Reich*, there is not a single mention of the Shoah. (Such an omission is reminiscent of Saul Friedländer's reservations regarding Martin Broszat's efforts to displace historiographical emphasis from the twelve years of Nazi rule to the *longue durée* of processes of modernization.)

Despite the rich analytical insight into the historical processes of modernization offered by Kluge's work, his texts and films provide a shaky foundation for the labor of mourning which has been my concern. In a sense, Kluge makes the same mistake made by a certain orthodox school of psychoanalysis. It is as if he believed that analytical insight into a complex of baleful relations were a sufficient basis for the working through and mastery of those relations. But to work through means, in a fundamental sense, to recuperate *affect*— the absence of which, as Freud claimed, is the real cause of traumatization. For all their evocations of tragedy, violence, and horror, Kluge's stories and films are in a very disturbing way lacking in affect. What remains is a deadpan irony spoken from a place strangely dissociated from human life and emotion. It is in part because of this a-pathetic analytical rigor that Kluge's work offers only a very modest contribution to the discussion I have presented.

Another cinematic example that comes to mind of the kind of anamnesis and mourning I have sketched out here, that is, the construction of an alternative legacy out of symptoms and parapraxes, is Helma Sanders-Brahms's 1979 film, *Deutschland, bleiche Mutter* (Germany, pale mother). The latter parts of this film are visually dominated by the pervasive image of Lene's facial paralysis, which very clearly—and indeed perhaps too obtrusively—represents the way that history has inscribed itself on the body of one of its players. The problem with this particular example is that the film predisposes viewers to read this symptom as an emblem of Lene's vocation not as a player but rather as a victim of history. (This allegorical direction is established from the very start with the film's title and introductory citation of the Brecht poem from which the title is taken.) The facial paralysis does indeed point to lost historical opportunities that the daughter-filmmaker recollects and mourns in and through her film, but these lost opportunities seem in the end to be limited to possibilities of female self-expression, autonomy, and agency which are repressed by a partriarchal social order. Her symptom thus becomes a sign not of ambivalent complicities but, rather, of a fundamental innocence with regard to the suffering of the Jewish victims who appear now and then at the margins of the film's narrative. How Lene chooses to remain blind to what is happening to the Jews is clear, but the film never invites the audience to make connections between these lost opportunities for empathy and solidarity on the one hand and the privileged sign of her own suffering on the other. Rather than providing an opening through which the second generation might catch a glimpse of a lost chance for resistance and solidarity with the Jewish victims, this symptom closes the blinds once more on this other suffering—on the suffering of the other—and becomes a sign pure and simple of a woman's suffering under a particularly oppressive form of patriarchy.[12]

Before concluding, I would like to comment very briefly on what may be the most successful performance by a postwar German artist of the Benjaminian mode of anamnesis and mourning which I have been proposing here as an alternative to the kinds of *Trauerarbeit* performed in the films of Reitz and Syberberg. It is not a work of cinematic art but a novel to which I have referred in passing, Christa Wolf's *Kindheitsmuster* (A model childhood).

II

In the middle of the seventh chapter of Wolf's novel, in one of the many passages in which the narrator engages in metafictional reflections on the labor of the imagination she has taken upon herself, readers are offered a compelling metaphor for the mnemonic procedures guiding these autobiographical researches into a childhood played out in a petit bourgeois milieu during the Nazi period[13]:

> Why, then, stir up settled, stabilized rock formations in order to hit on a possible encapsulated organism, a fossil. The delicately veined wings of a fly in a piece of amber. The fleeting track of a bird in once

spongy sediments, hardened and immortalized by propitious strat-
ification. To become a paleontologist. To learn to deal with petrified
remains, to read from calcified imprints about the existence of early
living forms which one can no longer observe.[14]

On the previous page are examples of what, in the context of the
memory work enacted by the novel, would correspond to such
traces of organic presences in petrified remains. It is a series of
symptoms exhibited by the narrator and members of her immediate
family in the course of their lives together:

> The childhood nights at the end of the long summer vacation. Sleep-
> less, but as yet without the headaches, which are now going to attack
> you without fail. Analgesic caffeine tablets suppress pain and sleep.
> My head is splitting—who was it that always used those words?
> Bruno Jordan [the narrator's father]. He takes aspirin. . . . It obviously
> wasn't migraine he was suffering from. . . . Tension, then. A kind of
> anxiety. . . . Possibly a cervical vertebra out of alignment. Increasing
> stiffness of the shoulder area can transfer painful pressure to the
> head. But inner conflicts, too, may find no other means of
> expression.[15]

In the course of the novel the narrator gathers together quite a
substantial archive of such symptoms. Along the way she offers
numerous demonstrations of the double act of forgetting which gen-
erates the sorts of symptoms that interest her. As the above passage
suggests, symptoms may be the traces of conflicts that have been
repressed, that is, forgotten by consciousness but remembered by
the body. The body, then, functions in this novel as a sort of writing
tablet and mnemonic device of the unconscious. But this act of forgetting comes in its turn to be subjected to a secondary act of
amnesia:

> The failure of language. Well-lit family pictures without words. Word-
> less pantomime on a tidy, dusted stage. When did Charlotte [the
> narrator's mother] reproach her husband for his smoking for the first
> time, when did she first press her left hand to her barely swollen
> neck, complaining accusingly that she had trouble breathing? . . .
> Charlotte, her hand on her gradually more and more swollen thyroid,
> slamming doors, cursing the store, was out of her mind, but she
> didn't know it and later was to forget it completely in her urgent wish
> to have had a happy life.[16]

Several pages further, reflecting on her parents' capacity to remain emotionally unaffected by the violence of historical events taking shape around them, the narrator reiterates the amnesic logic that had structured her family's "happiness": "Why didn't they suffer? The question is wrong. They suffered without knowing it, they raged against their bodies, which were giving them signals: My head is splitting. I'm suffocating."[17]

The chapter concludes with a recollection of the narrator's child-hood experience of witnessing the *Kristallnacht* in her home town. It is an object lesson in the formation of the symptom that would plague the narrator a good deal of her life, chronic anxiety attacks. But as this remarkable novel demonstrates, it is precisely such symptoms that can prove to be the most valuable resource in the labor of mourning and anamnesis that has been my concern here:

> Nelly couldn't help it: the charred building made her sad. But she didn't know she was feeling sad, because she wasn't supposed to feel sad. She had long ago begun to cheat herself out of her true feelings. . . . Gone, forever gone, is the beautiful free association [*die schöne freie Entsprechung*] between emotions and events. That, too, if you think of it, is a reason for sadness [*Trauer*]. . . . It wouldn't have taken much for Nelly to have succumbed to an improper emotion: compassion. But healthy German common sense built a barrier against it: anxiety [*Angst*].

The narrator then adds this parenthetical commentary: "Perhaps there should be at least an intimation of the difficulties in matters of 'compassion,' also regarding compassion toward one's own person, the difficulties experienced by a person who was forced as a child to turn compassion for the weak and the losers into hate and anx-iety."[18] Much of the paleontological work performed in the novel is dedicated to the recuperation of this central symptom, anxiety, so that it may be reconverted into what it at one time was or at least could have been: an opportunity for compassion and solidarity with the victims. By recollecting and deciphering the fossilized traces of her own emotional life, that is, by reestablishing contact with stranded parts of her own past, the narrator is able to reinvigorate her capacity for empathy and thereby ground anew her engagement in history.

In the chapter that follows the narrator quite dramatically seizes hold of a memory—and once more it is a memory of a symptom—as it flashes up at a moment of danger in the present. This moment is circumscribed by a series of events that preoccupy the narrator at the time of the composition of this particular chapter: the Vietnam War; military escalation in the Middle East; mounting repression by the junta in Chile. In the midst of the narrator's reflections on these world-historical events are the fitful beginnings of a very personal *Trauerarbeit* for the Austrian author Ingeborg Bachmann whose tragic death on October 17, 1973, cuts into the narrative like a wound, disrupting its focus and rhythm, and whose own distrust of the power of language to name what is essential in human affairs was of deep concern to the author of *Kindheitsmuster* (the difficult and highly elliptical passages dealing with Bachmann have been left out of the English translation). Under the pressure of these contemporary events and concerns, a strange memory of the narrator's father flashes up, a memory of his ashen face one November day in 1939. The narrator's father, Bruno Jordan, is home from the front (the war is only two months old); a phone call from a neighbor and member of Jordan's infantry unit interrupts the midday meal:

> They talked for a good five minutes. Charlotte Jordan was getting slightly annoyed about this disturbance right at mealtime and called the children to the table. Nelly stood in the door of her room, directly behind her father; she could see her father's face in the vestibule mirror; she heard him say a couple of words in a totally changed tone, questioning words mostly, which were being answered at greater length at the other end of the line.

At a certain point in the conversation the number five is mentioned:

> At this point, her father's ashen face appears. Nelly is sure she saw it in the mirror. A gray, sunken face. She insists: Her father reached for a sleeve of his battle-gray overcoat, to steady himself. He hurriedly ended the conversation with Leo Siegmann. Without paying attention to her, he walked into the dining room with buckling knees and dropped into a chair. From then on, words fail her.[19]

The gist of the conversation was that Jordan's unit had executed five Polish hostages two days earlier. It is, however, only years later that the narrator can begin to appreciate what she saw that November afternoon:

Only now are you able to see that the face Nelly saw for a few fleeting seconds in the vestibule mirror on that November day reappeared seven years later when he came back from captivity. It was the unrecognizable face of her own father that had devastated Nelly. It took her years to understand that in those short moments he had been recognizable.[20]

By blasting such moments out of the continuum of her family's history, the narrator can begin to recuperate the empathy and protest preserved, if only in distorted form, in them. These are moments in which one is shocked into synch with one's humanity. And it is in these moments in which she catches a glimpse of who she, or as in the present example her father, might have been, that the narrator begins to discover totemic resources that help to empower her in a present moment of danger.[21] (I should add here that I do not believe that this work of recuperation can succeed in all cases or perhaps even in the majority of cases. In numerous instances it may be that no amount of paleontological memory-work will hit on the fossilized traces of a once vital and intact solidarity with the victim. It may be the case, in other words, that the breach in solidarity with the victims was so thorough—the very existence of the extermination sites suggests that such a radical breach was in fact realized—that there is no residual empathic potential that could in any sense be recuperated. In these instances a boundary has been crossed from which there is no return, not even by way of the unconscious. In short, these are cases in which all elegiac resources fail.[22])

But the narrator is not only interested in assembling an archive of signs of an oppressed past. She has also set herself the task of working through the sociopsychological mechanisms that forced her, for so much of her life, to communicate in the language of symptoms. Where does this process begin? When does a person begin to cut him- or herself off from his or her own experience and therewith from history? In this model childhood it begins at the beginning, with the first inklings of what it means to be a "self" in this particular culture:

Yours is an authentic memory, even if it's slightly worn at the edges, because it is more than improbable that an outsider had watched the child and had later told her how she sat on the doorstep of her father's store, trying the new word out in her mind: I . . . I . . . I . . . I . . . I

. . . each time with a thrilled shock which had to be kept secret, that much she knew right away.

The danger inherent in this first experience of saying "I" is, as the narrator soon adds, that "a child that has felt the first thrill of her life at the thought of I . . . me . . . can no longer be pulled in by her mother's voice."[23] As I note at the beginning of this study, in saying "I" the child enters into an *unheimlich* order of relations and of relationality—call it the Symbolic—in which here and there, now and then, self and other, have boundaries, and in which all varieties of nonattunement—misunderstanding, disagreement, betrayal— become real and constant possibilities. It is also the opening up of a space of play and creativity. In the particular time and place in which the narrator found herself thrust into this adventure of human self-hood, the risks of nonattunement proved to outweigh the delights of play and to be a constant source of anxiety. Toward the end of the novel the narrator characterizes this *Grundangst* or core anxiety that has plagued her throughout her life and that has become especially acute in the course of writing these memoirs as a fear of "experiencing too much and being pushed into a zone of discord [*eine Zone der Nichtübereinstimmung*] whose climate you haven't learned to tolerate. . . . An anxiety from the deepest recesses of the past."[24]

Earlier in the novel the narrator describes the law of this anxiety in the language of paradox: "her anxiety expressed itself as a continuous penetrating feeling of inner alienation, whose very track consisted in the effacement of tracks. A person who wants to pass unnoticed soon stops noticing anything. The horrible wish for self-surrender [*Selbstaufgabe*] doesn't allow the self to emerge."[25] The ambiguity of the word "*Selbstaufgabe*" underlines the paradoxical nature of this anxiety. "*Aufgabe*" can mean "relinquish," "give up (as lost)," "surrender," but also "task" or "obligation."[26] The double bind named in this passage is, however, far from being a purely linguistic complication. Rather, Wolf implies, in the particular historical milieu in which she grew up, the imperative to discipline the self and to project an acceptable and harmonious self-identity—one in tune with the dominant social formation, with the *Volksgemeinschaft*—proved to be so powerful that one ended up abandoning the self (first meaning of *Selbstaufgabe*) in the compulsive and compulsory labor of (con)forming the self (second meaning of *Selbstaufgabe*).²⁷ A particular mode of constituting the self—call it specular or narcissistic—becomes the very thing that cripples the self and arrests it at a stage of paranoid fragility. In the name of a narrowly conceived self-identity the self expunges all traces of the *unheimlich*, past and present, from its psychic household. What remains is, one might say, a well-defined, well-defended, and vacant Heimat. Christa Wolf's remarkable novel is above all an attempt to work through this conundrum as it emerges in a particular historical context so that a different kind of self can be constituted, one that might be called, to return to Habermas's formulation, "postconventional." As the evocative final lines of the novel suggest, this will be a self that feels entitled to play with its boundaries (rather than denying them or reifying them), and it will be a self more consistently able to experience the vitality of that "free association between emotions and events" which ultimately grounds the human capacity to bear witness to history and to claim solidarity with the oppressed of history, past and present.

Notes

Preface

1. Cited in Saul Friedländer, "Some German Struggles with Memory," in *Bitburg in Moral and Political Perspective*, ed. Geoffrey Hartman (Bloomington: Indiana University Press, 1986), 28.

2. Peter Schneider, "Hitler's Shadow: On Being a Self-conscious German," trans. Leigh Hafrey, in *Harper's Magazine*, September 1987: 52.

3. Schneider, "Hitler's Shadow," 52.

Chapter 1 Postwar/Post-Holocaust/Postmodern

1. Alexander and Margarete Mitscherlich, *The Inability to Mourn: Principles of Collective Behavior*, trans. Beverley R. Placzek (New York: Grove Press, 1975), 26.

2. Sigmund Freud, "Mourning and Melancholia," in *The Standard Edition of the Complete Psychological Works of Sigmund Freud*, ed. James Strachey (London: Hogarth Press, 1953–74), 14: 244–45.

3. Freud, "Mourning and Melancholia," 245.

4. For the sake of economy, I ignore the whole range of distinctions among the various kinds of narcissistic personality and character disorders and their specific etiologies. My interest is in what unifies them: an incapacity to tolerate difference and separateness.

5. For a brilliant discussion of this more primitive mode of mourning as it figures in the experience of falling in love, see Anne Carson's *Eros the Bittersweet: An Essay* (Princeton: Princeton University Press, 1986).

6. Freud, "Mourning and Melancholia," 246.

7. A. and M. Mitscherlich, *Inability to Mourn*, 26.

8. A. and M. Mitscherlich, *Inability to Mourn*, 28.

9. Theodor W. Adorno, "What Does Coming to Terms with the Past Mean?" trans. Timothy Bahti and Geoffrey Hartman, in *Bitburg in Moral and Political Perspective*, ed. Geoffrey Hartman (Bloomington: Indiana University Press, 1986), 121–22.

10. A. and M. Mitscherlich, *Inability to Mourn*, 45–46.

11. A. and M. Mitscherlich, *Inability to Mourn*, 25.

12. In the following discussion, "postmodern" shall signify the general remapping of political, technological, cultural, economic, and sexual power that has taken place since World War II. These shifts and developments include: a redistribution of power and alliances within Europe as well as a general destabilization of European hegemony in the world; the ascendancy of the United States as a world power; the decolonization of the Third World (these three developments were recently the subject of a lecture by Cornel West entitled "Historicizing the Postmodernism Debate," at Princeton University, December 4, 1988); the women's movement and the emergence of gender issues more generally in the figuration and theorization of "otherness"; massive migrations of indigenous populations under political and economic pressures; a more international division of labor; the passage into a computer and information-based rather than industrial economy; the availability, with the computer, of vast memory banks allowing for the instant recall of unlimited "bits" of information; revisions within the sciences of the systems of logic considered to be natural; new forms of image consumption and spectacle; the availability, with nuclear weaponry, of technologies capable of eliminating life on the planet. These developments have put pressures on conventional, i.e., premodern and modern, notions of personal, sexual, and cultural identity which may be insupportable. The new discourses of cultural criticism which I am calling postmodern situate themselves at the points of tension in these notions of identity. As the perhaps all too familiar postmodern preoccupation with historical representations, images, and discourses may testify, these points of tension have proven to be those sites where identity begins to become legible as an effect of various signifying practices.

13. Jean-François Lyotard, "Ticket to a New Decor," trans. Brian Massumi and W. G. J. Niesluchowski, in *Copyright* 1 (Fall 1987): 10; 14–15. See also Lyotard, *The Postmodern Condition: A Report on Knowledge*, trans. Geoff Bennington and Brian Massumi (Minneapolis: University of Minnesota Press, 1984). In a recent essay, Peter Schneider, a German author who has written a great deal about the burdens of mourning and anamnesis in German society, has offered a similar reading of the tasks facing postmodern, post-Holocaust Europe. Commenting on the recent proliferation of conferences dealing with the question of Europe's future destiny, Schneider remarks: "The mood of these conferences is a little melancholy. You will find some who say that Europe must reassert itself. But the notion that, if there is such a thing as Europe, it must finally and in some reasonable way come into its own is obviously an idea born of decline. This idea stands on the realization that all the other—the 'intoxicating' and 'heroic'—European dreams have been dreamed out: the dream of colonial domination of the rest of the world; the dream of British, Spanish, Dutch, French, and finally German hegemony; the dream of unobstructed pillage in countries held to underdevelopment. The Old World only freed itself from the last and most fearsome nightmare vision of Europe, the German one, with the help of the non-European peoples. Sadly, Europe . . . never simply renounced and relinquished its dreams. No, those dreams were smashed by history." Postmodern, post-Holocaust Europe is thus—and here Schneider's view is identical with Lyotard's characterization of the postmodern—one that is to be constituted by a labor of mourning not only for past dreams and quests for hegemony but for dreams of redemption as such, even if they are cast in the rhetoric of liberation: "This Europe, then, is one not of intoxication but of withdrawal and freedom from addiction. It is shaped not by the heroic or triumphant or absolute but by the doubts and self-doubts of sinners who have not necessarily become wise through their suffering, but who are now at least cautious

and able to listen. Of course, Europe will not fully clear its head until it shakes itself from those other dreams, the ones we might call release or redemption dreams. . . . However we choose to evaluate the results that these liberation dreams have produced so far, their monstrous costs can no longer be denied. Above all, it has become evident that most of these liberation dreams, like dreams of European hegemony, are and have been, with shockingly few exceptions, dreams of mastery and power" ("Is There a Europe? After Empire, Yalta, and Malaise," trans. Leigh Hafrey, in *Harper's Magazine*, September 1988: 56).

14. Here see, for example, Andreas Huyssen, *After the Great Divide: Modernism, Mass Culture, Postmodernism* (Bloomington: Indiana University Press, 1986), 208; Craig Owens, "The Discourse of Others: Feminists and Postmodernism," in *The Anti-Aesthetic: Essays on Postmodern Culture*, ed. Hal Foster (Port Townsend: Bay Press, 1983), 67; Alice Jardine's introductory remarks in *Copyright* 1 (Fall 1987): 6. There one reads the programmatic statement: "Thus I have preferred to speak of our epoch as one of impossibility, and to call for an *ethics* of impossibility: im-possi-bility, the antithesis of *posse/potis/pátis*, the antithesis of that which relies on power, potency, possessors, despots, husbands, masters. The epoch of impossibility is . . . an epoch of extreme difficulty, a configuration of knowledge which causes some to long for the good ol' days when art was art, politics was politics, men were men, women were women, and Americans were Real Americans. . . . These individuals opt for the 'nostos,' the desire to return, and a general climate of nostalgia prevails for them within a larger postmodern logic of simulation."

15. "A Klee painting named 'Angelus Novus' shows an angel looking as though he is about to move away from something he is fixedly contemplating. His eyes are staring, his mouth is open, his wings are spread. This is how one pictures the angel of history. His face is turned toward the past. Where we perceive a chain of events, he sees one single catastrophe which keeps piling wreckage upon wreckage and hurls it in front of his feet. The angel would like to stay, awaken the dead, and make whole what has been smashed. But a storm is blowing from Paradise; it has got caught in his wings with such violence that the angel can no longer close them. This storm irresistibly propels him into the future to which his back is turned, while the pile of debris before him grows skyward. This storm is what we call progress" (Walter Benjamin, *Illuminations: Essays and Reflections*, trans. Harry Zohn [New York: Schocken, 1969], 257–58).

16. Jacques Derrida, *Speech and Phenomena and Other Essays on Husserl's Theory of Signs*, trans. David B. Allison (Evanston: Northwestern University Press, 1973), 96–97.

17. Jacques Derrida, "Signature Event Context," trans. Samuel Weber and Jeffrey Mehlman, in *Glyph* 1 (1977): 180.

18. Jacques Derrida, *Of Grammatology*, trans. Gayatri Chakravorty Spivak (Baltimore: Johns Hopkins University Press, 1978), 39.

19. Rainer Maria Rilke, *Duineser Elegien* (Frankfurt: Insel, 1977), 14. Translation by Stephen Mitchell in *The Selected Poetry of Rainer Maria Rilke* (New York: Vintage, 1984), 155.

20. Charles Bernheimer, *Flaubert and Kafka: Studies in Psychopoetic Structure* (New Haven: Yale University Press, 1982), 36.

21. Walter Benjamin, *The Origin of German Tragic Drama*, trans. John Osborne (London: NLB, 1977), 209.

22. Benjamin, *Origin of German Tragic Drama*, 175.

23. Terry Eagleton, who might be seen as representing a certain postmodern reception of Marxism, has remarked on Benjamin's insights into the elegiac structure

of language as it is revealed in the practice of the baroque allegorist: "Symbolism has denigrated allegory as thoroughly as the ideology of the speaking subject has humiliated script. . . . For the allegorical object has undergone a kind of haemorrhage of spirit: drained of all immanent meaning, it lies as a pure facticity under the manipulative hand of the allegorist, awaiting such meaning as he or she may imbue it with. Nothing could more aptly exemplify such a condition than the practice of writing itself, which draws its atomized material fragments into endless, unmotivated constellations of meaning. In the baroque allegory, a jagged line of demarcation is scored between theatrical object and meaning, signifier and signified—a line that for Benjamin traces between the two the dark shadow of that ultimate disjoining of consciousness and physical nature which is death." (Terry Eagleton, *Walter Benjamin: or, Towards a Revolutionary Criticism* [London: Verso, 1985], 6.) See also Craig Owens's use of Benjamin to characterize allegorical tendencies in postmodern artistic practice, "The Allegorical Impulse: Toward a Theory of Postmodernism," in *October* 12 (Spring 1980): 67–86.

24. See Huyssen, *After the Great Divide*, 210.

25. Benjamin, *Origin of German Tragic Drama*, 166.

26. Paul de Man, *Allegories of Reading: Figural Language in Rousseau, Nietzsche, Rilke, and Proust* (New Haven: Yale University Press, 1979), 296.

27. Jacques Derrida, *Memories for Paul de Man*, trans. Cecile Lindsay, Jonathan Culler, and Eduardo Cadave (New York: Columbia University Press, 1986), 22.

28. Paul de Man, *The Resistance to Theory* (Minneapolis: University of Minnesota Press, 1986), 64; 70.

29. De Man, *Allegories of Reading*, 47.

30. Paul de Man, *The Rhetoric of Romanticism* (New York: Columbia University Press, 1984), 81.

31. The phrase is from Baudelaire: "Is it not the necessary garb of our suffering age, which wears the symbol of a perpetual mourning even upon its thin black shoulders? Note, too, that the dress-coat and the frock-coat not only possess their political beauty, which is an expression of universal equality, but also their poetic beauty, which is an expression of the public soul—an immense cortège of undertaker's mutes (mutes in love, political mutes, bourgeois mutes . . .). We are each of us celebrating some funeral" (Charles Baudelaire, "The Salon of 1846," in *Art in Paris 1845–1862: Salons and Other Exhibitions*, trans. and ed. Jonathan Mayne [Oxford: Phaidon, 1981], 118; I am grateful to Richard Sieburth for this reference).

32. Jacques Derrida, "Like the Sound of the Sea Deep within a Shell: Paul de Man's War," trans. Peggy Kamuf, in *Critical Inquiry* 3 (Spring 1988): 590–652. The full set of the wartime writings has appeared as *Wartime Journalism, 1933–43, by Paul de Man*, ed. Werner Hamacher, Neil Hertz, and Thomas Keenan (Lincoln: University of Nebraska Press, 1988).

33. One reads sentences such as: "The war will only bring about a tighter union of these two things—the Hitlerian soul and the German soul that, from the start, were so close together—until they have been made one single and unique power. This is important, because it means that one cannot judge the phenomenon of Hitler without judging at the same time the phenomenon of Germany and that the future of Europe can be envisioned only in the frame of the needs and possibilities of the German spirit. It is not a matter only of a series of reforms but of the definitive emancipation of a people which finds itself called upon to exercise, in its turn, a hegemony in Europe" (*Le Soir*, October 28, 1941). Or: "The necessity of action which is present in the form of immediate collaboration is obvious to every objective mind" (*Le Soir*, October 14, 1941). I am grateful to Stanley Corngold for letting me use his translations.

34. Geoffrey Hartman, "Blindness and Insight," *New Republic*, March 1988: 29.
35. Hartman, "Blindness and Insight," 29; 30; 31.
36. Werner Hamacher, "A Continuous Work of Mourning—Paul de Man's Complex Strategy," in *Frankfurter Allgemeine Zeitung*, February 24, 1988: 35.
37. Hamacher, "Continuous Work of Mourning," 35.
38. Derrida, "De Man's War," 638.
39. Derrida, "De Man's War," 634; 650; 647; 648; 649. These themes and approaches may be found in all of the recent efforts to make sense, from a perspective sympathetic to de Man, of the connections between de Man's past and his later work as a literary theorist. I will limit myself here to a very brief survey of some of the more interesting responses that appeared in newspapers and journals in the months immediately following the discovery of the earlier writings. (A number of more comprehensive responses may now be found in *Responses: On Paul de Man's Wartime Journalism*, ed. Werner Hamacher, Neil Hertz, and Thomas Keenan [Lincoln: University of Nebraska Press, 1989].) In his essay "Paul de Man's Past" (*London Review of Books*, February 4, 1988), Christopher Norris insists that "deconstruction evolved, in de Man's case at least, as a form of rigorous ideological critique directed against precisely that seductive will to treat language and culture as organic, quasi-natural products rooted in the soil of some authentic native tradition," i.e., as a critique of the "aesthetic ideology" that ostensibly provides the rhetorical and phantasmic underpinnings of fascism. According to Norris, de Man's mature work is singularly dedicated to the project of demystifying "the sources of aesthetic ideology in its various forms, especially where these lend credence to the illusion of history as a process of predestined organic evolution." In a letter to the *London Review of Books* (May 19, 1988), Cynthia Chase criticizes some of Norris's claims about the historical development of de Man's ideas only to put in more radical terms his argument regarding the relationship between the wartime writings and de Man's subsequent preoccupations as a literary theorist and deconstructor of "aesthetic ideology" (this term, as Chase notes, is taken from the title of a forthcoming volume of essays by de Man circulating at present only as typescripts, dealing with Kant, Schiller, and Hegel). De Man's mature writing is, in her view, an even more powerful critique of fascism—her phrase is "aestheticist totalitarianism"—than Norris or Hartman have indicated: "de Man's concept of 'formalisation'—the aesthetification, as a satisfying, recognisable form, of the formal, mechanical, arbitrary and contradictory process of language—gets at *both* aspects of Nazism, the combination of which has puzzled and appalled political analysts: the Nazis' romantic aestheticism, an ideology of organic form, and at the same time unparalleled total commitment to sheer mechanical technological power." As such de Man's work represents "the resource . . . for a non-authoritarian, non-totalitarian, non-aesthetic politics." In a brief essay with the provocative title, "It's Time to Set the Record Straight about Paul de Man and His Wartime Articles for a Pro-Fascist Newspaper" (*Chronicle of Higher Education*, July 13, 1988), Jonathan Culler argues that de Man's wartime activities were, to a very large extent, aligned with the side of resistance, and that where they do indicate collaboration this is to be understood as rather unexceptional behavior typical of many in Belgium "from editors of newspapers to the printers who produced them, from railway executives to the engineers and brakemen." As for the one flirtation with a suave anti-Semitism, Culler relies on the judgment of Jewish friends of de Man from the period in question who "suggest that the anti-Semitic column was an aberration, that the young man stupidly consented to write it to please his employers." (Similar testimonies have been documented by James Atlas in his article "The Case of Paul de Man," *New York Times Magazine*, August 28, 1988.) Despite this demonstration of the relative harmlessness

of the wartime activities, Culler goes on to claim that the "discovery of his wartime juvenilia does, however, add a new dimension to his later writing." At this point Culler invokes, as Hartman did previously, the name of Walter Benjamin and his well-known dictum that fascism may be seen as the introduction of aesthetics into politics. "De Man's critique in his later work," Culler continues, "of what he called 'the aesthetic ideology' now resonates also, in the light of his early writings, as a critique of ideas and underlying fascism and their deadly quest for unity and the elimination of difference." Culler then makes the very powerful claim that deconstruction, as a form of analysis dedicated to the disarticulation of what one had taken to be natural and inevitable, is that mode of *Ideologiekritik* which may best undo the narcissisms and nostalgias—and the totalitarian tendencies that ostensibly flow from them—informing the Western tradition: "What makes Nazism the worst excess of Western civilization is the fact that it took to an appalling extreme the process of constituting a group by opposing it to something else and attempting to exterminate what it falsely defined as a corrupting element. Nazism sought to construct a 'pure' Aryan German nation by setting up Jews as its opposite and then slaughtering them. Never has there been so clear a case of how horrendously a culturally constructed opposition can function. Deconstruction seeks to undo (to deconstruct) oppositions that in the name of unity, purity, order, and hierarchy try to eliminate difference." In his contribution to the debate, Hans-Thies Lehmann reiterates the by now familiar argument: de Man's later work represents a singular project directed against the organicist ideologies that aestheticize politics and that are overdetermined by the compulsion to eliminate difference ("Paul de Man: Dekonstruktionen," in *Merkur* 6 (June 1988): 445–460). But more radically, Lehmann accuses de Man's accusers of themselves having failed to assume their (postmodern) decenteredness, a failure that amounts to a serious act of repression and inability to mourn in its own right. The desire to identify the empirical subject who signed his name "Paul de Man" in 1941 with the authorial instance of theoretical texts produced decades later amounts to an indulgence in "narrative psychological certainties of the past century" (457); the naive belief in the myth of the self-identical ego is complicitous in an ideology of the subject the political consequences of which it claims to want to prevent: "The empirically acting subject is not identical to the subject of its theoretical or aesthetic discourse. This discrepancy is the insight that may not be repressed" (459). By focusing so vigilantly on *this* discrepancy in its multiple forms and manifestations, de Man's work earns its exemplary status as a work of *Vergangenheitsbewältigung* or working through of the past. For some very interesting critiques of these positions see Roger Kimball's "Professor Hartman Reconstructs Paul de Man," in the *New Criterion*, May 1988: 36–43, as well as Stanley Corngold's contributions to the debate in the *Chronicle of Higher Education* (September 1, 1988) and the *Times Literary Supplement* (August 26, 1988).

40. As Richard Sennett has noted: "In the present century, the clinical data on which psychoanalysis was founded have gradually eroded. Hysterias and hysterical formations still exist, of course, but they no longer form a dominant class of symptoms of psychic stress. . . . This shift in ordinary symptomology has challenged psychoanalytic thinking to find a new diagnostic language, and to expand terms which in the early years of psychoanalysis were poorly thought out, because the then dominant clinical experiences of distress did not demand their articulation" (*The Fall of Public Man: On the Social Psychology of Capitalism* [New York: Vintage, 1978], 323–24). See also Julia Kristeva, "On the Melancholic Imaginary," trans. Louise Burchill, in *Discourse in Psychoanalysis and Literature*, ed. Shlomith Rimmon-Kenan (London: Methuen, 1987), 106–7: "However, with the treatment of narcissistic personalities, modern analysts have been led to comprehend a different modality of depres-

sion. . . . Far from being a dissimulated assault upon another—imagined hostile because frustrating—sorrow would be the signalling of an incomplete, empty and wounded primitive ego. Such a person doesn't consider himself as injured but as stricken by a fundamental lack, by a congenital deficiency. . . . In this context, suicide is not a camouflaged act of war but a reuniting with sorrow and, beyond it, with that impossible love, never attained, always elsewhere."

41. Kristeva, "The Melancholic Imaginary," 108.

42. For a provocative discussion of this term in a literary context, see Bernheimer, *Flaubert and Kafka.*

43. Samuel Hahnemann's *Organon der rationellen Heilkunde,* first published in 1810, is still the cornerstone of homeopathic medical practice. One reads there, for example: "It follows . . . that substances become remedies and are able to destroy disease only by arousing certain manifestations and symptoms, i.e. particular artificial disease conditions, which are capable of eliminating and destroying the symptoms that already exist, i.e. the natural disease being treated" (*Organon of Medicine,* trans. Jost Künzli, Alain Naude, and Peter Pendleton (Los Angeles: J. P. Tarcher, 1982), 24). And further: The homeopathic therapy "uses in appropriate dosage against *the totality of symptoms* of a natural disease a medicine capable of producing, in the healthy, symptoms as similar as possible" (70).

44. Angus Fletcher, *Allegory: The Theory of a Symbolic Mode* (Ithaca: Cornell University Press, 1964), 189.

45. Peter Sacks, *The English Elegy: Studies in the Genre from Spenser to Yeats* (Baltimore: Johns Hopkins University Press, 1985), 11–12.

46. Juliet Mitchell, *Psychoanalysis and Feminism: Freud, Reich, Laing and Women* (New York: Vintage, 1975), 397. See also Sacks, *English Elegy,* 15: "The oedipal resolution also governs the creation of a superego; and here, too, we find an important relation to the work of mourning and the elegy. At the most obvious level, we recall Freud's suggestion that the superego is made up of the 'illustrious dead,' a sort of cultural reservoir, or rather cemetery, in which one may also inter one's renounced love-objects and in which the ruling monument is the internalized figure of the father. Since the father, as Freud suspected in *Totem and Taboo,* and as Lacan has stressed, intervenes and governs precisely as a *figure,* a totemic metaphor or name—the *Nom du Père*—any actual father thus has himself been displaced by a substitutive image with which the child seeks to identify. This displacement of the actual father by an idealized totemic figure involves an act very much like the child's castrative creation or adoption of the phallus."

47. Sacks, *English Elegy,* 7.

48. Sacks, *English Elegy,* 33.

49. Sacks, *English Elegy,* 8. As Sacks goes on to point out, the imagery of empowerment and survival, especially sexual survival, so important in the performance of mourning, has an even more ancient model and resource in the fundamentally elegiac mythology associated with the rites of vegetation deities. These rites, already cited by Freud as enactments of oedipally structured totemic procedures, are characterized by the homeopathic pattern. In these rites the sexual martyrdom of the deity provides for the regeneration of nature and thus the transference of a legacy of fertility and power across the barrenness of winter; the castrative or thanatotic moment performed within the liminal or transitional space of the ritual allows for the construction of a figure that may be manipulated and resurrected, thus guaranteeing the refertilization of the matrix (see *English Elegy,* 28).

50. As I have already indicated, much of the discourse of bereavement I have addressed thus far would seem to derive its imagery, particularly its metaphors of

sexual martyrdom and empowerment, from masculine patterns of psychosexual development. It is beyond the scope of this investigation to address the very important question of the possible differences between male and female patterns of mourning. Despite the differences that may obtain, however, I would expect that female mourning, insofar as its patterns and rhythms are laid down during the primal scenes of the constitution of the self, will also unfold as a homeopathic procedure, though it might make little sense to call the negativity to be integrated "castration." That is, the female child too must endure the passage into the realm of difference and separateness—the place where things and words, where "I" and "you" have edges—and must, in order to be able to thrive in this order of difference, learn to identify with totemic figures of power, though it might make little sense to think of these totems as instantiations of the "phallus." For a very powerful critique of utopian feminist texts that seem to suggest that the constitution of female identity does not include the thanatotic moment of triangulation (one thinks of the writings of Hélène Cixous), see Toril Moi's excellent study, *Sexual/Textual Politics: Feminist Literary Theory* (London: Methuen, 1985), esp. 102–16. See also Sacks, *English Elegy*, 12–13, as well as Celeste Schenck's "Feminism and Deconstruction: Re-Constructing the Elegy," in *Tulsa Studies in Women's Literature* 1 (Spring 1986): 13–27. Schenck's arguments for distinguishing between inherently male and female elegiac patterns are vulnerable to many of the same criticisms that Moi directs against Cixous, since Schenck situates female mourning within the closure of the Imaginary rather than at the site of its chastening. For a discussion of gender issues as they impinge on the cinematic performance of *Trauerarbeit* in the postwar German context that will be the focus of the next chapters, see Angelika Bammer's "Through a Daughter's Eyes: Helma Sanders-Brahms' *Germany, Pale Mother*," in *New German Critique* 36 (Fall 1985): 91–109.

51. Freud, *Beyond the Pleasure Principle*, in *Standard Edition*, 18: 32.

52. D. W. Winnicott, *Playing and Reality* (London: Tavistock, 1971), 15.

53. Winnicott, *Playing*, 97. One finds in Winnicott quite programmatic statements regarding the importance of the facilitating environment; consider the following: "It is hoped that psychoanalysts will be able to use the theory of transitional phenomena in order to describe the way in which good-enough environmental provision at the very earliest stages makes it possible for the individual to cope with the immense shock of the loss of omnipotence" (71).

54. Winnicott, *Playing*, 97.

55. Winnicott, *Playing*, 97.

56. The same emphasis on the role of the environment in which, or the audience before which, the scenes of mourning are to be staged may be found in the work of another neo-Freudian psychoanalyst, Heinz Kohut. In Kohut's metapsychological theories of optimal frustration and transmuting internalization, it is the "psychological oxygen" provided by empathic "selfobjects" (this is Kohut's technical term for the function performed by the supportive witness) which permits the consolidation of the self out of disruptions of primary narcissism. See especially his *Restoration of the Self* (Madison: International Universities Press, 1977), as well as his posthumously published *How Does Analysis Cure?* ed. Arnold Goldberg (Chicago: University of Chicago Press, 1984). The role of the empathic witness/analyst who must accompany the analysand to the sites of loss, fragmentation, and trauma is the central focus of Alice Miller's trilogy of studies of narcissistic character disorders: *Das Drama des begabten Kindes und die Suche nach dem wahren Selbst* (Frankfurt: Suhrkamp, 1979); *Am Anfang war Erziehung* (Frankfurt: Suhrkamp, 1980); *Du sollst nicht merken: Variationen über das Paradies-Thema* (Frankfurt: Suhrkamp, 1981). All of these works have become available in English translations.

57. De Man, *Resistance to Theory*, 80.
58. De Man, *Resistance to Theory*, 84.
59. De Man, *Resistance to Theory*, 85.
60. De Man, *Resistance to Theory*, 85–86; 96.
61. De Man, *Resistance to Theory*, 96.
62. See Bernheimer, *Flaubert and Kafka*. Speaking about the "lack of affective language in deconstructive discourse," Bernheimer remarks: "It often seemed as if they [deconstructive critics] had managed to remove all anxiety from the fantasy prevalent among schizophrenics of the body fragmented into pieces and to consider the unifying force of narcissistic identification simply a fictional illusion with no compelling power. Their desire to assimilate everything to textuality makes of the human psyche a kind of avoidance machine, constantly displacing, substituting, replacing, sliding and slipping away. A-void-dance, a dance around the void" (4). See also Stanley Corngold's critique of poststructuralist readings of the canon of German Romanticism and Modernism in *The Fate of the Self: German Writers and French Theory* (New York: Columbia University Press, 1986).
63. It is in this context that I understand Jameson's various critiques of postmodern critical discourse. What is lacking in much of this discourse is a notion of the collective, of the social solidarity without which all efforts to decenter anything become double binds. See, for example, his *Political Unconscious: Narrative as a Socially Symbolic Act* (Ithaca: Cornell University Press, 1981), 125: "From a Marxist point of view, this experience of the decentering of the subject and the theories, essentially psychoanalytic, which have been devised to map it are to be seen as the signs of the dissolution of an essentially bourgeois ideology of the subject and of psychic unity or identity (what used to be called 'individualism'); but we may admit the descriptive value of the poststructuralist critique of the 'subject' without necessarily endorsing the schizophrenic ideal it has tended to project. For Marxism, indeed, only the emergence of a post-individualistic social world, only the reinvention of the collective and the associative, can concretely achieve the 'decentering' of the individual subject called for by such diagnoses; only a new and original form of collective social life can overcome the isolation and monadic autonomy of the older bourgeois subjects in such a way that individual consciousness can be lived—and not merely theorized—as an 'effect of structure.'"
64. De Man, *Resistance to Theory*, 92. As should now be obvious, much of this critique could be directed equally against Heidegger.
65. Culler, "It's Time to Set the Record Straight"; Derrida, "De Man's War," 650.

Chapter 2   Germany and the Tasks of Mourning in the Second and Third Generations

1. Saul Friedländer, *Reflections of Nazism: An Essay on Kitsch and Death*, trans. Thomas Weyr (New York: Harper and Row, 1984), 14–15. See also Alvin H. Rosenfeld's *Imagining Hitler* (Bloomington: Indiana University Press, 1985) for a discussion of representations of Hitler in both high and popular culture in the last few decades.
2. This is, of course, the literal translation of the title of Wolf's remarkable novel about growing up under fascism: *Kindheitsmuster* (Darmstadt: Luchterhand, 1979). I will return to this novel in the Epilogue.
3. Margarete Mitscherlich, *Erinnerungsarbeit: Zur Psychoanalyse der Unfähigkeit zu trauern* (Frankfurt: S. Fischer, 1987), 114.
4. Margarete Mitscherlich, "Rede über das eigene Land," in *Reden über das eigene*

Land: Deutschland 3 (Munich: C. Bertelsmann, 1985), 61. Or as one of the few pub lished psychoanalytic case studies focusing on the particular traumas of the children of Nazis has concluded: "In order to establish the situation in which an ideology can flourish, the longing for regression must be stimulated in the masses—regression to the immature symbiotic state of grandiose omnipotence. Children are even more vulnerable than regressed adults. The children in the second generation, therefore, whose mothers transmitted the ideology through the early object relationship, were not only influenced but cumulatively traumatized" (Anita Eckstaedt, "A Victim of the Other Side," in *Generations of the Holocaust*, ed. Martin S. Bergmann and Milton E. Jucovy [New York: Basic Books, 1982], 222).

5. Eckstaedt, "Victim," 225. Regarding this notion of a memory "engraved" but not "integrated," see Nicolas Abraham, "Notes on the Phantom: A Complement to Freud's Metapsychology," trans. Nicholas Rand, in *Critical Inquiry* 2 (Winter 1987): 287–92. I strongly disagree with Abraham's assessment of the role of mourning in such a configuration.

6. A somewhat anomalous text in this series is Peter Schneider's *Vati* (Daddy; Darmstadt: Luchterhand, 1987), a fictional autobiographical account of Rolf Mengele's visit to his father in Brazil. Another quite interesting work of fiction about a son coming to terms with deep psychological wounds resulting from a relationship to a mother who was herself in many ways a victim of fascism, is Hanns-Josef Ortheil's novel *Hecke* (Frankfurt: Fischer, 1983).

7. Michael Schneider, "Fathers and Sons, Retrospectively: The Damaged Rela-tionship between Two Generations," in *New German Critique* 31 (Winter 1984): 3–51.

8. See Sacks's excellent discussion of Hamlet as mourner in *The English Elegy: Studies in the Genre from Spenser to Yeats* (Baltimore: Johns Hopkins University Press, 1985), 82–89.

9. Schneider, "Fathers and Sons," 37.

10. Schneider, "Fathers and Sons," 43. See once more Kristeva, "On the Melan-cholic Imaginary," trans. Louise Burchell, in *Discourse in Psychoanalysis and Literature*, ed. Shlomith Rimmon-Kenan (London: Methuen, 1987), 106–7.

11. Peter Sichrovsky, *Born Guilty: The Children of the Nazis*, trans. Jean Steinberg (London: I.B.Taurus, 1988). Further references will be made in the text.

12. "Not far from us lived a group of Jewish emigrants, all Germans. Half of the kids in some of our classes were Jews and the other half non-Jews, mostly the children of old Nazis" (Sichrovsky, *Born Guilty*, 44).

13. Paul Celan, "Deine Augen im Arm," in his *Gesammelte Werke* (Frankfurt: Suhrkamp, 1986), 2: 123.

14. A. and M. Mitscherlich, *The Inability to Mourn: Principles of Collective Behavior*, trans. Beverley R. Placzek (New York: Grove Press, 1975), 220–21.

15. This essay has been republished in, among other places, an anthology of the key essays and statements generated in the course of the so-called historians' debate: *Historiker-Streit: Die Dokumentation der Kontroverse um die Einzigartigkeit der na-tionalsozialistischen Judenvernichtung*, ed. Ernst Reinhard Piper (Munich: Piper, 1987): 62–76.

16. Ernst Nolte, "Vergangenheit, die nicht vergehen will" (A past that will not pass away), *FAZ* 6, June 1986; reprinted in *Historiker-Streit*, 39–47. The essay was originally intended as a contribution to the Frankfurt Römerberg-Colloquium. For a summary of the events surrounding Nolte's publication of his essay see his letter to *Die Zeit*, August 1, 1986, republished in *Historiker-Streit*, 93–94, as well as Hilmar Hoffmann's introduction to *Gegen den Versuch, Vergangenheit zu verbiegen: Eine Diskus-sion um politische Kultur in der Bundesrepublik aus Anlaß der Frankfurter Römerberg-gespräche 1986* (Frankfurt: Athenäum, 1987).

17. Nolte, "Vergangenheit," in *Historiker-Streit*, 45.

18. Nolte, "Vergangenheit," 46. A recent effort to historicize the Final Solution by an American historian, Arno Mayer, makes a powerful argument for the importance of the connections between antibolshevism and anti-Semitism in Nazi ideology. Unlike Nolte, however, Mayer does not use the former to displace or absorb the relative autonomy of the latter, nor does he posit the sorts of mechanical causalities that interest Nolte. In Mayer's reading, Nazi antibolshevism is not defensive in the sense in which Nolte presents it but is, rather, part of an ultimately maniacal crusading ideology. See Arno J. Mayer, *Why Did the Heavens Not Darken? The "Final Solution" in History* (New York: Pantheon, 1988).

19. Ernst Nolte, "Between Myth and Revisionism? The Third Reich in the Perspective of the 1980s," in *Aspects of the Third Reich*, ed. H. W. Koch (New York: St. Martin's Press, 1985), 28.

20. See Nolte, "Zwischen Geschichtslegende und Revisionsimus? Das Dritte Reich im Blickwinkel des Jahres 1980," in *Historiker-Streit*, 33; "Vergangenheit," 46.

21. Nolte, "Vergangenheit," 42. One might also add to this summary of Nolte's remarkable capacity to equalize distinct historical phenomena the rather bizarre lesson he manages to learn from Claude Lanzmann's film *Shoah*, namely that the film "makes plausible that the SS men in the death camps were victims in their own right and that . . . a virulent anti-Semitism was not foreign to the Polish victims of National Socialism" (42).

22. Nolte, "Vergangenheit," 45.

23. Nolte, "Between Myth and Revisionism," 21. For an insightful analysis of the "pseudo-interrogative mode" of such reflections, see Charles S. Maier's book on the historians' debate, *The Unmasterable Past: History, Holocaust, and German National Identity* (Cambridge, Mass.: Harvard University Press, 1988), 83. These sorts of comparisons and analogies are, of course, by no means new, nor are they necessarily clear markers of membership in a particular political or ideological camp. For as Margarete Mitscherlich, Peter Schneider, and others have pointed out, the German left has deployed such rhetorical strategies quite as much as neoconservative historians, and also, one might assume, out of interest in reducing the pressures of the historical burdens weighing on the postwar generations in Germany. Commenting on Helmut Kohl's comparisons of Mikhail Gorbachev's public relations skills with those of Goebbels and the work camps for political prisoners in East Germany with Nazi concentration camps, Peter Schneider points to similar rhetorical moves on the part of the German left: "One has to concede that long before Kohl began formulating his hair-raising comparisons for Goebbels and the death camps, the children of the postwar period had dehistoricized the concept of Nazism. After 'fascism' had become a generalized term of opprobrium in Germany it served hardly at all to refer to the twelve years that gave it its concrete meaning. The term was used mainly to denounce one's political opponents. The rebels of 1968 were as uninterested as today's revisionist historians in the uniqueness of the Nazi crimes. They were after comparisons, though for the students the term of the comparison was capitalist democracy, not Soviet communism. Only now has it become apparent that the Leftist misuse of the accusation of fascism is an equally reflexive attempt at relief: for the reduction of the historical profile of Nazism to general and transferable characteristics also had, apart from its instructive value, an unburdening function. If National Socialism was the 'conspiracy' of a couple of powerful industrialists, our parents, no matter what they had done, were the victims of the conspiracy" ("Hitler's Shadow: On Being a Self-conscious German," trans. Leigh Hafrey, in *Harper's Magazine*, September 1987: 52). Not surprisingly, one area that has become a key site for this process of political and psychological unburdening on the part of the German left has been Israel and its

relations with the Palestinians. See, for example, Margarete Mitscherlich's remarks regarding the vehemence with which the German left has taken up the Palestinian cause, i.e., that of the "victim" against the Jewish, "fascist" oppressor (*Erinnerungsarbeit*, 102–3). Yet another site where the boundaries between left and right became somewhat blurred was the controversy over the attempt to stage Fassbinder's play, *Trash, City, and Death*, at the Schauspielhaus in Frankfurt in the fall of 1985. There it was generally the left that supported the staging of the play over the protests of the Jewish community which—for good reason, I think—found the play to be full of undigested and unanalyzed anti-Semitism, and it was generally from conservative circles, with the *Frankfurter Allgemeine Zeitung* at the forefront, that one heard the strongest public outcry against the staging of the play. These were the very circles that had more or less warned the Jewish community not to interfere with Reagan's visit to the cemetery at Bitburg. The controversy demonstrated, among other things, how the fundamental desire for normalcy in Germany is able to attach itself to a great variety of ideological positions both from the left and the right. For an excellent summary of the debates surrounding the Fassbinder play see *New German Critique*'s special issue on the German-Jewish controversy, 38 (Spring/Summer 1986); see also Margarete Mitscherlich's remarks in *Erinnerungsarbeit*, 28–30.

24. Michael Stürmer, "Geschichte in geschichtslosem Land," in *Historiker-Streit*, 38.

25. Stürmer, "Geschichte," 38.

26. Stürmer, "Geschichte," 36–37. See also Stürmer's *Dissonanzen des Fortschritts* (Munich: Piper, 1986). Martin Broszat, who has at times been associated with the revisionist camp of historians, has noted Stürmer's tendency to overburden historiography with quasi-theological social functions it can never fulfill. Broszat points to parallels with cruder, more explicitly political versions of the same vision of the task of the historian in the remarks of Alfred Dregger, parliamentary leader of the Christian Democratic Union. Broszat cites the following example: "We are deeply disturbed by the lack of historical awareness and consideration vis-à-vis one's own nation. Without a fundamental patriotism, which is a given for other peoples, our own people will not be able to survive. Whoever misuses the process of 'coming to terms with the past,' as some have chosen to call it and which no doubt had its place, as a way of foreclosing the future of our people, must face our firm opposition" (quoted in Broszat, "Wo sich die Geister scheiden: Die Beschwörung der Geschichte taugt nicht als nationaler Religionsersatz," in *Historiker-Streit*, 194).

27. "Looking back at the catastrophe of the winter of 1944–45, the historian is left with only one position, even if it is difficult to assume when it comes to the particulars of the case: he must identify with the concrete fate of the German population in the East and with the desperate efforts of the German forces on land and at sea, suffering casualty upon casualty. These efforts were dedicated to protecting the population of the eastern parts of Germany from the Red Army's orgies of revenge, the mass rapes, the arbitrary murders and deportations, and to keeping escape routes to the West open in those last moments of the war" (24–25). In the narrative sections of the book this pathos of identification leads to some remarkable passages: "In these events, in which everyone was consumed by the single task of saving what could be saved, the destruction of entire armies stands side by side with the courage and selflessness of individuals; the loss of cities with the protection of river crossings upon which the fate of entire trains of refugees depended. In the catastrophe that was enveloping everyone and everything, many a nameless soldier and citizen found new strength and courage" (36). And further: "Among the National Socialist authorities, there were those who proved themselves in the hour of need . . . while others failed, at times pathetically" (37).

28. As Maier remarks about this asymmetry: "The sufferings of Jews are not evoked: no sealed freight cars, purposeful starvation, flogging, degradation, and final herding to 'the showers' parallels the accounts of the evacuation of East Prussia. If indeed these two experiences are two sorts of destruction, one is presented, so to speak, in technicolor, the other in black, gray, and white." Maier goes on to characterize Hillgruber's elegiac evocation of the lost center as the "geopolitics of nostalgia" (*The Unmasterable Past*, 23).

29. Habermas, "Eine Art Schadensabwicklung," in *Historiker-Streit*, 73.

30. Habermas, "Eine Art Schadensabwicklung," 75. The notion of a postconventional identity that Habermas has deployed in the historians' debate has been a key term in his thinking for some time. See especially his "Können komplexe Gesellschaften eine vernünftige Identität ausbilden?" in Jürgen Habermas, *Zur Rekonstruktion des historischen Materialismus* (Frankfurt a.M.: Suhrkamp, 1976), as well as in the same volume his attempt to use the psychological theories of Jean Piaget and Lawrence Kohlberg to theorize the formation of postconventional identities. See also most recently, "Geschichtsbewußtsein und posttraditionale Identität: Die Westorientierung der Bundesrepublik," in his *Eine Art Schadensabwicklung: Kleine politische Schriften VI* (Frankfurt: Suhrkamp, 1987).

31. See Konrad H. Jarausch, "Removing the Nazi Stain? The Quarrel of the German Historians," in *German Studies Review* 2 (May 1988): 293.

32. For a somewhat different reading of this repetition compulsion, see Dan Diner, "The Historians' Controversy—Limits to the Historization of National Socialism," in *Tikkun* 2, 1: 74–78.

33. See Habermas, "Vom öffentlichen Gebrauch der Historie: Das offizielle Selbstverständnis der Bundesrepublik bricht auf," in *Historiker-Streit*, 247: "Now as before we are faced with the simple fact that those born later also grew up in a form of life [*Lebensform*] in which *that* was possible. Our own life is not contingently but in its very essence, tied together with that life-context in which Auschwitz was possible. Our form of life is connected with the form of life of our parents and grandparents by way of a tightly woven fabric of familial, geographical, political, and also intellectual traditions that would be most difficult to untangle; we are part of a historical milieu that has made us into the people we are today. No one can escape from this milieu because our identity as individuals and as Germans is indissolubly tied up with it. That reaches from the level of mimicry and bodily gesture to that of language and into the capillary ramifications of one's intellectual habitus." The question that follows is the one I have been addressing all along: "But what are the consequences of this existential link with traditions and forms of life which have become poisoned by unspeakable crimes?" This question is, of course, the central and ultimately suicidal core of Paul Celan's poetry.

34. For an excellent discussion of the debates surrounding the plans for these museums as well as the best evaluation to date of Habermas's interventions here and in the historians' controversy, see Maier, *The Unmasterable Past*.

35. Winnicott, *Playing and Reality* (London: Tavistock, 1971), 71.

36. Martin Broszat, "Plädoyer für eine Historisierung des Nationalsozialismus," in *Merkur* 39 (May 1985): 373–85.

37. Broszat, "Plädoyer," 384–85; 384.

38. Broszat, "Plädoyer," 375.

39. For a collection of these responses see *Ist der Nationalsozialismus Geschichte? Zu Historisierung und Historikerstreit*, ed. Dan Diner (Frankfurt: Fischer, 1987).

40. Saul Friedländer and Martin Broszat, "Um die 'Historisierung des Nationalsozialismus': Ein Briefwechsel," in *Vierteljahrshefte für Zeitgeschichte* 2 (April 1988): 339–372. For Friedländer's initial response to Broszat's "Plädoyer," see his essay

"Überlegungen zur Historisierung des Nationalsozialismus," in *Ist der National-sozialismus Geschichte?* ed. Diner, 34–50; this essay has been published in English as "Some Reflections on the Historicization of National Socialism," in *German Society and Politics* 13 (February 1988).

41. See for example the so-called *Bayern-Projekt* conducted under Broszat's direction by the Institut für Zeitgeschichte, *Bayern in der NS-Zeit*, 6 vols. (Munich: R. Oldenbourg, 1977–83).

42. The *Ordensburgen*, or "castles of a knightly order," were training centers for Nazi party leaders. As David Schoenbaum has noted, "Not only a kind of Party university, it was to be the institutional core of a band of brothers, united in mystic union and remote from the more prosaic world to which they were to return" (*Hitler's Social Revolution: Class and Status in Nazi Germany, 1933–1939* [New York: W. W. Norton, 1980], 269). Schabbach is of course the fictional village in which Edgar Reitz's film *Heimat* takes place.

43. Friedländer and Broszat, "Um die 'Historisierung des Nationalsozialismus'," 358–59.

Chapter 3 Screen Memories Made in Germany

1. The film's title actually underwent several transformations. Under pressure from the television producers, the film's offical title was changed from *Heimat* to *Made in Germany* primarily because of the loaded ideological genealogy of the word "Heimat." It was thought that one generation had not had sufficient time to thin out the residue of "blood and earth" connotations still associated with the word from the Nazi period. Throughout the two years of production, however, *Heimat* was retained by the production crew as the unofficial working title. After the film was completed, the title was debated once more and the compromise version, which includes the subtitle: *A Chronicle in Eleven Parts*, was agreed on. Reitz has written that his own personal title had always been *Geheischnis*, a Hunsrücker word signifying the trust, security, and warmth one feels amongst the members of a small, tight-knit community (see Edgar Reitz, *Liebe zum Kino: Utopien und Gedanken zum Autorenfilm, 1962–1983* [Cologne: Verlag Köln 78, 1984], 206). Given the great resonance that the film found in Germany, this film might be said to represent the next most significant discursive event since the Nazi period with regard to the genealogy—the history of the various emotional and ideological "occupations"—of the word Heimat. See Anton Kaes's excellent summary of this genealogy in his *Deutschlandbilder: Die Wiederkehr der Geschichte als Film* (Munich: Edition Text und Kritik, 1987), 174–77.

2. According to ARD (the First West German Television Network) press releases, the series was seen by more than nine million viewers, or 26% of the viewing public, while some twenty-five million or 54% saw at least one episode. These figures are cited in Michael Geisler, "*Heimat* and the German Left: The Anamnesis of a Trauma," in *New German Critique* 36 (Fall 1985): 25–66.

3. Edgar Reitz and Peter Steinbach, *Heimat: Eine deutsche Chronik* (Nördlingen: Greno, 1985). Reitz has also published a coffee table book for those who want a souvenir of their sixteen hours in the Hunsrück: *Heimat: Eine Bildchronik* (Munich: C. J. Bucher, 1985).

4. See Ingrid Scheib-Rothbart and Ruth McCormick, "Edgar Reitz: Liberating Humanity and Film," in *New German Filmmakers*, ed. Klaus Phillips (New York: Frederick Ungar, 1984), 284.

5. The true master of the aesthetics of the "body politic" as the politics that is

inscribed on the body was to be, of course, Rainer Werner Fassbinder. See also Reitz's notes on hands in his study for *Mealtimes,* in *Liebe zum Kino,* 95–97.

6. Edgar Reitz, quoted in Scheib-Rothbart and McCormick, "Edgar Reitz," 258.

7. Scheib-Rothbart and McCormick, "Edgar Reitz," 258.

8. In his study of German films of the seventies and eighties dealing with fascism and the postwar era, Kaes positions *Deutschland im Herbst* at the turning point in the preoccupations of the New German Cinema toward memory and mourning, noting that Kluge, Schlöndorff, Fassbinder, Sinkel, and Reitz, all of whom contributed to the film, went on to make major films dealing with recent German history. See *Deutschlandbilder,* 34.

9. Edgar Reitz, interview with author, July 1987.

10. Mikhail M. Bakhtin, *The Dialogic Imagination: Four Essays,* ed. Michael Holquist, trans. Caryl Emerson and Michael Holquist (Austin: University of Texas Press, 1981), 225.

11. Bakhtin, *Dialogic Imagination,* 227.

12. Reitz and Steinbach, *Heimat,* 25.

13. Thomas Elsaesser, "Heimat (Homeland)," in *New German Critique* 36 (Fall 1985): 23.

14. Kaes, *Deutschlandbilder,* 188–89.

15. Victor Shklovsky, "Art as Technique," in *Russian Formalist Criticism: Four Essays,* trans. Lee T. Lemon and Marion J. Reis (Lincoln: University of Nebraska Press, 1965), 12.

16. T. G. Ash, "The Life of Death," *New York Review of Books,* December 19, 1985: 26.

17. Benjamin, *Illuminations: Essays and Reflections,* trans. Harry Zohn (New York: Schocken, 1969), 83; 84.

18. Reitz, interview with author, July 1987.

19. See Geisler, "*Heimat* and the German Left," 38–42, and Kaes, *Deutschlandbilder,* 181–83, for good discussions of the sociopolitical context within which this ethnographic gesture may best be understood.

20. Benjamin, *Illuminations,* 86–87.

21. For a discussion of the "hyperreal," see Jean Baudrillard, *Simulations,* trans. Paul Foss, Paul Patton, and Philip Beitchman (New York: Semiotext(e), 1983).

22. This term has its own troubled history in the texts of Benjamin and Adorno; in the present discussion I will limit myself to the sense given the term in the "Storyteller" essay.

23. Benjamin, *Illuminations,* 94.

24. Benjamin, *Illuminations,* 97.

25. Benjamin, *Illuminations,* 94.

26. Rainer Maria Rilke, *The Notebooks of Malte Laurids Brigge,* trans. M. D. Herter Norton, in *Rainer Maria Rilke: Prose and Poetry,* ed. Egon Schwarz (New York: Continuum, 1984), 6.

27. Benjamin, *Illuminations,* 93–94.

28. In one of John Berger's stories about life in a rural community in France, a dying woman refuses to go to the hospital: "If she was going to die, she wanted death to pass by the things she knew" (*Pig Earth* [New York: Pantheon, 1979], 32). Though they have much in common, Berger's stories offer, I think, a far less sentimental version of peasant life and of the world of the storyteller, than does Reitz's film.

29. Reitz, interview with author, July 1987.

30. Reitz, *Liebe zum Kino,* 128.

31. Reitz, *Liebe zum Kino,* 131; 127; 129.

32. Kaes, *Deutschlandbilder*, 190–91.

33. Susan Sontag, *On Photography* (New York: Dell, 1977), 15. See also Kaes, *Deutschlandbilder*, 190–91. Sontag's remarks regarding the use of the "photography effect" in Robert Siodmak's 1929 film *Menschen am Sonntag* also describe Reitz's technique of evoking the pathos of the still photograph: "Some working-class Berliners . . . are having their pictures taken at the end of a Sunday outing. One by one they step before the itinerant photographer's black box—grin, look anxious, clown, stare. The movie camera lingers in close-up to let us savor the mobility of each face; then we see the face frozen in the last of its expressions, embalmed in a still. The photographs shock, in the flow of the movie—transmuting, in an instant, present into past, life into death" (70).

34. John Berger, *Another Way of Telling* (New York: Pantheon, 1982), 86–87. See also Roland Barthes's *Camera Lucida: Reflections on Photography*, trans. Richard Howard (New York: Hill and Wang, 1981). There Barthes characterizes the *noeme* of photography as the "'That-has-been,' or again: the Intractable" (77), and stresses the "pure deictic language" (5) of the photograph: "In the Photograph, the event is never transcended for the sake of something else: the Photograph always leads the corpus I need back to the body I see; it is the absolute Particular, the sovereign Contingency, matte and somehow stupid, the *This*" (4). See also my own narratological discussion of photography in Santner, *Friedrich Hölderlin: Narrative Vigilance and the Poetic Imagination* (New Brunswick: Rutgers University Press, 1986), 19–24.

35. The German word *"Bauer"* can signify farmer as well as peasant; Reitz's interest in evoking premodern modes of production and social relations suggests that one should treat the word as a palimpsest and read the earlier signification beneath its more recent layer of meaning.

36. Reitz, *Liebe zum Kino*, 130.

37. Sontag, *On Photography*, 71. See once more in this context Saul Friedländer, *Reflections of Nazism: An Essay on Kitsch and Death*, trans. Thomas Weyr (New York: Harper and Row, 1984).

38. See, for example, Elie Wiesel's remarks in the *New York Times*, April 16, 1978.

39. For good discussions of the reception of *Holocaust* in West Germany, see *New German Critique* 19 (Winter 1980) and Kaes's remarks in *Deutschlandbilder*, 35–42.

40. Reitz, *Liebe zum Kino*, 101–2 (I have drawn on Elsaesser's translation in Thomas Elsaesser, "Memory, Home and Hollywood," in *New German Critique* 36 [Fall 1985]: 11).

41. "Normally a person only cries about the things that happen to him or remind him of his own life. Emotions tend to be resistant to attempts to make them uniform, and remain stubbornly centered within their own *Lebensraum*. It is already disastrous that in spite of this it is possible to universalize and de-individualize in this way people's sentiments, their capacity to be moved by stories projected on a screen" (Reitz, *Liebe zum Kino*, 99–100).

42. Reitz, *Liebe zum Kino*, 141; 102 (I have drawn on Elsaesser's translation in Elsaesser, "Memory, Home and Hollywood," 12; for some strange reason, Reitz fails to italicize *Holocaust* in his essay).

43. The classic statement regarding the hegemony of the American culture industry in postwar Germany was spoken by Robert in Wim Wenders's *Kings of the Road*: "'The Yanks have colonized our unconscious.'"

44. See again Geisler, *"Heimat* and the German Left," 38–43.

45. Reitz, *Liebe zum Kino*, 99 (Elsaesser renders "Urteil" as "opinion"; see Elsaesser, "Memory, Home and Hollywood," 12).

46. Thomas Mann, "Gedanken im Krieg," in *Schriften zur Politik* (Frankfurt: Suhrkamp, 1970), 7–23.

47. Jacques Derrida, "Plato's Pharmacy," in *Dissemination*, trans. Barbara Johnson (Chicago: University of Chicago Press, 1981).

48. Derrida, "Plato's Pharmacy," 70; 124.

49. See Eric Rentschler's chapter on the *Heimatfilm* in his *West German Film in the Course of Time: Reflections on the Twenty Years since Oberhausen* (Bedford Hills, N.Y.: Redgrave, 1984).

50. Derrida, "Plato's Pharmacy," 133.

51. Reitz, *Liebe zum Kino*, 142.

52. Reitz, quoted in Geisler, "*Heimat* and the German Left," 63.

53. Reitz, *Liebe zum Kino*, 141; 142.

54. Reitz, *Liebe zum Kino*, 145–46 (I have drawn on the translation in Gertrud Koch, "How Much Naiveté Can We Afford? The New *Heimat* Feeling," in *New German Critique* 36 [Fall 1985], 15). Perhaps one should add here that gypsies (Appolonia) and refugees (Klärchen), i.e. those other people who since time immemorial have "gone away," would also fit well into this American culture.

55. Reitz, interview with author, July 1987.

56. As Gertrud Koch has quite aptly noted, the equation of the "plague of commercialization . . . with 'the Jews' (had) been a staple of anti-Semitic critiques of civilization already in prefascist Germany" (Koch, "How Much Naiveté," 15).

57. This remarkable exchange of positions is no doubt part of the larger context of strategies of exorcism identified by Friedländer in his *Reflections of Nazism*. There he analyzes a similar "inversion of signs and the beginnings of a new discourse about Evil" (107) in a number of recent works of fiction and cinema dealing with fascism and the Holocaust. Summarizing, for example, George Steiner's strategy of reversals in his novel *The Portage to San Cristobal of A.H.*, Friedländer notes, "Jewish fanaticism, which rests on the assurance of being the chosen people, a unique conception in antiquity, gave birth to a tide that finally led to another chosen race, the Nazis. In a natural reaction and proper reversal, they turn against the Jews and destroy them" (112). Another important mode of reversal is the representation of the triumphant Jew who emerges out of the destruction (one thinks of the "rich Jew" in *Trash, City, and Death*, and the Mendelsohn clan in *Lili Marleen*).

58. Frederic Morton, *Crosstown Sabbath: A Street Journey through History* (New York: Grove Press, 1987).

59. Morton's recent novel *The Forever Street* (Garden City, N.Y.: Doubleday, 1984) documents in epic breadth, much as Reitz's film does for Schabbach, the destruction of his Viennese "shtetl" existence.

60. Morton, *Crosstown Sabbath*, 14.

61. See, for example, Martin Heidegger, "Die Frage nach der Technik," in *Vorträge und Aufsätze* (Pfullingen: Neske, 1967), vol. 1.

62. Morton, *Crosstown Sabbath*, 14–15; 13; 15–16.

63. Morton, *Crosstown Sabbath*, 15–16; 17–18; 31.

64. Morton, *Crosstown Sabbath*, 26.

65. Reitz and Steinbach, *Heimat*, 11.

66. See Bakhtin, *Dialogic Imagination*, 234.

67. "One aspect of this process of destruction is the transformation of historical forms of interaction through technological change. The introduction of the means of mass communication (radio, telephone, television) jolts the village out of its isolation, but also cuts through the protective layer of marginality, leaving it more susceptible to the levelling influences of hegemonic culture. They also replace the actual, physical social communication of the kitchen and the village square with the passive, atomized participation of media culture" (Geisler, "*Heimat* and the German Left," 46). These remarks reiterate Benjamin's reflections on the differences between historical

forms of communication. In "On Some Motifs in Baudelaire," for example, one reads: "Historically, the various modes of communication have competed with one another. The replacement of the older narration by information, of information by sensation, reflects the increasing atrophy of experience. In turn, there is a contrast between all these forms and the story, which is one of the oldest forms of communication" (*Illuminations*, 159).

68. James Clifford, "Of Other Peoples: Beyond the 'Salvage' Paradigm," in *Discussions in Contemporary Culture*, ed. Hal Foster (Seattle: Bay Press, 1987), 122. See also Raymond Williams, *The Country and the City* (New York: Oxford University Press, 1973).

69. Clifford, "Of Other Peoples," 122. See also George Marcus, "Contemporary Problems of Ethnography in the Modern World System," in *Writing Culture: The Poetics and Politics of Ethnography*, ed. James Clifford and George Marcus (Berkeley: University of California Press, 1986). Marcus distinguishes between two related narrative paradigms that have shaped the ethnographic imagination: "The two most common modes for self-consciously fixing ethnography in historic time are what I shall call the salvage mode and the redemptive mode. In the salvage mode, the ethnographer portrays himself as 'before the deluge,' so to speak. Signs of fundamental change are apparent, but the ethnographer is able to salvage a cultural state on the verge of transformation. . . . In the redemptive mode, the ethnographer demonstrates the survival of distinctive and authentic cultural systems despite undeniable changes. The redemption of cultural authenticity is often undertaken and measured against some imputed pre-modern or pre-capitalist state—the 'golden age' motif—or else a spatial, rather than temporal, preserve is found for cultural authenticity amidst transformation—the anthropologist's odyssey up-river or to the back country to situate fieldwork where 'they still do it'" (165).

70. Clifford, "Of Other Peoples," 126. Reitz is by no means oblivious to the dangers posed by his own narrative strategies. In the diary Reitz kept during the making of *Heimat*, he notes on January 27, 1981: "Once he [*der Weggeher*] has gone away, he regards his home as immutable. . . . House and surrounding nature are frozen in the fantasy of a man plagued by homesickness. He doesn't permit the people back home a life subject to change. Nostalgia seeks stasis in the things left behind and is inconsolable in the face of every sign of innovation." Reitz then adds: "A theme for *Heimat*, which is a period film, must be noted right off: period films tend to be nostalgic when they limit their vision to purely historical scenes. Our task will be to sublimate this compulsion [*diesen Zwang aufzuheben*] and to allow some of our present day reality to come into view so that we can thematize this compulsion" (excerpted in *Liebe zum Kino*, 151–52). I have been arguing that this effort was largely unsuccessful and that Reitz falls victim to exactly the sort of nostalgia he ascribes to the *Weggeher*.

71. Clifford, "Of Other Peoples," 126.

72. In this same vein, numerous critics have pointed to the simplistic portrayal of the Nazification of Schabbach as a process that begins with contamination in Berlin.

73. I take this term from Geisler, "*Heimat* and the German Left."

74. Eric Rentschler, "The Use and Abuse of Memory: New German Film and the Discourse of Bitburg," in *New German Critique* 36 (Fall 1985): 82. It is also interesting to note that in the "Storyteller" essay, Benjamin suggests that the processes that led to the disintegration of experience began to accelerate around the time of World War I and that this was the primary reason why so many returned soldiers appeared to be mute. See *Illuminations*, 84. The final scene of Michael Cimino's *The Deer Hunter* bears certain resemblances to this scene in *Heimat*.

75. Further examples offered by the film for the lack that begins at home are

allusions to those who were forced to leave the Hunsrück for economic reasons. Quite early in the film the audience hears of a line of Simons who live in Brazil; later Katharina's relatives in Bochum are introduced. Maria mentions that many Hunsrücker migrated to the industrial Ruhr valley because their Heimat was unable to nourish them. Reitz himself has relatives in Texas whose forebears, along with thousands of other Germans, left their homeland in the nineteenth century.

76. Reitz, *Liebe zum Kino*, 168.

77. It comes as no great surprise then that the sequel to *Heimat* currently in production, this time twenty hours long and bearing the title *Die zweite Heimat*, focuses primarily on Hermann's development as an artist against the backdrop of Munich bohemian life and student revolts.

78. Reitz and Steinbach, *Heimat*, 150. See also Kaes, *Deutschlandbilder*, 182–83. The literature of and about oral history has become vast since the beginning of the discipline, usually dated with Allan Nevins's first interviews in 1948 at Columbia University. To the titles mentioned by Kaes (see his bibliographical note, p. 245) should be added the important journals, *International Journal of Oral History*, *History Workshop Journal*, *Oral History: The Journal of the Oral History Society*; a by now standard oral history manual is Paul Thompson's *Voice of the Past: Oral History* (Oxford: Oxford University Press, 1978); an important collection of articles on the use of oral history within the public history movement may be found in *Radical History Review* 25, "Presenting the Past: History and the Public" (1981); for a good survey of the uses of oral history in a variety of disciplinary settings, see also *Oral History: An Interdisciplinary Anthology*, ed. David K. Dunaway and Willa K. Baum (Nashville: American Association for State and Local History, 1984); finally, for a work more directly relevant to the uses of oral testimonies in the reconstruction of the history of fascism, see Luisa Passerini's *Fascism in Popular Memory: The Cultural Experience of the Turin Working Class*, trans. Robert Lumley and Jude Bloomfield (Cambridge: Cambridge University Press, 1987). This is, of course, only a tiny sampling of the literature.

79. Alessandro Portelli, "The Peculiarities of Oral History," in *History Workshop Journal* 12 (Autumn 1981): 105–6.

80. Walter Benjamin's critique of Döblin's recourse to the conventions of the *Bildungsroman* at the conclusion of *Berlin Alexanderplatz* is interesting in this context. See "Krisis des Romans: Zu Döblin's 'Berlin Alexanderplatz,'" in *Die Gesellschaft* 7 (1930): 562–66.

81. Kaes, *Deutschlandbilder*, 183. In this context, see also Linda Shopes, "Beyond Trivia and Nostalgia: Collaborating in the Construction of a Local History," in *International Journal of Oral History* 3 (November 1984): 153: "Community oral history projects . . . generally do not explore the way the internal experience of the community is shaped by the economic and social forces external to it, the way the action of banks, employers, landlord, schools, planners, and developers have structured the dynamics of the place." Of course Reitz does demonstrate such interconnections, from Paul's first radio experiments, to the building of the Hunsrücker highway, to the attempt by a multinational corporation to buy out Anton's company; but as I have suggested, these interconnections with the larger world—with modernity—are coded within the narrative as catastrophic intrusions of linear time into a world otherwise organized by the natural cycles of pastoral time, or to put it in terms suggested by Reitz: intrusions of judgment into the preserve of experience. Regarding this binary opposition, one does well to recall Christa Wolf's remarks in *Kindheitsmuster* on the role of judgment in the work of memory and mourning: "Thus Nelly has her first opportunity to learn in a deeply personal way how long it takes before one is ready to regard the unthinkable as a possibility. One never learns it once and for all.

Those moments in which she didn't risk drawing the appropriate conclusions from what she was seeing with her own eyes are marked . . . by a special form of loss: the loss of inner memory. . . . It is as if a wall had been pushed between her observations and her attempts to interpret them. . . . Her inner memory, whose task it is to transmit the judgments one has made about events, was immobilized. It remained mute" (*A Model Childhood*, trans. Ursule Molinaro and Hedwig Rappolt [New York: Farrar, Straus and Giroux, 1980], 278–79). The novel was reissued by Farrar, Straus and Giroux in 1984 under the title *Patterns of Childhood*. Here and in the Epilogue, where I offer an interpretation of Wolf's novel, I have cited the earlier edition. I have noted all places where I thought it necessary to modify the translation, as in the passage just cited.

82. Koch, "That's Why Our Mothers Were Such Nice Chicks," a discussion among several critics reprinted in *New German Critique* 36 (Fall 1985): 16–17.

83. Reitz and Steinbach, *Heimat*, 148.

84. Reitz, *Liebe zum Kino*, 151.

85. Yet a third example that might be included in this series is the curious fact that Anton never seems to have any nightmares about the executions he witnessed on the Eastern Front. See J. Hoberman, "Once upon a Reich Time," in *New German Critique* 36 (Fall 1985): 9.

86. Reitz and Steinbach, *Heimat*, 299.

87. I am very grateful to Clare Rogan for bringing the full significance of this scene to my attention.

88. Reitz, interview with author, July 1987.

89. See Reitz, *Liebe zum Kino*, 170–71.

90. Reitz and Steinbach, *Heimat*, 230–31. Eduard's melancholic prayer recalls his earlier remark to Lucie, who in contrast to her husband can think only of the future, after the visit of Frick, Rosenberg, and Ley: " 'We'll remember this momentous day for a long, long time' " (201).

91. For a sampling of documents that might have crossed a small-town mayor's desk, see the monumental nine-volume study of Jews in Rhineland-Palatinate, especially volume 6, *Dokumentation zur Geschichte der jüdischen Bevölkerung in Rheinland-Pfalz und im Saarland von 1800 bis 1945* (Koblenz: Selbstverlag der Landesarchivverwaltung Rheinland-Pfalz, 1972–82). Volume 5, a compilation of statistical material on Jewish populations in the region, offers data that may help to put in perspective Reitz's claim regarding the paucity of memories of Jews among Hunsrücker. For example, in 1925 in the town of Rhaunen there were 70 Jews professing the Jewish faith from an overall population of 1,074. By 1933 the Jewish population was down to 58, in 1938 to 30. Some figures for villages and cities in the general region covered by the film are as follows (the figures are for 1925):

Town	Jewish population	General population
Hermeskeil	45	2,795
Kirchberg	73	1,591
Koblenz	709	58,322
Simmern	87	3,123
Boppard	97	6,513

The total figures for the combined administrative districts of Koblenz and Trier for 1927 count 9,944 Jews from a total population of 1,392,129. Among the towns and villages that still have Jewish cemeteries (at least until 1972 when these statistics were gathered) are Rhaunen, Simmern, Kirchberg, Sohren, Rheinböllen, Oberwesel, Laufersweiler,

Gemünden, Kastellaun, Bacharach, Bad Kreuznach, Bengel, Bernkastel-Kues, Bingen, Boppard, Hermeskeil (see volume 7, *Dokumente des Gedenkens*). For further information concerning Jewish life in small towns and villages see also: E. G. Lowenthal, "In the Shadow of Doom—Postwar Publications on Jewish Communal History in Germany," in *Leo Baeck Institute Yearbook* 23 (1984): 283–308; Werner J. Cahnmann, "Village and Small-Town Jews in Germany—A Typological Study," in *LBI Yearbook* 21 (1978): 107–30; Hans Heß, *Die Landauer Judengemeinde* (Landau: Verlag Pfälzer Kunst, 1983); Hildegard Kattermann, *Das Ende einer jüdischen Landgemeinde: Nonnenweier in Baden, 1933–1945* (Freiburg: Verlag Wolf Mersch, 1984). This is only a partial listing of relevant titles.

92. Reitz, *Liebe zum Kino*, 102.

93. Quoted in Kaes, *Deutschlandbilder*, 198.

94. Reitz, interview with author, July 1987.

95. Reitz, interview with author, July 1987.

96. Reitz, *Liebe zum Kino*, 208. Though primarily reserved to signify family members, some of the emotional resonances of the word *Geheischnis* are found in the Yiddish word *mishpokheh*. Indeed, one of the things that makes Reitz's—and his characters'—lack of curiosity about Jews and their fate so uncanny is the numerous parallels between Reitz's turn to his rural origins and the work of a great many twentieth-century Central European Jewish writers in their searches and researches in the culture of *Yiddishkeit*. A number of the themes of *Heimat* are anticipated, for example, in the work of the Austrian writer Joseph Roth. Though it does not deal primarily with a Jewish milieu, Roth's most articulately and intelligently nostalgic work, *Radetzkymarsch*, shares many of the concerns and much of the ethos of *Heimat*. Here, for example, the estrangement from one's own language plays a central role. Roth is also interesting in this context because of his view, presented in his essay *Juden auf Wanderschaft* (Wandering Jews), that the journey west, away from the shtetl, was the beginning of the end of what was most valuable in European Jewish culture, as well as his disgust with what he called *Hölle-Wut* (literally, the "fury of hell").

97. It is understandable, then, that the entire film has been described as "a panorama of mourning. . . . For the peasant culture of the Hunsrück is irrevocably lost. Rather than celebrating this culture, the film honors it with a farewell song—a requiem, an exquisite dirge" (Karsten Witte, "Of the Greatness of the Small People: The Rehabilitation of a Genre," in *New German Critique* 36 [Fall 1985]: 11–12). According to this view, the film's celebration of the culture of oral tradition echoes Benjamin's sober words of leave-taking in the "Storyteller" essay. Speaking of the decline of the art of storytelling, Benjamin admonishes: "And nothing would be more fatuous than to want to see in it merely a 'symptom of decay,' let alone a 'modern' symptom. It is, rather, only a concomitant symptom of the secular productive forces of history, a concomitant that has quite gradually removed narrative from the realm of living speech and at the same time is making it possible to see a new beauty in what is vanishing" (*Illuminations*, 87). I have been arguing that Reitz fails to achieve this more sober mode of nostalgia and that his own work of mourning is hindered by a narrative form that reinscribes an archaic search for the pharmakos.

98. In *The Pastoral Elegy: An Anthology*, ed. Thomas Perrin Harrison (New York: Octagon, 1968), 203.

99. Sacks, *The English Elegy: Studies in the Genre from Spenser to Yeats* (Baltimore: Johns Hopkins University Press, 1985), 5.

100. Bakhtin, *Dialogic Imagination*, 234.

101. Once more, see Baudrillard, *Simulations*. The use of fashion and furnishings to simulate identity within a world complete with the traces of a family history—a

bloodline—may be studied in the remarkable success story of the American designer Ralph Lauren. Lauren's fashions offer mirrors in which the consumer may see him- or herself as a complete, "orthopedic" self within a harmonious vision of home. Here to look like one lives a particular life is the key. Much as one can change one's name from Lifshitz to Lauren, anyone can cite this or that past as one's own. And as Holly Brubach has remarked in an essay entitled "Ralph Lauren's Achievement" (*Atlantic*, August 1987: 70–73), his particular vision of "the whole atmosphere of the good life," as he has called the aura his clothes are designed to evoke, was itself most likely constructed from a different order of simulations, namely projections on the silver screen first seen during a Bronx adolescence: "One imagines that his Paris is the Paris of *Gigi*, his Wild West that of *High Noon*, his Main Line Philadelphia the house where Katherine Hepburn lived in *The Philadelphia Story*. His career may indeed be the Great American Success Story, not so much because he rose from hand-me-downs to vast riches as because he has re-created the world according to his imagination and then recreated himself as the sort of person who would live in it." Essential to Lauren's designs is the evocation of a lived-in-world, somewhat worn, washed out, like an old family photograph displaying several generations of one's (someone's) clan: kinship is simulated by a line of products. Lauren's ads are therefore, Brubach remarks, "always photojournalistic, persuading us that this world we see before us actually exists, that events are taking place in it even as we peruse a magazine. These pictures are the visual equivalent of eavesdropping." Here one is reminded of the fact that after the telecast of *Heimat* the Hunsrück experienced a flurry of tourism: people came in search of the fictive village of Schabbach. Lauren *creates* new stranded objects from the fantasized world of the landed gentry and leisure classes and lets anyone who can pay the price appropriate these bits of aura-off-the-rack as if one had found a long lost piece of one's own past. Lauren's stores and advertisements are in turn something on the order of consumer *Gesamtkunstwerke*. As Brubach puts it, "With tiny fires burning in every grate, the beds (on the top floor, the home furnishings department) turned down for the night, the teacups on the end table, the house looks lived in, like a home." An article on trends in American home construction (Carol Vogel, "Clustered for Leisure: The Changing Home," *New York Times Magazine*, June 28, 1987) registered parallel tendencies in the marketing of the new American home. Peter Rowe of the Harvard Graduate School of Design is quoted as saying, "the name of the game is to sell an image people can easily identify with. A modern house simply won't do." And Stan Eckstat, one of the architects and planners of Manhattan's Battery Park City, makes the further claim about that planned community's 'neighborhood'-like design: "it gives people an instant feeling of identity." Each of these examples demonstrates a perhaps peculiarly postmodern paradox: the salvage paradigm is deployed here not to recuperate the old but, rather, to fashion the new.

102. See especially the seventh and ninth *Duino Elegies* for Rilke's version of the poetic and human significance of such objects and traces.

103. Eagleton, *Walter Benjamin; or, Towards a Revolutionary Criticism* (London: Verso, 1985), 33.

104. Miriam Hansen, Introduction to "Dossier on *Heimat*," in *New German Critique* 36 (Fall 1985): 5. For these reasons Hermann's music ultimately fails to fulfill the modernist role to which it is assigned. That is, though Hermann's music is associated with a modernist aesthetic of fragmentation—I believe it is Schönberg's photograph in the studio in which Hermann works on his first piece, "*Bindungen*"—its sentimentality bends it back into a distinctly premodernist, pastoral sensibility.

105. Geisler has pointed to one of Reitz's strategies of circumventing this entire complex of issues: the world of *Heimat* is presented as an essentially fatherless society. See his "*Heimat* and the German Left," 60–62.

106. These issues become all the more urgent when one recalls that one of the effects of *Heimat* was the beginning of a wave of memory-work in the general population. After the telecast of the film Reitz received numerous letters, memoirs, and even autobiographical screenplays in which people offered their own recollections after the pattern of the story of the Simon family. In this context see Kaes's provocative concluding remarks in *Deutschlandbilder*.

Chapter 4 Allegories of Grieving

1. The most important essays on Syberberg in English, all of which discuss the mourning performed in his films, are: Susan Sontag, "Syberberg's Hitler," in Sontag, *Under the Sign of Saturn* (New York: Vintage, 1981); Thomas Elsaesser, "Myth as the Phantasmagoria of History: H. J. Syberberg, Cinema and Representation," *New German Critique* 24–25 (Fall/Winter 1981–82): 108–54; Russell A. Berman, "Hans Jürgen Syberberg: Of Fantastic and Magical Worlds," in *New German Filmmakers*, ed. Klaus Phillips (New York: Frederick Ungar, 1984); Timothy Corrigan, "The Exorcism of the Image: Syberberg's *Hitler, A Film from Germany*," in Corrigan, *New German Film: The Displaced Image* (Austin: University of Texas Press, 1983); Fredric Jameson, "'In the Destructive Element Immerse': Hans-Jürgen Syberberg and Cultural Revolution," in *October* 17 (Summer 1981): 99–118; and Anton Kaes's chapter on Syberberg in his *From Hitler to "Heimat": The Return of History as Film* (Cambridge: Harvard University Press, 1989), a translation of his *Deutschlandbilder: Die Wiederkehr der Geschichte als Film* (Munich: Edition text und kritik, 1987).

2. Published works of Syberberg to which I refer are: *Syberbergs Filmbuch* (Frankfurt: Fischer, 1979); *Hitler, ein Film aus Deutschland* (Reinbek: Rowohlt, 1978)—this volume contains essays along with the entire script of the *Hitler* film and has been published in English as *Hitler, A Film from Germany*, trans. Joachim Neugroschel (New York: Farrar, Straus, Giroux, 1982); *Die freudlose Gesellschaft: Notizen aus den letzten Jahren* (Frankfurt: Ullstein, 1983; first published with Hanser in 1981); *Parsifal: Ein Filmessay* (Munich: Wilhelm Heyne, 1982); *Der Wald steht schwarz und schweiget: Neue Notizen aus Deutschland* (Zurich: Diogenes, 1984).

3. The film was distributed in the United States by Francis Ford Coppola under the title *Our Hitler*. See Syberberg's remarks concerning this change of title in *Freudlose Gesellschaft*, 109.

4. Kaes's criticism of Syberberg focuses on this very strategy: "The posture of cultural pessimism . . . allows the concrete guilt of the German people to be absorbed by the general malaise of the *post-histoire*" (*Deutschlandbilder*, 163–64).

5. Syberberg, *Freudlose Gesellschaft*, 91.

6. Syberberg often uses formulations familiar from the discourse that has emerged over the years regarding the subject of the Holocaust to describe his own treatment in Germany. When a manuscript of his was rejected by publishers he made the rejection public with the warning: "So that later no one can claim that he didn't know" (*Wald*, 498). And he concludes one of the many parables he has written about his treatment in Germany: "And if he didn't exist, he would have to be invented. Every country and every age and thus every generation too has its own Jews, especially in Germany" (*Freudlose Gesellschaft*, 355). One finds numerous other examples in Syberberg's writings of a deeply ambivalent identification with Jews as victims.

7. See Max Horkheimer and Theodor W. Adorno, *Dialektik der Aufklärung: Philosophische Fragmente*, in Adorno, *Gesammelte Schriften*, vol. 3, ed. Rolf Tiedemann (Frankfurt: Suhrkamp, 1981).

8. This was the title of Sontag's essay on *Hitler* when it was first published in the *New York Review of Books*, February 21, 1980.

9. Much of this biographical information is taken from Syberberg's *Filmbuch*, interviews with Syberberg, and Berman's essay.

10. See Syberberg, *Filmbuch*, 63.

11. Syberberg has come to understand his affinity to Sedlmayr at least in part as a function of their both having grown up on country estates, Sedlmayr in the Balkans and Syberberg in Pomerania. It was the aristocratic equilibrium of such a life that, according to Syberberg, made both men especially sensitive to the imbalances of modernity: "Growing up in a hierarchical, rural culture as it still existed until 1945 in East Germany and still predominated in Slavic regions at that time, instills a sense of world-responsibility totally unknown to urbanites and which today even people in the country can no longer learn, since wherever you go, East or West, agriculture is now for the most part industrialized" (interview with author, July 1987). Years later Syberberg was unable to get funding to make a documentary about Sedlmayr. See his *Wald*, 259–60; 466.

12. Syberberg, *Wald*, 257.

13. See Syberberg, *Filmbuch*, 47.

14. See Syberberg, *Filmbuch*, 60.

15. Syberberg, *Filmbuch*, 85.

16. See Syberberg, *Filmbuch*, 86.

17. Sontag has remarked that Syberberg is "incapable of writing an essay that is not a manifesto" ("Syberberg's Hitler," 154).

18. The history of Syberberg's relationship to the German press and to the quasi-national system of film subsidy and distribution in the Federal Republic is a study in its own right. Each of Syberberg's publications contains lengthy documentations—rhetorically and stylistically occupying a place somewhere between Krausian polemics and a legal brief—of his mistreatment and persecution primarily at the hands of what he calls the "leftist establishment" that he sees as controlling the machinery of film support, distribution, and criticism in Germany. Perhaps the most bizarre example of such self-documentation is the "Dictionary of the German Film Critic," published in his *Filmbuch*, which contains a collection, in alphabetical order, of the various epithets German critics have used to characterize, and for the most part disparage, Syberberg's work (this "dictionary" is in part so remarkable for some of the absurd and outright sadistic language German critics have used to discuss Syberberg and his work). Syberberg then juxtaposes these bite-sized attacks with longer excerpts from French reviews of his films in which he is for the most part celebrated as the true genius of the New German Cinema. Syberberg has also written several brief parables that tell the story of his relationship to his country and its cultural establishment. The language of these little narratives, based no doubt on real experiences, is marked by rage, self-pity, and a strong dose of Nietzschean grandiosity. See for example his *Wald*, 332.

19. Syberberg, *Filmbuch*, 56–57.

20. See Berman, "Hans Jürgen Syberberg," 363; Sontag, "Syberberg's Hitler," 161.

21. Syberberg, *Filmbuch*, 310–11.

22. Syberberg, *Filmbuch*, 75–76. Peter Handke has also recently found his way back to Stifter's "gentle law," which both implicitly and explicitly informs his tetralogy *Langsame Heimkehr* (Slow homecoming). Handke is, interestingly, one of the cultural figures whom Syberberg expressly thanks "for his separatist meditations regarding the productive work of resistance of an oppositional art" against the forces of the "joyless society" (*Freudlose Gesellschaft*, 384).

23. Syberberg, *Filmbuch*, 50. Berman has remarked on Syberberg's affinity here to *Death in Venice*, the most famous version of the familiar story of the dissolution of cold, northern calculation in the voluptuousness of the south. See Berman, "Hans Jürgen Syberberg," 364.

24. Berman, "Hans Jürgen Syberberg," 364.

25. Syberberg, *Filmbuch*, 54. Syberberg's most recent meditation on terrorism is a brief essay, "Im Herbst sterben die Eltern nach den Kindern" (In autumn the parents die after the children) in *Wiener*, September 9, 1986.

26. Syberberg, *Filmbuch*, 55.

27. Walter Benjamin, *Illuminations: Essays and Reflections*, trans. Harry Zohn (New York: Schocken, 1969), 257–58.

28. For a description of Syberberg's technique of back projection see Corrigan, "Exorcism," 149.

29. See Elsaesser, "Myth as the Phantasmagoria of History," 120.

30. Syberberg, *Filmbuch*, 15.

31. Elsaesser, "Myth as the Phantasmagoria of History," 120.

32. Elsaesser, "Myth as the Phantasmagoria of History," 121. See also Jameson, *The Political Unconscious: Narrative as a Socially Symbolic Act* (Ithaca: Cornell University Press, 1981), for an excellent discussion of desire and the production of ideology.

33. See Syberberg, *Filmbuch*, 20.

34. Terry Eagleton, *Walter Benjamin: or, Towards a Revolutionary Criticism* (London: Verso, 1985), 38.

35. Elsaesser, "Myth as the Phantasmagoria of History," 121.

36. Eagleton, *Walter Benjamin*, 34–35.

37. In a later work, human sexuality seems to occupy the position which Syberberg otherwise associates with the commodity. See Syberberg, *Parsifal*, 264–65: "There are the tears of Eros, but there is also an Eros of tears. In *Parsifal* by Richard Wagner are we not once again faced with a . . . rare and successful attempt to overcome the small death that is part of love, our life, and our worlds, by searching for the eternal life of the Grail while simultaneously pronouncing damnation upon earthly love as embodied by woman and her profane arts of seduction that keep us from the glory and success of the beyond? And out of this grow the rapacious efforts to glorify, and thereby redeem, the great death of all earthly life by way of sublimation, exaltation, mythologization; to overcome ourselves for the eternal life of the moment of art. To win life by sacrificing life—this is what keeps us alive—in the murderous pleasure of our pain, the last or already lost radiance of the Eros of tears." (I have tried here as elsewhere to capture something of Syberberg's often convoluted syntax; these sentences are as strange in German as they are in English.)

38. Syberberg, *Filmbuch*, 92–93. In his brief review of Edgar Reitz's *Heimat*, Syberberg shifts his conception of Heimat from a Blochian to a Heideggerian framework: "Now that the word 'Heimat' has suddenly become fashionable again, I think more in terms of the 'Heimat' of which Heidegger spoke, when he quoted Hölderlin, and understood the word as meaning the abode of the gods" (*Sight and Sound* 54 [Spring 1985]: 125).

39. Jameson, *Political Unconscious*, 142.

40. Susan Sontag has suggested that the film was inspired by Brecht's unfinished novel about the life of Julius Caesar as told by a slave. See "Syberberg's Hitler," 156.

41. Elsaesser, "Myth as the Phantasmagoria of History," 122.

42. Syberberg, *Filmbuch*, 35; see also Elsaesser, "Myth as the Phantasmagoria of History," 121–23.

43. May's popularity, seventy-five years after his death, continues unabated (it is

estimated that his total circulation comprises some 80 million volumes). The Nörd-lingen publishing house in West Germany has recently published the first volume of a ninety-nine-volume critical edition, edited by Hermann Wiedenroth and noted author and Joyce translator Hans Wollschläger, who has also written a monograph on Karl May.

44. Syberberg, *Filmbuch*, 39.

45. An American clothing retailer, Banana Republic, has recently made a business out of recycling the phantasmagoria and garments of the colonial era. Each store bears a certain resemblance to May's cluttered Saxon villa and seems to be based on the same patterns of fantasy production, only now deployed, with self-conscious cynicism, at one postcolonial nostalgic remove.

46. Syberberg, *Filmbuch*, 46. Nearly all of these elements may be found in Jameson's analysis of the writings of May's contemporary Joseph Conrad. See Jameson, *Political Unconscious*, 206–80.

47. See Syberberg, *Filmbuch*, 38; 188.

48. Berman, "Hans Jürgen Syberberg," 368; see also Syberberg, *Filmbuch*, 45; 224–25.

49. In an essay on Karl May, Frederic Morton reiterates much of Syberberg's filmic argument: "By the 19th century Germans knew themselves to be respectable, reliable, thorough, knowledgeable and not particularly heroic. At this juncture Richard Wagner and Karl May, born a year apart, went to work. . . . Pulling the Nibelungs out of medieval mists, Wagner charged them with Teutonic grandeur. But it was May who made patriotism mythic for the man in the street. For every German who can hum a Siegfried aria, 10 will recite Old Shatterhand's sallies. True, there is much more to Wagner's vision than *Herrenvolk* propaganda, and in his final books May preached a mystical pacifism. Yet both men, on different esthetic levels, helped shape the collective German dream of feats far beyond middle-class bounds—a dream Hitler mobilized into mania" ("Tales of the Grand Teutons: Karl May among the Indians," in *New York Times Book Review*, January 4, 1987: 16).

50. Benjamin, *Illuminations*, 189.

51. Trans. by C. F. MacIntyre, in *French Symbolist Poetry* (Berkeley: University of California Press, 1958), 12.

52. See Frank Kermode, *The Sense of an Ending: Studies in the Theory of Fiction* (Oxford: Oxford University Press, 1967).

53. Benjamin, *Illuminations*, 183; 190.

54. Eagleton, *Walter Benjamin*, 39.

55. See Elsaesser, "Myth as the Phantasmagoria of History," 128.

56. I take this notion of "your-face–my-face" communality from Morton, *Crosstown Sabbath: A Street Journey through History* (New York: Grove Press, 1987). In this context, Jameson's remarks on modern recuperations of the religious impulse—including the attempt to make a religion out of art—are quite interesting: "Religion is the superstructural projection of a mode of production, the latter's only surviving trace in the form of linguistic and visual artifacts, thought systems, myths and narratives, which look as though they had something to do with the forms in which our own consciousness is at home, and yet which remain rigorously closed to it. Because we can no longer think the figures of the sacred from within, we transform their external forms into aesthetic objects, but also monuments, pyramids, altars, presumed to have an inside, yet housing powers that will forever remain a mystery to us" (*Political Unconscious*, 252).

57. The double binds described here were first theorized by Hegel in his description of the master/slave dialectic in the *Phenomenology of Spirit*, trans. A. V. Miller (Oxford: Oxford University Press, 1977), 111–19.

58. Hölderlin's poem "Hälfte des Lebens" (Half of life) distributes these oppositions across two halves of life (and the two strophes of the poem):

> With its yellow pears
> And wild roses everywhere
> The shore hangs in the lake,
> O gracious swans,
> And drunk with kisses
> You dip your heads
> In the sobering holy water.
>
> Ah, where will I find
> Flowers, come winter,
> And where the sunshine
> And shade of the earth?
> Walls stand cold
> And speechless, in the wind
> The weathervanes creak.

Trans. Richard Sieburth, *Hymns and Fragments by Friedrich Hölderlin* (Princeton: Princeton University Press, 1984), 47. See my reading of the poem in Santner, *Friedrich
Hölderlin: Narrative Vigilance and the Poetic Imagination* (New Brunswick: Rutgers University Press, 1986), 83–91.

59. Eagleton, *Walter Benjamin*, 42.

60. As should be clear from this discussion of the gaze, I am also shifting the
framework of analysis of cinematic pleasure from oedipal scenarios and their attendant voyeurism and fetishism to the pre-oedipal and questions of narcissism. This
shift is, as I noted earlier, part of a more general shift in recent psychoanalytic theory
from a study of drives to that of the constitution of the self.

61. Jameson, *Political Unconscious*, 260–61.

62. Syberberg, *Filmbuch*, 260–61.

63. Syberberg, *Filmbuch*, 286. And as Winifred says elsewhere in the film: "'It is
simply impossible to portray Hitler's personality to someone who didn't know him. It
simply can't be done. It's . . . just as impossible to describe in words the performance
of a singer. . . . And . . . a person's charisma [*Ausstrahlung*], that's really so important. You can't simply think it out of existence'" (*Filmbuch*, 278).

64. Wagner claims, for example, that she felt no great sadness when Mahler's
music was forbidden because she never cared for his music anyway. When Toscanini
canceled his engagement to conduct in Bayreuth, Wagner claims that she had no time
or interest "to mourn his absence [*ihm nachzutrauern*]" because of the pressures of
finding a last minute substitute (Richard Strauss). And predictably she thinks, like so
many of her contemporaries, of Willy Brandt as a man who abandoned his country in
a time of need. One is reminded of a recent documentary by Irmgard von zur
Mühlen, *The Children of the 20th of July*, in which the children of the conspirators in the
plot to assassinate Hitler speak of the years of being regarded with contempt by other
Germans for being members of traitor families.

65. Syberberg, *Filmbuch*, 281.

66. Syberberg, interview with author, July 1987.

67. Syberberg, *Hitler*, 64 (all quotations from *Hitler* are from Neugroschel's
translation).

68. Fletcher, *Allegory: The Theory of a Symbolic Mode* (Ithaca: Cornell University
Press, 1964), 360–61.

69. Berman, "Hans Jürgen Syberberg," 372–74.

70. See Fletcher, *Allegory*, 108–20. See also Sontag on Syberberg's use of *kosmoi* that the audience cannot even see, in "Syberberg's Hitler," 159.

71. Sontag, "Syberberg's Hitler," 151.

72. Syberberg, *Hitler*, 126.

73. A similar Friedell quotation closes *Winifred Wagner*.

74. Syberberg, *Hitler*, 128.

75. See Hans R. Vaget, "Syberberg's *Our Hitler*: Wagnerianism and Alienation," *Massachusetts Review* 23 (Winter 1982): 593–612, for a detailed account of the use of *Rienzi* in the film.

76. Syberberg, *Hitler*, 129.

77. See Vaget, "Wagnerianism," 597.

78. Syberberg, *Hitler*, 118.

79. Syberberg, *Hitler*, 124–25.

80. Syberberg, *Hitler*, 69.

81. Elsaesser, "Myth as the Phantasmagoria of History," 137.

82. Fletcher, *Allegory*, 59; 40; 65; 55.

83. Benjamin's study of baroque *Trauerspiel* is, in many ways, a demonstration of the emergence of the allegorical agent out of the "maimed rites" of mourning.

84. Syberberg, *Hitler*, 200.

85. Elsaesser has pointed to the tendency of the mass media to create what I have been calling, following Baudrillard, simulacra of intimacy and presence: "Technology tends to be used not to produce new forms of social interaction, but [to] reproduce ones charged with (nostalgic) affectivity, and thus binding the consumer libidinally, through the secondary narcissism of a sense of loss. This is the essence of kitsch, whether it is fascist art or formica tables looking like solid pine" ("Myth as the Phantasmagoria of History," 138).

86. See Syberberg, *Hitler*, 145. In his discussion of the more contemporary form of gossip about the lives of the stars, Morton reminds us of the genealogy of that discursive practice: "The history of the word 'gossip' leads to its collective origins. It derives from 'God's sibb'—'sibb' being the Gothic word for the clan that gathers at the godly rite of baptism to exchange family news around the crib. Around the birth of a new star crystallizes an ad hoc kinship group of applauders and gossipers" (*Crosstown Sabbath*, 114–15). Martin Scorsese's *King of Comedy* is a brilliant study of the narcissistic foundations of a contemporary psychotic fan.

87. See Elsaesser, "Myth as the Phantasmagoria of History," 135.

88. Corrigan, "Exorcism," 160. One is reminded of Karl May's four years of blindness as a child and his lifelong quest to undo that early trauma of deprivation. May's last words also echo Kane's "rosebud": "Rosen, rosenrot."

89. Syberberg, *Hitler*, 70.

90. Syberberg, *Hitler*, 18.

91. Elsaesser, "Myth as the Phantasmagoria of History," 147.

92. The crumbling letters of "The Grail" anticipate the slab of stone bearing the inscription/epitaph "Made in Germany" that is shown at the beginning of each episode of *Heimat*.

93. Joachim Neugroschel's translation of Celan, cited with slight modifications in Joel David Golb, "Celan and Hölderlin: An Essay in the Problem of Tradition," Ph.D. diss., Princeton University, 1986, 240. This fissured apotheosis seems also to take place in the same time as Syberberg's film: in the *Eulenflucht* (owl's flight). Yet a third figure to consider here would of course be Anselm Kiefer whose monumental canvases move through similarly poisoned mythic and historical landscapes.

94. Part 4 of the film contains a long, bitterly sarcastic sequence in which the

mayor of Berchtesgaden and an entrepeneur discuss the great successes of a new Hitler theme park that would include the obligatory memorial services for the victims of Nazism. In an open allusion to Celan's "Todesfuge" (Death fugue), Syberberg calls "progress," which includes the production of these sorts of spectacles, the new "Meister aus Deutschland" (*Freudlose Gesellschaft*, 354). For two disturbing accounts of the Hitler industry, see once more Friedländer's study, *Reflections of Nazism: An Essay on Kitsch and Death*, trans. Thomas Weyr (New York: Harper and Row, 1984) and Alvin H. Rosenfeld's *Imagining Hitler* (Bloomington: Indiana University Press, 1985).

95. Fletcher, *Allegory*, 174; 176.

96. Syberberg, *Hitler*, 242. As Joel Golb has quite dramatically demonstrated in his dissertation on Paul Celan, each of Celan's poems may be thought of as an obsessive effort to master the fallenness of the German language, and in particular the language of the Romantic tradition after Auschwitz. Golb points to the remarkably concentrated way in which Celan engages in this struggle by highlighting Celan's strategic word choices. Each word seems to become a site of a nearly intolerable ambivalence; collectively the words represent something on the order of the new antithetical primal words of post-Holocaust history. The sixth strophe of "Engführung" contains, for example, a series of adjectives descriptive of both plant and mineral properties. Golb points out the various ambivalent—utopian/dystopian—resonances of each adjective, an exegetical labor that delves deeply into the at times obscene genealogies of these words. Of the first adjective, *körnig*, Golb remarks: "Along with an abstract connotation, similar to Mallarmé's, of purity, clarity, self-reflective illumination, and also . . . of its polar nullity in death, there is a concreter thantic reference at work in Celan's allegorical crystal: both to the *Kristallnacht*, and . . . apocalyptically, to the crystalline *Zyklon B*." Golb turns to the Grimm dictionary to discover yet another archeological layer of the word: *Kornjude*, the pejorative term for the Jew who speculated in grain. Golb concludes: "Celan the poet is a sort of *Kornjude*, expressing his desire for a vanished origin by means of a fragmented language . . . steeped in the tradition responsible for its extinction . . . hence itself polarized between the corrupt nature of its materiality and the transcendence towards which it strives" (Golb, "Celan and Hölderlin," 30–31).

97. Fletcher, *Allegory*, 207.

98. Syberberg, *Hitler*, 271. See Sontag, "Syberberg's Hitler," 162: "Science fiction is precisely the genre which dramatizes the mix of nostalgia for utopia with dystopian fantasies and dread; the dual conviction that the world is ending and that it is on the verge of a new beginning. Syberberg's film about history is also a moral and cultural science fiction. Starship Goethe-Haus." Eagleton's remarks on the messianic impulse in Benjamin's *Trauerspiel* book are also relevant to Syberberg's vision of the black hole: "As the petrified stage-properties are ritually shuffled, time is almost folded back into space, dwindled to a recurrence so agonizingly empty that some salvific epiphany might indeed just be conceived to tremble on its brink." And further: "The rich profusion of mundane objects is seen as a kind of plundering of the hereafter: the more history is thoroughly secularized, the less possible it is to characterize heaven in its terms. Heaven, accordingly, is reduced to a pure signifier, an empty space, but this vacuum will one day engulf the world with catastrophic violence" (*Walter Benjamin*, 11; 21). The black hole is also affiliated with Heidegger's conception of *die Kehre* (the turn) and Celan's poetological conception of the *Atemwende* (breath's turn). Both concepts, familiar in European mystical traditions, go back in a more direct way to Hölderlin's notion of the *Kata-strophe* in his theory of the modulation of tones. For a good discussion of "the turn" in Celan, Hölderlin, and Heidegger, see Golb, "Celan and Hölderlin."

99. See in this context Leon Wieseltier's excellent review of the film in the *New Republic*, March 8, 1980. There Wieseltier notes, for example: "This brazenly eschatological interpretation will be construed by many to be an apology for Hitler, when in fact it is an apology for eschatology. Syberberg is determined to show that Parsifal survived Hitler's impersonation."

100. Sontag is wrong, I think, when she claims that the Mitscherlichs had diagnosed the Germans as being afflicted by mass melancholia in the postwar period. See Sontag, "Syberberg's Hitler," 153.

101. Syberberg's next two films, *Parsifal* and *Die Nacht*, are beyond the scope of the present study. Each film does, however, in its own way continue and concentrate even further the saturnine lament of the previous cycle. Syberberg claims, for example, that *Parsifal* represents "utopia as a society of the dead [*Totengesellschaft*] . . . the liberation, finally the myth of remembrance, myth as memory. Once again the journey into the interior, the world after its decline" (*Parsifal*, 13). And indeed, Syberberg stages Wagner's last work in a gigantic model of Wagner's death mask—Syberberg calls it a "*Kopftempel*" (97)—of which every part has a particular allegorical meaning. The opera is performed as a vast, final "eschatological ritual" (219), an "ascetic apotheosis" (247), in which all separations, injuries, restlessness—embodied by the wandering Jew and the "evil" of woman—are overcome in the final sabbath celebrated by the death cult of the grail: "What was divided for so long is thus finally reunited, at the cost of dissolution in the icy loneliness of this utopia of our last stage of knowledge" (228). The wedding at the end of this "comedy"—Syberberg has, as noted earlier, insisted that *Parsifal* is a comedy—is one in which all difference and alterity are extinguished in the conjugal bliss of death. In *Parsifal*, Syberberg's strategy of universalizing the wounds of recent history, already apparent in *Hitler*, becomes programmatic. As Syberberg says of Amfortas's wound, which in the film becomes a disembodied fetish object, "bleeding in the manner of reliques or medieval allegorical representations": "A wound rich in mythical resonances and associations with the reality of our world, of the nineteenth century, and of the story and its author, resonating further with all wound-mysticisms since the fall from paradise, since man is born in pain as punishment for woman's betrayal, or the symbol of Christ's wound, applicable to every human being and to all times and nations, emblem of . . . the fall as the source of the flowing blood of our polymorphic longings. Woman's betrayal in paradise, the Jews' betrayal of Christ, the wound continues to bleed and cries out for salvation" (*Parsifal*, 102; see also *Wald*, 166). Syberberg stages his next film, *Die Nacht*, even more explicitly in the tense of the future perfect: when the Occident will have been. In this film Syberberg openly recants his previous cinematic techniques of back projection and the crowding of the visual field, and opts instead for a single actress, Edith Cleaver, who speaks a six-hour monologue—an "oratorio for one voice" (*Wald*, 561)—in a dark room that appears to be the last, ruinous dwelling after the end of civilization. Cleaver herself seems to stand in for the last member of many civilizations: the last American Indian, the last Greek, the last German, the last European, the last human. The monologue is a tapestry of textual citations primarily from Western literature and philosophy including, in a central position, the German metaphysical and Romantic tradition. Among the texts Syberberg includes are those of Hölderlin, Goethe, Novalis, Jean Paul, Heine, Wagner, and Heidegger. One is made to feel that Cleaver's words will be the last words spoken in and of Western culture. And indeed, Syberberg has referred to this work as his testament, his swan song for Europe, his final lament.

102. Syberberg openly recanted the term *Trauerarbeit* in an interview with me in September 1986. His review of Bernhard's novel appears in the *Tageszeitung*, October

1, 1986. The novel is Syberbergian in a number of ways, most obviously in being a relentless monologue that fills some 650 pages and that attempts to cancel out a personal and collective history by the sheer force of a verbal spell and by the rhetorical technique of exaggeration.

103. Walter Benjamin, *Illuminationen: Ausgewählte Schriften* (Frankfurt: Suhrkamp, 1980), 352.

104. The series of videos Syberberg produced after *Die Nacht* indicates that he has begun to move beyond the eschatological terms of his previous work. And indeed, Syberberg has suggested that to continue in this manner would be *"Größenwahnsinn"* (megalomania) (interview with author, July 1987). Not unlike Hölderlin's turn to the *"fester Buchstab"* (firm letter) of scripture, Syberberg's last few works, produced in the mid- to late 1980s, are primarily interpretive, staged readings, performed by Edith Cleaver, of texts by Joyce, Schnitzler, and Kleist. As a more recent essay by Syberberg suggests, however, he has not lost his taste for apocalyptic pronouncements (see "Seeing the Light," in *New Republic*, October 3, 1988: 32–36).

Epilogue

1. Habermas, "Geschichtsbewußtsein und posttraditionale Identität: Die Westorientierung der Bundesrepublik," in his *Eine Art Schadensabwicklung: Kleine politische Schriften VI* (Frankfurt: Suhrkamp, 1987), 171. That this excessive hunger for stable and authoritative cultural values is not limited to the Federal Republic of Germany may be seen, for example, in the great popularity in the United States of a work such as Allan Bloom's *Closing of the American Mind* (New York: Simon and Schuster, 1987), in the intensity of debates around issues of cultural literacy and canon formation in and outside the academy, and in a more general sense in the enormous successes of that great simulator of stable cultural values and meanings, Ronald Reagan.

2. Benjamin, *Illuminations: Essays and Reflections*, trans. Harry Zohn (New York: Schocken, 1969), 255; 262–63.

3. Regarding the use of this new term signifying behaviors situated somewhere between outright resistance and outright collaboration, see once more the so-called *Bayern-Projekt* conducted by the Institut für Zeitgeschichte under the direction of Martin Broszat. For a powerful critique of this new historiographical category, see Friedländer, "Überlegungen zur Historisierung des Nationalsozialismus," in *Ist der Nationalsozialismus Geschichte? Zu Historisierung und Historikerstreit*, ed. Dan Diner (Frankfurt: Fischer, 1987), 45.

4. Walter Benjamin, *One-Way Street and Other Writings*, trans. Edmund Jephcott and Kingsley Shorter (London: NLB, 1979), 243.

5. See once more Eagleton, *Walter Benjamin; or, Towards a Revolutionary Criticism* (London: Verso, 1985), 33.

6. Andreas Huyssen, "An Analytic Storyteller in the Course of Time," in *October* 46 (Fall 1988): 121.

7. The battle of Stalingrad is, of course, one of Kluge's obsessions. See his *Schlachtbeschreibung* (Frankfurt: Suhrkamp, 1983).

8. Alexander Kluge, *Die Patriotin: Text / Bilder 1–6* (Frankfurt: Zweitausendeins, 1979), 58.

9. Kluge, *Die Patriotin*, 171.

10. David Roberts, "Alexander Kluge und die deutsche Zeitgeschichte: Der Luftangriff auf Halberstadt am 8.4.1945," in *Alexander Kluge*, ed. Thomas Böhm-Christl (Frankfurt: Suhrkamp, 1983), 103.

11. Kluge, *Die Patriotin*, 171.

12. As Angelika Bammer has remarked, "In the end it makes little difference whether she is choosing to close her eyes or is truly blind to what is going on around her. The fact is, she does not see and, in not seeing, allows what is happening to continue, unchallenged and unchecked. Lene ignores the atmosphere of horror, the gas chambers and ovens, in the building where she and her child find shelter. In much the same way she had earlier ignored the anti-Semitic violence of the *Kristallnacht* pogrom, seemingly oblivious to the danger in which she puts both herself and the elderly Jewish shop owner to buy some silk thread for the new blouse she is embroidering. While these scenes seem intended to plead Lene's essential innocence (she is guiltless because she is ignorant), I think that, instead, they beg the essential questions of guilt and responsibility" ("Through a Daughter's Eyes: Helma Sanders-Brahms' *Germany, Pale Mother*," in *New German Critique* 36 [Fall 1985], 108). See also Kaes's chapter on the film in *Deutschlandbilder: Die Wiederkehr der Geschichte als Film* (Munich: Edition text und kritik, 1987).

13. The novel's action occupies three different time frames: the narrator's childhood and adolescence during fascism, the war, and the immediate postwar period; a trip taken by the narrator along with her brother, husband, and daughter to her home town (now in Poland) on the tenth and eleventh of November 1971; the present, i.e., the time of the composition of the manuscript, 1972–75.

14. Christa Wolf, *A Model Childhood*, trans. Ursule Molinaro and Hedwig Rappolt (New York: Farrar, Straus and Giroux, 1980), 151. As noted earlier, this translation has been republished as *Patterns of Childhood* (New York: Farrar, Straus and Giroux, 1984).

15. Wolf, *Model Childhood*, 150.

16. Wolf, *Model Childhood*, 152.

17. Wolf, *Model Childhood*, 156.

18. Wolf, *Model Childhood*, 161, modified translation.

19. Wolf, *Model Childhood*, 178.

20. Wolf, *Model Childhood*, 184–85; modified translation.

21. For further examples of the language of symptoms in the novel, see also 193; 280; 348–49; 392.

22. This is of course a huge and difficult issue that has occupied the hearts and minds of all who have concerned themselves with these matters. It is part of the larger question of the comprehensibility and representability of the Shoah. Even in such lucid and bold attempts to contextualize and historicize the Final Solution such as Arno Mayer's *Why Did the Heavens Not Darken?*, one comes up against this boundary line across which no metaphor seems to afford safe passage. Speaking, for example, of the four out-and-out extermination sites, Chelmno, Belzec, Sobibor, and Treblinka, Mayer says: "The executioners carried out their infamous deeds without public ceremony, and the victims suffered their dehumanization in terrifying silence. . . . *There were no bonds of common humanity between them* [my emphasis]. Theirs was an encounter of radical mutual exclusion and enmity which precluded both reintegration into society and defection from it. . . . Seemingly discontinuous with the intrinsic social amalgam and tactical ambiguity of the Nazi project, as well as uninformed by precedent, the extermination sites defy explanation. The historian faces them with a poverty of critical theory and imagination. This analytic and speculative inadequacy is compounded by his deficient empathic understanding of the behavior of both executioner and victim" (376–77). My own feeling is that these boundaries need to be understood more broadly as marking those real as well as imaginary "sites" where "bonds of common humanity" have been irreparably torn asunder, or to use Celan's phrase once more: "*auseinandergeschrieben.*" Here see also

Friedländer, "Um die 'Historisierung des Nationalsozialismus': Ein Briefwechsel," in *Vierteljahrshefte für Zeitgeschichte* 2 (April 1988): 371–72, as well as his "Überlegungen zur Historisierung des Nationalsozialismus," 49–50. Recall also Christa Wolf's insistence on the limits of her own labor of mourning and anamnesis. In the chapter that begins with the phrase "The Final Solution," the narrator writes: "You've forgotten when you first heard those words. When you gave them their proper meaning; it must have been years after the war. But way after that—to this day—every tall, thickly smoking smokestack forces you to think 'Auschwitz.' The name cast a shadow which grew and grew. To this day, you can't bring yourself to stand in this shadow, because your otherwise lively imagination balks at the suggestion that you might take on the role of the victims. For all eternity, an insurmountable barrier separates the sufferers from those who went free" (*Model Childhood*, 233).

23. Wolf, *Model Childhood*, 5; 6.

24. Wolf, *Kindheitsmuster*, 346 (this section has been omitted from *Model Childhood*).

25. Wolf, *Model Childhood*, 231, modified translation.

26. See once more de Man, *Resistance to Theory*, 80.

27. One thinks here as well of the language of "reason" cited early in the novel: "Understanding and listening to reason. Thus: to come to one's senses (Come to your senses!) [*Zu sich kommen. (Komm zu dir)*]" (92).

Index

Adorno, Theodor, 5, 8–9, 104
Artenfels, Rainer von, 138
Ash, Timothy Garton, 61

Bachmann, Ingeborg, 159
Bakhtin, Mikhail, 60
Bammer, Angelika, 194n12
Barthes, Roland, 178n34
Baudelaire, Charles, 166n31; Benjamin
   on, 123–24; de Man on, 14, 15; "Cor-
   respondances," 123
Benjamin, Walter, 121, 168n39, 179–
   80n67; on baroque Trauerspiel, 11–12,
   143, 191n98; essay on the storyteller,
   62–63, 65–67, 180n74, 183n97; essay
   on Walser, 148; on philosophy of his-
   tory, 15, 111, 112, 114, 122–24, 151–
   53, 154
Berger, John, 71, 177n28
Berman, Russell, 109, 110, 122, 132,
   187n23
Bernheimer, Charles, 171n62
Brecht, Bertolt, 107, 136
Broszat, Martin, 54–56, 90, 155, 174n26,
   193n3
Brubach, Holly, 184n101

Celan, Paul, 13, 101, 175n33, 191n94,
   191n96, 191n98; "Engführung," 144–
   45, 191n96

Chamberlain, Houston Stewart, 129
Chase, Cynthia, 167n39
cinema. See film; New German Cinema
Cleaver, Edith, 192n101, 193n104
Cleaver, Eldridge, 110
Clifford, James, 85, 86
Corrigan, Timothy, 142
Culler, Jonathan, 30, 167–68n39

de Man, Paul: assessments of, 15–17,
   30, 167–68n39; Derrida on, 14, 15,
   17–18, 30; essay on Benjamin, 16, 26–
   30; and rhetoric of bereavement, 13–
   15, 17–19; wartime writings, 15–17,
   30, 167–68n39
Derrida, Jacques, 9–11, 14; on de Man,
   14, 15, 17–18, 30; on pharmakon, 76–
   78
Dürer, Melencolia, 26, 132

Eagleton, Terry, 99–100, 115, 124, 125–
   26, 153, 165–66n23, 191n98
Eckstat, Stan, 184n101
Edel, Alfred, 133–34, 136
Ellerkamp, Fritz, 139, 140–41
Elsaesser, Thomas, 60, 113, 115, 139,
   144

Fassbinder, Rainer Werner, Trash, City,
   and Death, xi, 174n23

Library of Congress Cataloging-in-Publication Data

Santner, Eric L., 1955–
    Stranded objects : mourning, memory, and film in postwar Germany / Eric L. Santner.
        p.   cm.
    Includes bibliographical references.
    ISBN 0-8014-2344-9 (alk. paper)
        1. Motion pictures—Germany (West)—History.   2. Motion pictures—Social aspects—Germany (West)   3. World War, 1939–1945—Motion pictures and the war.   4. Holocaust, Jewish (1939–1945), in motion pictures.   5. Germany—History—Allied occupation, 1945–   6. Reitz, Edgar—Criticism and interpretation.   7. Syberberg, Hans Jürgen, 1935–   —Criticism and interpretation.   I. Title.   II. Title: Title: Mourning, memory, and film in postwar Germany.
    PN1993.5.G3S33   1990
    791.43'0943'0945—dc20   89-38522